STOP HURTING

START HEALING

Raquel

Stop Hurting, Start Healing

Raquel Kirszenbaum

Copyright © 5785 / 2025: Raquel Kirszenbaum

All rights reserved
ISBN: 978-1-962522-19-9

Printed in Israel

To contact the author,
email: *raqueldidio@gmail.com*

To discuss publishing your material — self-publishing or regular publishing — email: *submissions@AdirPress.com* or visit us at *www.AdirPress.com*

No part of this publication may be translated, reproduced, stored in a retrieval system or transmitted in any form or by any means; electronic, mechanical, photocopying, recording or otherwise without prior permission from the publisher — except for a reviewer wishing to quote brief passages in connection with a review for inclusion in a magazine or newspaper.

I highly recommend the book "Stop Hurting, Start Healing" by Raquel Kirszenbaum. In this deeply moving and insightful memoir, Raquel vulnerably shares her many profound emotional and psychological challenges, detailing respectfully, the trials and tribulations that tested her faith and inner strength to the core.

Through Raquel's narrative, readers witness her struggles with adversity, loss, and uncertainty, as she navigates life's darkest moments, supported by deep insights into Rabbinic teaching & with unwavering belief in Hashem and the resilience of the human spirit. Instead of viewing her challenges as obstacles to overcome, Raquel reframes them as opportunities for growth and transformation, embracing each trial as a stepping stone toward personal enlightenment and spiritual awakening.

What sets "Stop Hurting, Start Healing" apart is Raquel's unwavering faith in the meaning and purpose of her journey, even in the face of seemingly insurmountable odds. With Hashem's guidance and grace, she finds solace in the knowledge that her struggles have not been in vain but have paved the way for profound growth, self-discovery, and a renewed appreciation for the beauty of life.

As Raquel emerges stronger, happier, and more resilient from her experiences, she embodies a beacon of hope and inspiration for others facing their own challenges. Through her candid reflections and heartfelt wisdom, she imparts a message of love, faith, and perseverance, demonstrating that true growth is not in spite of adversity *but because of it.*

I highly recommend it,
Respectfully,
Rabbi Shimon Russell

SHEVET AHIM
COMUNIDAD HEBREA DE PANAMÁ
Fundada en 1933

ב"ה

Panamá, 1 de octubre de 2024
28 de Elul 5784

CARTA DE REFERENCIA
"STOP HURTING, START HEALING"

Es un honor redactar esta carta de referencia para el libro **"Stop Hurting, Start Healing"** de nuestra querida y respetada morá, Raquel Didio, quien ha destacado por transmitir la sabiduría de la Torá y sus enseñanzas de manera práctica y dinámica.

En esta obra, la morá Raquel nos invita a un viaje profundo y personal, compartiendo su corazón y ofreciéndonos una perspectiva transformadora sobre cómo enfrentar los desafíos de la vida. A través de sus páginas, nos guía en un proceso de sanación que nos enseña a sobrellevar las dificultades con una fortaleza que combina la fragilidad y la genuina Emuná.

Su enfoque, enriquecido con ejemplos de nuestras sagradas enseñanzas, ofrece una brújula para encontrar serenidad, paz interior, comprensión y fortaleza al enfrentar las pruebas que Hashem nos presenta. Esta obra es una guía que inspira a encontrar sentido y apoyo en cada experiencia que vivimos.

Confío en que las palabras de esta publicación serán una fuente de bendición para quienes lo lean, llenándolos de fe y confianza, y recordándonos que, detrás de cada reto, La Mano de Hashem está presente, apoyándonos y guiándonos hacia nuestro bienestar, crecimiento y superación personal.

Berajá Vehatzlajá!

Rabino David Perets
Rabino Oficial de Shevet Ahim
Comunidad Hebrea de Panamá

TEL: 225-5990 • FAX: 227-1268 • E-mail: info@shevetahim.com • Apartado: 0816-00068 Panamá, Rep. de Panamá

SHEVET AHIM
COMUNIDAD HEBREA DE PANAMÁ
Fundada en 1933

Panama, October 1, 2024
28th of Elul, 5784

REFERENCE LETTER
"STOP HURTING, START HEALING"

It is an honor to write this reference letter for the book "Stop Hurting, Start Healing" by our dear and respected Mora, Raquel Didio, who has distinguished herself by conveying the wisdom of the Torah and its teachings in a practical and dynamic manner.

In this work, Mora Raquel invites us on a profound and personal journey, sharing her heart and offering us a transformative perspective on how to face life's challenges. Through its pages, she guides us through a healing process that teaches us how to overcome difficulties with a strength that blends fragility with genuine Emuná (faith).

Her approach, enriched with examples from our sacred teachings, provides a compass to find serenity, inner peace, understanding, and strength when facing the trials that Hashem places before us. This book serves as an inspiring guide to find meaning and support in every experience we go through.

I trust that the words of this book will be a source of blessing for all who read it, filling them with faith and confidence, and reminding us that behind every challenge, the hand of Hashem is present, supporting and guiding us toward our well-being, growth, and personal development.

Berajá Vehatzlajá!

Rabbi David Perets
Official Rabbi of Shevet Ahim
Hebrew Community of Panama

Michtav Bracha

Cheshvan 5784

Raquel Kirszenbaum has written a very powerful book detailing how to deal with emotional pain, suffering and abuse from a Torah perspective. Because this book arose out of the circumstances of her own life, it is a cry from the depths of her soul which may be difficult to read. I believe, however, that there are many insights in the book that will help people struggling with these issues. She eloquently articulates R.Tzadok's famous teaching that just as one needs to have emunah in Hashem ,they must also have emunah in themselves, that if God gave us a challenge, He gave us the kochot and the ability not only to surmount the challenge but to grow from it. So although there is much sadness in Raquel's story, the message is ultimately one of hope, courage, optimism, faith—giving those in need the strength to go on by connecting to the source of all strength.

May Raquel's message reach all who need chizuk and comfort.

With Admiration and Bracha,
Yitzchak A. Breitowitz
Rav, Kehillat Ohr Somayach

Rabbi Zev Leff

Rabbi of Moshav Matityahu
Rosh HaYeshiva—Yeshiva Gedola Matityahu

בס"ד

הרב זאב לף

מרא דאתרא מושב מתתיהו
ראש הישיבה—ישיבה גדולה מתתיהו

D.N. Modiin 71917　　Tel: 08-976-1138 טל'　　Fax: 08-976-5326 פקס'　　ד.נ. מודיעין 71917

כב כסלו תשפ"ד
December 5, 2023

Dear Mrs. Raquel Kirszenbaum,

    I read portions of your book and was impressed with your ability to convey your trials and tribulations in a very refined and Torah oriented fashion. Also impressive is your knowledge of Torah ideas concerning emunah, bitachon and mussar. Your book not only serves the purpose of coping with one's difficulties by conveying them to others but, will definitely be an aid to others in dealing with their own trials and tribulations - especially in dealing with oppressive marriages and divorces.

    May Hashem Yisborach bless you with life and health and may you see much nachas from your children and in your own personal life's situations. May Hashem reward you richly for helping others to deal with their trials and tribulations in a true Torah fashion.

Sincerely,
With Torah blessings

Rabbi Zev Leff

Rabbi Zev Leff

One of the aspects of life that sets Judaism and the Jewish community apart from a significant percentage of the modern world, is the importance and sanctity of marriage. We know that the fairy-tale "and they lived happily ever after" is not only false, but creates an unrealistic image which many people find themselves comparing their own marriage to, and find it lacking. In reality, a great marriage is something that develops over time, and in most cases, is commensurate to the amount of effort and self-work put into it.

Nevertheless, there are occasions where, despite hard work and significant self development, and after direction from therapists and spiritual mentors, it is correct for a couple to seek separation and divorce. We even see that an aspect of the divorce process is a Mitzva, i.e. the Torah is telling us that there are times when this is the positive next step in the two people's emotional and spiritual path in this world.

Unfortunately, because there is rightly such a stress within our community on making a marriage work, people who need to take the crucial step out of a marriage can find themselves alone, voiceless, judged and abandoned. When this is placed on top of the real and significant pain that a person may well be carrying internally, the feelings of embarrassment, worry for the future, and even a misplaced sense of failure, the weight can feel too much to carry.

The author of this superb book, 'Stop Hurting, Start Healing', has done a tremendous service to those in the Jewish community who need support and direction when carrying the weight of suffering on their shoulders, whether it be divorce or any other of the myriad challenges that people have to navigate during their time on this temporary world. Not only has she given a voice to those suffering in silence, acknowledging both their pain and their right to feel that pain, she has more importantly provided a roadmap that lays out how one moves forward – through faith, growth and love.

While it would be understandable for an account of a life of tribulations to contain blame and Lashon Hara, with the person's negative perspectives laid out for all to see, this author has demonstrated that living in that mode is actually often self-destructive and blocks the necessary healing. It is true that one of the permitted types of Lashon Hara L'Toelet – negative speech for a constructive purpose – is when a person who is going through a difficulty speaks out their troubles for their own emotional support (and only when the conditions for such speech are fulfilled), it is rare that there is a Toelet in such a public forum. Instead she has chosen to write a work without blame or recrimination, fully focused on the closeness she has built with her Father in Heaven, as she scaled the walls of challenge.

When I read the book, I cried at times and at others I felt uplifted and even in awe of the clear vision of life's purpose. As a colleague of the author, I can attest that the concepts in this book are not just words and ideals, they are the real life processes that she has gone through to build her resilience, personal happiness, and closeness to the Creator, and she is kindly sharing them so that so many others who are carrying their own troubles can learn from her practical experience.

I would like to end with a bracha: May Hashem give the author all the strength she needs to inspire others and continue her journey of personal healing, and to you, the reader, may He help you find in the words of this book the insights you need to pick yourself up and start climbing the ladder of personal greatness.

Rabbi Menachem Salazsnik,
author of *Words Change Worlds*

Rebbetzen Tziporah Heller-Gottlieb

"Knowing that others suffer brings you to feeling as though half of your burden has been lifted."

Many people are afraid to deal with their vulnerabilities, their painful life situations, their failures and those of others in a n unending and futile effort to seem perfect. people living perfect lives. No one is perfect. We are all works in progress living with challenges that are designed with love and care by the One who knows us best.

We sometimes succeed brilliantly, and sometimes have to start again from the bottom up. We are all nonetheless beloved by Hashem, and this book may help you recognize both how imperfection, love and faith are not contradictory. The author lives with both and is an example to all of us.

Raquel Kirszenbaum has written a fantastic book, packed with powerful chizuk — it is wise, relevant and deeply inspiring.

Raquel courageously shares many of her life struggles in a candid way, showing her readers how her life-line of Emunah continually pulled her from darkness into light.

This book truly is like a huge burst of Emunah.

Chana Levitan M.S.,
Author, Couples Therapist, International Speaker

Raquel Kirszenbaum has written an unbelievably honest, insightful and inspirational book about the meaning of pain and struggle. What is unique about this book is how real it is. Raquel does not pontificate on matters of philosophy from a high perch of safety and security, but rather from the very trenches of which she speaks. Her heart is wide open to share her deepest insecurities and lowest points, and yet what we take out of the book is her incredible bravery. We are amazed at how tenaciously she clings to faith no matter what. This book is part memoir, part "how-to" on maintaining faith in the most trying of times, part Torah text, and part therapy. It is an honor to call Raquel a friend, because actually, she is one of our nation's greatest unsung heroes.

    Ruchi Koval
    Founder and Director,
    Jewish Family Experience of Cleveland
    Author
    Parent Coach

Dear Raquel

What can the heart of a father and mother say to their children but give them support, resilience, love and above all perseverance.

Let us not let our hardships define us, but use it as the impulse to get up higher and higher and know that Hashem is with you in everything you decide.

Count on our unconditional support and love, keep going because God is ahead of you. Keep taking advantage of life. Continue to illuminate souls, and we hope that you can — through these words that came from a suffering heart — reach other hearts and awaken in them feelings of bravery and courage.

With love, your parents

In the honor of my beautiful children Batsheva, Shira Bracha, Adina Malka and Yosef Yehuda. May Hashem continuously give you unlimited reason to smile, may we dance and sing through all the seasons together. May I merit to see you in the chuppah with a person full of heart and Yiras Shamaim and may you continue to be strong, resilient and reach all heights.

May we one day look back, laugh, and be grateful with a heart full of hope and understanding.

In the honor of the beautiful community in Panamá who have filled me with love and embraced me through all the years, lifting me up from all situations and helping me swim all waves, constantly inspired and strengthened by all the beauty and Torah that comes Out of this beautiful community. I am personally grateful forever.

In the honor of all my students around the world! You inspire me to inspire, to always keep going to strive for better.

You have given me wings to fly and a heart full of love and the desire to give. Thank you for all you have done through out the years, I wouldn't be here without you. I am blessed to be able to be a guide and a friend and to infuse in you the greatest love of all, the love of Hashem.

This book is dedicated to all those who are hurting, who feel unseen, undeserving, unwanted, who feel stuck and worry they won't and can't make it. To the hundreds and thousands who have shared their hearts with m4 under the year I SEE YOU, this is for you, I won't let you give up, I won't let you get used to it! It can be better, it will be better, not because it was what it was it means it has to be what it is!

Trust ,hope ,we will make it together and we will burst in joy when we realize "הינו חולמים"

Let us hold hands and hold on to the one above who loved us and had never forsaken us

Dedicated to everyone who supported this book, every campaign, those who I know and those who I don't! All the angels that have taken care of us in a meaningful dignified way עולם חסד יבנה, it is your constant chessed that continues strengthening me to rebuild my world and those of others.

For the refuah shelema of Ezra ben Sarina, Batsheva bat Rajel and Ivette bat Rajel.

May Hashem continue to strengthen you and you should have a healthy strong life and 120.

Raquel

ספר זה מוקדש ומוקטר לעלוי נשמת הורי היקרים שהקדישו כל רגע וכל מאמץ לגדל אותנו , לחנך אותנו על־ידי תורה ומסרת ישראל ובפרט על־ידי מעשים טובים

ליאון בן רחל

רבקה בת שרינה

יהי זכרם ברוך ונשמתם צרורה בצרור החיים לנצח

אנחנו אסירות תודה להם

In memory of my grandmothers,
two beautiful *neshei chayil*:

**Faiga bat Avraham and
Devora Leah Leeba bat Chaim Akiva**

And in memory of all the victims of October 7th and the fallen soldiers. Their neshamas should have the highest *aliyahs*,

With love,
Rachel Shnay

Dedicated to all the strongest of women who journey towards healing.

With love
Liraz Blank

In honor of all of the young women that Raquel has changed their lives forever — to live a life of *emunah* and closeness to HaShem!

Thank you, Raquel, for inspiring me and so many others to see HaShem in every challenge.

In honor of Raquelita, friend and teacher.

May this book be a channel of blessings
for a long, healthy sweet life.

Harry and Dina Dornbusch

מוקדש לע"נ

ירמיה בן אברהם ז"ל

פרל אולגה בת אריה לב ז"ל

En honor a una gran mujer, mora y ejemplo mi amiga Raquel, que Hashem siempre te mande berajots, alegrias y najat de sus hijos. Que siempre tenga el privilegio de transmitir tora, con cariño Sarina Silvera

In honor of Raquel, a shining example of what happens when you're brave enough to be vulnerable.

And in the *zchut* of the safety of our *chayalim* and the immediate return of our *chatufim*.

To the single mothers who face each day with courage and determination. Your strength and love for Hashem are a beacon of hope and inspiration.

May we "Drink in" the lessons of this book. This is for you.

Jordana (Baruchov) Greenfield

Para que cada una de las personas que donamos podamos ver nuestra Yeshua en lo que necesitemos con mucha salud y todas las bendiciones de H.

Raquel sabemos que con tu libro, en el cual expresarás tu sabiduría, podrás ayudar a cientos de personas como has hecho con nosotras.

Te queremos mucho:

Tus queridas alumnas

I want to publicly thank Hashem for all that He has given to me and continues to give to me BH!

For my amazing teachers, one of them being the beautiful Raquel.

In honor of

Raquel Didio

Bezrat Hashem she should have the חוכמה ורוח הקודש לגדל את כל ילדיה לגדולה הצלחה ומעשים טובים צדיקים גדולים

In honor of
Chaim ben Mashiach v'Shoshana
and
Aharon ben Yosef v'Tova, who are always in our hearts, our thoughts and our memories.

לעילוי נשמת חיים בן משיח ושושנה ואהרן בן יוסף וטובה. זכרונם לברכה.

ת.נ.צ.ב.ה.

Para haztlaja y beraja de nuestros hijos,

Gaby y Karen Ashkenazi

Dedicated to the brave soldiers of the IDF, whose unwavering courage and resilience defend our homeland and uphold our values. May your dedication inspire healing and peace for all.

With deepest gratitude and admiration to you and your families.

Sammy and Reyna Simnegar

A mis padres,

Jaime y Olga Cohen;

que me han enseñado a ver siempre lo bueno en la vida" con cariño.

Jessica Rajek

Dedicated *l'iluy nishmas*

Miriam bas Yosef

from
Katie and Eric Goldstein

This book is dedicated with love and affection to:

Chava bat Avraham
by her children, grandchildren and great grandchildren

Eliyahu Raphael Ben Tzvi Aryeh
by his children and grandchildren

Shalom ben Harael
by your grateful parents and siblings.

We love you all and pray for your neshamos to have a constant aliyah to Hashem.

In honor of the life force of my family,

Miriam bat Raquel

& for the aliya of the neshamot of Am Israel that were returned to Hashem

---

Dedicated to

Raquel Kirzenbaum

for her tireless efforts on behalf of her family, her students and Klal Yisrael.

May Hashem bless her efforts with Siyata Dishamya and success.

With love,
Debby & Ari Winter

To all women who tirelessly protect and nurture, may HKBH turn tears of suffering into joy!

To Raquel a true inspiration!

In the merit they we should all feel Hashem's love, light, and presence in our life.

Sara bat azzizolah and Davood Ben Chaim

Refua Shelema de mi madre Jaffa Golda bat Chana Lea

Beraja para Elias, Ivette Levy y familia

Le'ilui nishmat luisa leah bat victoria. Beraja y hazlaja para Raquel y sus hijos. Ve ilui nishmas Eliezer Alter Ben Shaul and Zlata bas Yaakov

Refua shlema to Yehuda ben miriam hacohen

Le'ilui nishmat Shlomo Joseph ben Regina, Leah bat sara, Yosef ben Aziza, Aviva bat Naomi

Dedicated to the hundreds of students of Michlelet Esther through the years. May you all continue to make an impact on Hashem's world. "With love, Debby & Ari Winter

En agradecimiento a nuestros padres:
Abraham Ico y Vicky Eshkenazi
Moris y Rebeca Sasson
para su beraja, briut y hatzlajá
De Rab. Moi y Sophie Eshkenazi e hijos

ACKNOWLEDGMENTS

Where to begin? I didn't think I would be publishing a book, especially after the hardest year of my life, and certainly not on the topic of hurting and healing. I did not think I could heal, smile again, dance again, live again. Therefore, I have to start and end by thanking Hashem, Who gives me life daily and "returns my soul with so much faithfulness." Thank you, Hashem, for always believing in me more than I could ever believe in myself, for dreaming much bigger dreams for me than I ever thought possible, and for gifting me with incredible resilience, willingness to live, hope, and positivity. Your kindness is incredibly abundant! Thank you for the darkness; it is through it I have learned to find and generate light. Thank you for all the challenges that have made me stronger and given me the gift of being able to help and guide others. "From bitterness, sweetness has come" — thank You for never giving up on me, and for opening my eyes and ears to Your truth even when I was stubborn and didn't want to see it. Thank you for so many incredible gifts and for the opportunity to use them, hopefully, in Your service and for the sake of the Jewish people.

I want to thank my Rabbi, Rabbi Yonah Refson, who has been an incredible source of support, positivity, empathy, and compassion throughout all this time, who believed in me and cheered me on when I couldn't see what he saw; who read the book over and over again and saw what it could be and what it could do.

To Rabbi Ari Winter, who started me on this journey and still accompanies me 20 years later, with the will and availability to help, listen, advise, and so much more.

To Rabbi Menachem Nissel and his wife, for not only having very important and sensitive input on the book and its direction, but for all the love, care, and support they constantly give our family.

Mrs. Chana Levitan, your friendship and guidance have been huge in this journey; you went over and beyond. Thank you for believing in me. Thank you for reading and re-reading this book and making sure it is the best it could be.

Rabbi Menachem Salasnik! Wow, I asked a question about lashon hara letoelet, and you got involved in every detail: reading the entire manuscript, taking notes, and giving me a lot of your time! You understood the value and need of this book and helped me achieve it in the most precise and kosher way.

Rabbi Abraham Edelestein, thank you for our long discussions, for hearing all my doubts, complaints, hopes, and goals for the Jewish people, and thank you for being honest, caring, sensitive, and real!

Thank you, Rebetzin Tzipora Heller Gotlieb, for your clarity of vision and sensitivity so this book can not only help the Jewish people but protect and be the best resource for me and my family.

I want to thank Rabbi Breitowitz for supporting this book when it was raw and looked very different; for understanding the need for it in this world and in our society, for his humility and attention; and if I may add, bravery and zealousness for truth.

Thank you, Rabbi Shimon Russel, for the strong, delicate advice that ultimately perfected the direction and purpose of this book. Thank you for reading it and re-reading it, and for all your support.

Thank you so much to the Chief Rabbi of Panamá, Rab Peretz; what an honor to not only have had you read the book, but for giving me your time and advice, with sensitivity and emet. Thank you for guiding our community to become as great and united as it is.

I want to thank my first editor, Blimi Segal, for taking on this project when it was written as one big long paragraph, for being an extension of my voice and my heart, knowing and understanding how to write it in a clean, beautiful, elegant way, but without losing my voice and essence.

Thank you to the amazing publisher, Adir Press; when we say that Hashem makes shidduchim, we mean it. No one could have done a better job in editing and bringing this book to reality! And to the head of Adir Press, Rabbi Moshe Kormornick. Wow! You really took this project under your wing, making it from good to great! You were so sensitive, kind, and patient with all my doubts and choices. You saw the big picture and took the book to a place where it would do the greatest service to the Jewish people while caring incredibly for me and my family. I'm so grateful Hashem brought you as the editor and publisher; this book would not be where it is and how it is without you. Your insights, wisdom, and sensitivity are incredible. Thank you.

Thank you to every Rabbi, therapist, mentor, and colleague who took their precious time to not only read and give advice on the book but also for the lengthy discussions and conversations! They did it in such a sensitive way, having concerns and considerations for the book that I could not initially see. Thinking about the welfare of my family, my children, and myself; looking at the greater picture of what would be most beneficial for the Jewish people, worrying about the toelet of everything that had been written and caring for the honor of those who had previously been mentioned. Discussing with me back and forth even when I was being stubborn and helping me understand that for something to reach its greatest impact it needs to be done in the most kosher, pure way, possible; even if that means letting go of what was written originally.

Thank you to my beautiful students from different walks of life who proofread the manuscript and allowed me to realize we all need this, and it reaches all of our hearts.

Thank you to my incredible community in Panama, my international community of students, and my family in Neve Yerushalayim, as well as the other institutions I'm blessed to be a part of and consider family. I wouldn't be where I am without you! You have always believed in me, supported me, and carried me through the most difficult paths that life has taken me.

My students, your belief and support for me is what keeps me going every day; the need to keep strong and hold on to Hashem because I know you see me as a role model of emunah and strength, and I want to model those middot for you. Thank you for your constant excitement around everything I try to create and for your incessant support: emotionally, physically, and economically, thank you!

To my parents, thank you for showing me it is never too late to change, as Reb Yisrael Salanter said, "The entire time that the candle is still lit, there is time to fix." I know this book may have generated conflicting feelings but you still supported me in my decision.

To my siblings for being strong, resilient, and choosing a path in life that is dignified and makes us proud.

To the ones that have been there in any way they could and sometimes even beyond, thank you for having my back.

To all the angels that have made me feel less alone, taken care of, hugged, and helped me... to all those who went way above the letter of the law, I will forever remember the kindness and pray that Hashem multiplies it your way.

To my ex-husband, thank you for being part of the greatest gift I have in my life, which is our beautiful children. These very high and special souls had to come to this world through you; that says a lot. I have you in my mind, in my prayers, may Hashem also allow us to heal in every way and find our unique path.

To my children, this is for you! You are the reason I live, the oxygen to my soul! This book is a gift for you so that you can grow up in a better world where there is more compassion and understanding. This book is so that one day you know that I wanted to give up, but you inspired me and gave me the strength to keep going. You teach me every day that life is beautiful; there are some dark shades but it is mostly colorful. You teach me to love, to forgive, to fight, to believe, and to hope. It's been a challenge but the greatest gift to raise you, much more so now that I am on my own.

You have taught me who I am, that I can give, that I'm enough, and you have taught me the real meaning of resilience! You are warriors, holy, wholesome souls, I don't know how you keep giving and forgiving; you are so considerate and loving, and I promise that I will continue to heal and become the best version that I can be so that I can help provide for you a life full of growth, opportunities, and happiness. It is an honor and the greatest calling of my life to be your mother. I will never be deserving of such precious gifts.

Hashem, I have to thank You again. Thank You for making me Jewish, for allowing me to reflect and change my ways, and for giving me the gift of dedicating my life to Torah! Thank You for all the times You call in to say I love you throughout the day! This book is my response to You.

I love You, I accept, I forgive, I let go, and I will continue to love you "בכל לבבך ובכל נפשך ובכל מאדך, *with all your heart, with all your soul, and with all your might.*"

Thank you

Raquel

PUBLISHER'S PREFACE

Rav Avigdor Miller related the story of a man who bemoaned to his rebbe that Hashem had caused him to miss a flight to a crucial business meeting, resulting in a significant loss of money for the upcoming year. The rebbe asked him, "If you would have heard that the plane had crashed, what would your reaction have been?" The man answered that he would have made a gala kiddush the likes that the community had never seen, so that he could publicly acknowledge the open miracle that Hashem had done for him. "Tell me," responded the rebbe, "Why do 140 people have to die for you to acknowledge that Hashem runs the world and has your best interest in mind, let them live and you can still acknowledge that Hashem runs the entire world with great precision!"

The principle that Hashem runs the world to perfection is known, understood and often repeated by us, but when difficulties actually occur, does that knowledge move from our head to our heart? Do we calmly thank Hashem for the challenge, despite the pain, because we know that it is for our best? Without doubt, such a mentality would take superhuman strength, require constant *chizzuk*, and need careful guidance and support.

Endorsed by leading Torah figures who have read through the full manuscript, *Stop Hurting, Start Healing* serves as a guidebook for anyone facing struggles and looking for strength, support, and advice in getting out of the rut they may find themselves in. Moreover, this unique book serves as a manual to actually *grow* through the challenges, not merely *cope* with the hurdles in the way.

The author, Raquel Kirszenbaum, is a highly-regarded international lecturer and teacher to thousands, and after facing significant challenges throughout her life, she has penned her own methods of growth, prayer and success in this honest portrayal of her journey to healing and personal development. And in doing so, she brings us along with her in the quest for strength and emunah.

It is my sincere *tefilla* that the goals of this book are achieved; that people heal from their past traumas and current challenges, gain strength and wisdom to develop a closer connection to Hashem, and *use* the hurdles in their way to climb to unimaginable heights of greatness.

    Rabbi Moshe Kormornick
    Adir Press

CONTENTS

Acknowledgments	. . . .	23
Publisher's Preface	. . . .	29
Prologue	. . . .	33
Introduction	. . . .	39
Chapter One:	*Hitting Rock Bottom*	49
Chapter Two:	*The Darkest Hour is Right Before the Dawn*	59
Chapter Three:	*The Gift of Brokenness*	73
Chapter Four:	*Don't Be Afraid of the Pain*	81
Chapter Five:	*My Inheritance Doesn't Have to Be My Legacy*	93
Chapter Six:	*Tailor-Made for You with Love*	109
Chapter Seven:	*God Doesn't Give You More than You Can Carry*	123
Chapter Eight:	*Fear and Control*	137
Chapter Nine:	*Dancing in the Rain, Singing through Darkness*	149
Chapter Ten:	*Choosing to Live*	165
Chapter Eleven:	*Self Awareness in the Image of God* . .	181
Chapter Twelve:	*Let It Go, There Is Nothing Holding Us Back Except for Us* . . .	193
Chapter Thirteen:	*Ready to Enjoy*	207
Chapter Fourteen:	*Becoming Godly by Choosing Good* . .	229
Chapter Fifteen:	*Learning to Listen*	243
Epilogue	. . . .	259

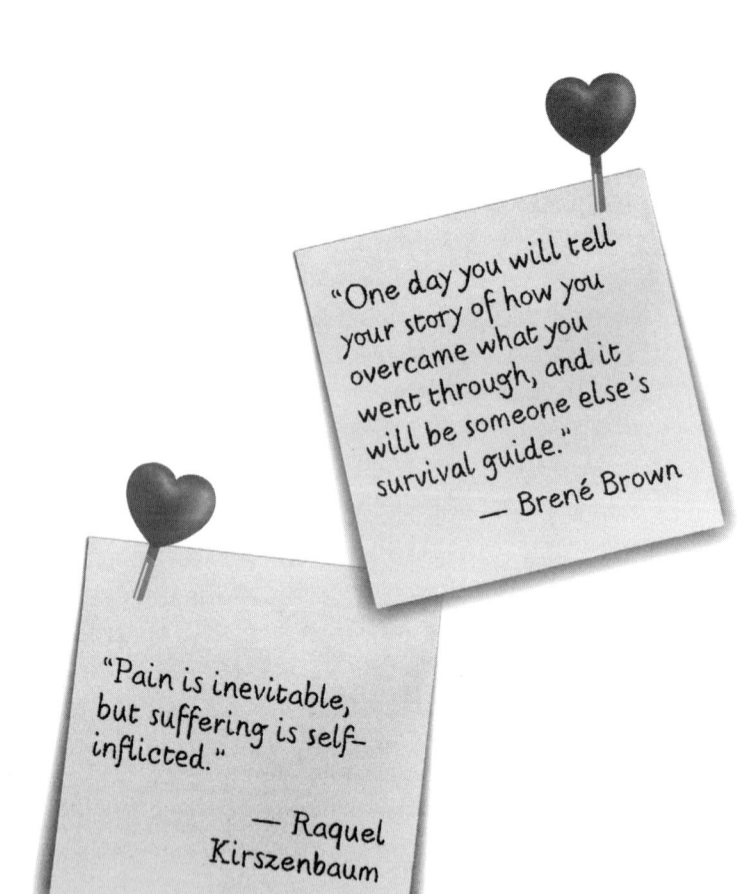

"One day you will tell your story of how you overcame what you went through, and it will be someone else's survival guide."
— Brené Brown

"Pain is inevitable, but suffering is self-inflicted."
— Raquel Kirszenbaum

PROLOGUE

One of my favorite quotes as a child was always, "Life is like a box of chocolates; you never know what you're going to get." That one sentence made life seem like an exciting treat, something to look forward to. I mean, I do love chocolate. And really, what could be better than life just giving you more and more of what you love? Chocolate is sweet and gratifying. Who wouldn't want more of that in their lives? That famous line taught me to hope for and crave sweetness in life.

But I was fated to discover that my life was more like dark chocolate: intense and bittersweet, which, despite its rich and complex flavor, is not the creamy and dreamy goodness of the milk chocolate I expected. I was quick to understand that my life was going to have a lot of that concentrated bitterness, and it was my job to find the subtle sweetness in it—to appreciate it and even derive some sort of pleasure from it. After all, milk chocolate isn't even real chocolate, right? It's a combination of bitter cacao mixed with sweet sugar and velvety cream. It's the ultimate example of mixing the bad with the good to get something incredible. So that was my goal: to take the bad, add the good, and create something fantastic out of this life.

My life, I always say, has pretty much offered me a sample of everything on the menu—or every chocolate in the box, so to speak. But I've come to appreciate that we don't get to decide which chocolates go into that box, just if and how we get to enjoy them. To switch metaphors for a moment—we don't get to choose the hand of cards we're dealt, but we do get to choose how to play them. We can choose to be smart, quick, and astute in our gameplay. And even though a good set of cards might give us an advantage, it doesn't guarantee a win. We have to learn how to play the game; how to use and outsmart the system. As Roger Crawford said, "Being challenged in life is inevitable; being defeated is optional." So I decided I'm not only not going to be defeated, but I'll use my challenges to propel me to greatness.

I had the idea for this book when I was going back and forth in my mind about sharing my most recent challenge on social media: *divorce*. As you will see in later chapters, it's much more complicated than just that one word. It's the culmination of eleven years of living in extremely challenging circumstances. I don't want to share the whole story with the world, but I felt the need to share what I can to help others, despite the obvious difficulties of making myself very vulnerable. I couldn't live a life of keeping up appearances anymore, overly concerned with what people thought about me and my life. I needed to set things straight—to be honest. To represent that which I honor and value so much: the truth.

You may be wondering what the purpose of this book is. To be honest, as I was going through so much pain, I thought I couldn't take it anymore, and I wanted to give up on life. But then I realized I have been "uniquely positioned and chosen" for so many challenges. I can't just turn away; I have to use it, to grow from it, and to inspire from it. Our rabbis teach us, *"Ein chacham k'baal nisayon*—there is no wise person as the one who has experience," and therefore I have to use my experience to share my wisdom. When we have a "why," it is much easier and more meaningful to go through difficult experiences. Sometimes we think we have to know the exact why, but the truth is, we don't need to know the exact why in order to understand that there is a why. Maybe this is my why… maybe this is my calling.

I'm sure you will read the book and have so many questions, be very curious, and rightfully so; at times, you may wonder and even think that the feelings I write are exaggerated. But in all honesty, even though we don't all share the same challenges, we probably have shared the same feelings. I wanted to do the right thing for my family, for all those who have played a role in my life—for better or worse—and for you, the reader. This book is a gift for you; therefore, although I initially wrote many more details of my life story, I have decided not to include many of the difficult details, and to just function as a channel to express godliness and divinity in this world. I am choosing to let go of my attachment to my challenges and set myself free to help you in your journey toward the same goal. I believe we all want to do good; we are made in the image of God, and it is not fair to define people and limit them through their difficult and sometimes horrible choices. I am choosing forgiveness and compassion even when it is super hard, and in this way, hoping I can help you do the same; and who knows, maybe heal, let go, and ultimately forgive and accept.

I have gone through unimaginable challenges; at times, I thought the weight would crash me. I'm choosing not to spell them out in detail in order to avoid engaging in lashon hara, even if it might have been *leto'elet,* for a constructive purpose. But most importantly, for the innocence and purity of my children and the goodness that is within all of us. I don't want to be remembered for all that I've been through, but rather for all that I have overcome and striven to be. I don't want others to be remembered for the worst chapters in their lives. I hope you respect and value that choice and understand that for this book to be a vessel for all we can be, I have to become a channel and not the spotlight.

Any student of mine will tell you that when it comes to being honest about life struggles, I am an open book. I always say you don't have to be ashamed of not having it together, so don't convince yourself or others that you do. But I wasn't exactly practicing my own preaching. You see, like many others who suffer in silence, on the outside, it seemed like we were doing well, my husband and I. On the outside, we managed. And there were even many days when we managed, so it seemed, on the inside as well. There were moments when we both thought we were a great team, and if only we could "fix ourselves," then we could have a better marriage. I had been told that most couples struggle with their marriages the first ten years anyway. I just kept wondering, when does it get easier?

The truth is, it wasn't always obvious that there was a real problem. In many ways, it seemed like things were kind of normal for a young marriage. We hosted for Shabbat, he supported me in my dreams, we had a great dynamic and structure with household duties, the children, and the division of roles… But it felt like there was constant chaos surrounding us. Our marriage was very much a construction zone. You might even say it was a war zone at times, with all its clamor and complexities. Over the years, I thought most of the issues were my fault. After all, I do come from an immeasurably problematic background. I carry lots—and I mean lots—of baggage. It wasn't in my nature to be the most caring or sensitive person. Maybe it just wasn't easy to be married to me. I told myself that I could give it just one more chance. And again, one more chance. And another. Concentrate on the positive. Maybe give up on some dreams. Get used to disappointment. Then maybe, just maybe, we could reach a middle point, and at the very least, do just fine. I had to stay. I had to make it work. I was willing to let go of my own personal dreams of happiness for the sake of my children. And, let's be honest here, for the sake of what others would think. I was absolutely consumed with how I might disappoint the world. At the same time, marriage is the most sacred entity in Judaism; we all aspire to build a home, a family, to emulate Hashem by creating life. Not only the concept of a happy marriage but the reality of it is the paradigm of a happy life. So, of course, it was worth fighting for. We went to therapy for so long; I went to therapy on my own, with so many different therapists. But it was to no avail. I wanted to make it work; I hoped, prayed, cried, and tried. Marriage is something that we have to be willing to constantly work on, to sacrifice for. Most times, couples can work through it and grow through it; but not us.

It just wasn't happening. I couldn't understand why we weren't getting better. I couldn't see how we would ever close the distance and cross the victory line together. My marriage was a cascade of story after story, excuse after excuse, breaking point after breaking point. There were times I felt like I was being knocked down over and over again, unable to get up before being knocked down again. I felt alone, living in constant panic and fear, feeling so guilty and ashamed of who I had become.

Everything that is valuable in life requires hard work and constant investment. Mine wasn't about the work anymore; I was choking. I remember so many classes where I heard about divorce; the metaphor was, "If your finger hurts, do you chop it off? What about if it›s broken? Blue, black? When do you chop it off? And the answer was, when it is either your finger or the rest of your body!" Sometimes you have to amputate a limb in order to survive, and the loss is huge, but the other option is to lose it all. I didn't know I had to amputate, but *Hashem* made a decision for me that I wasn't brave enough to make on my own.

The first step was confronting the truth and confronting myself. I had to do that which I feared the most and share the truth with those around me. So being the person I am, there was no question that it was something only I could do for myself. "*Im ein ani li mi li*,*" if I am not for myself, who will be?" So, I published a post on Facebook, and in that one moment, so much weight was lifted off my shoulders. I felt my heart open, my hands extend; and suddenly everyone was coming toward me, reaching for me and embracing me. All of my fears of rejection and desertion never came to fruition. The outpouring of love and support, of sheer admiration, was astonishing. I was flooded with messages: "You are so brave," and, "If I admired you before, I admire you now so much more." The post hadn't even included the details of what was happening in my life, only an articulation of what was happening in my heart. Yet, through that expression alone, it felt like I had opened a door for everyone else to open up and give voice to their own hearts. How desperately people want to feel heard and understood but are all so afraid of being ignored and rejected. So, suddenly there I was, a voice for the voiceless. A voice for so many who aren't in the public eye, but suffer so much with no public outlet. An honest and open tribute to the pain and suffering that we all feel at times. And that's when it hit me. I had always thought I would one day write a book, but about what and how? Suddenly I knew, this was it. This is the reason for my pain: to share with you, be there for you, and for all of us who so often feel like there is no one who sees us or understands us, no one that gets it.

But I get it. I get all of it.

INTRODUCTION

I've realized that there is a need for raw honesty, for role models who aren't afraid of their human frailty, and for real talk about real issues. Let's normalize pain and fragility. We all go through so much in our lives; why not go through it together? We live in a world full of photoshopped images of perfection, but life is real and flawed, and we can't live trying to emulate our so-called models of perfection or even trying to keep up with what's expected of us when we are breaking on the inside. Life is not about keeping up appearances; it's not about who we seem to be on the outside, but rather who we actually are on the inside. Every one of us performs in front of an audience, but what's going on behind the scenes when the cameras aren't rolling?

The Torah speaks about how everyone experiences hardship and documents life challenges so heavy that they would definitely be censored in today's world. In fact, the greatest people in the Torah were those who experienced the hardest trials in their lives. Great and holy figures like *Yosef* and King David, whose lives involved so much family conflict, so many difficult relationships, and so much lying and hurting, became pillars of the Jewish people. So why do we think we need to be perfect in order to make it in life? And even more so, why do we think we need to be ashamed of the challenges God has sent our way? Why do we automatically assume that it reflects character flaws and deficiencies in us? Maybe we are also meant for greatness, and these hardships are meant to help us develop our sensitivity, understanding, compassion, love, and humility. Maybe if some topics weren't such a taboo or if we weren't so afraid of what others would say and think, we would speak up sooner and get the help we need.

When Moshe received the Torah and the Jewish people sinned with the golden calf, Hashem commanded him, "Go down." Most people understand this as "go down and see what they are doing." But it also means "go down spiritually." Hashem is telling Moshe, "You can't be up here on such a holy level while your generation is down there sinning." Sometimes we need to "go down" to help others come up. I am no *tzadekes*, but I have been thrown down many times, and as I go up, I want to take you with me so that we can rise together.

One of my favorite ideas in the Torah is about this concept of helping others by helping yourself, an idea exemplified by Queen Esther. Esther was one of the greatest women that ever existed, one of only seven prophetesses in the whole of *Tanach*. Let's take a look at who Queen Esther really was: We know she was married to Achashverosh, forced to live with one of the most wicked men in history. But what we often forget is that she was the crème de la crème of the Jewish people, top of her class, designated by her peers as "most likely to succeed," so to speak. And just like that, it seemed that all was lost when she was taken as the wife of a *rasha*. Yet, look at what became of her! Who doesn't know about *Megillat Esther*? And the thing is, Esther herself asked that her story be written down. She wanted to make sure everyone knew how hard it was for her in the king's palace, how she saw no light at the end of the tunnel, and how much she had to sacrifice! Look at where she ended up—thanks to her, the Jewish people were saved. She wanted the story to be written down so that she may bear witness to the fact that we don't know how our lives are supposed to turn out. We may think we know, but God takes us from one place in life to another, moving us around without a clue as to the destination. And only at the end, when we get there, do we suddenly understand.

This is why the Megillah is so named, from the word *l'galot*, to reveal. We are often thrust into the dark, and we don't understand what's flying, but ultimately everything becomes revealed. Suddenly, light shines upon the situation and we understand: that's just life. The main mitzvah of Purim is *"likro hamegillah,"* to read the Megillah, teaching us that everything in life depends on how we read our lives—how we understand it, our perception of it, and the choices we make as a result.

There is a powerful idea which relates that at the time of Nechemia, most of the Jewish people had assimilated and intermarried. But Nechemia was able to rebuke the nation, and they left their wives and repented. The Torah teaches us that this was in the merit of Queen Esther and that the Jewish people continuously derived strength from her. What is the connection?

Tehillim 22, often interpreted in connection with the story of Purim, bemoans the distancing of Hashem. The psalm references Esther crying out to Hashem, "Why have You abandoned me? I see Your salvation far from me!" What happened that Esther felt a removal of Hashem's presence? This was right before Esther presented herself in front of Achashverosh to invite him and Haman to the feast she was to prepare for them. The *pasuk* says she was dressed in *"livush malchut,* royal dress," which we understand as *ruach haKodesh*. As she walked through the castle plaza, which was full of idols, she lost all *ruach haKodesh*.

Esther cries out to Hashem, "What is happening? Why are You doing this to me? I am fasting and giving my everything, approaching the king even though I haven't been called. Don't you see I'm sacrificing my life for the sake of the Jewish people? And this is how You respond?"

Hashem says to her, "Esther, My daughter! I have such big plans for you! Many generations will flourish in your merit. I want you to give strength and inspiration to all of the Jewish people, but in order to do that, I have to leave you on your own. You think I am not with you, but I am. However, you need to do this on your own in order to give strength to all of those who feel they are on their own—to support them, encourage them, and show that they can rise from their lowest lows!"

You see, the Gemara teaches, "*ze haclal, kol sh'eino mechuyav b'davar, eino motzei acherim m'yadei chovatam.*" This means that a person can only be *motzei*, fulfill someone else's obligation in a mitzvah, when he himself is obligated in the mitzvah. However, if the mitzvah is optional for me, I can perform it for myself but can't fulfill someone else's obligation through my own voluntary fulfillment. But our rabbis read this differently. *Mechuyav* can also mean obligated in punishment, as with doing something wrong. In other words, if you did not correct a wrongdoing of your own, you can't help someone who is in the midst of overcoming their own transgression. If you yourself aren't guilty of anything, then you can't relieve someone else of their guilt; you cannot understand them on the deepest of levels. Similarly, with life struggles—if a person hasn't gone through what we are going through to some degree, then how could they possibly relate to us? How can they possibly connect and empathize with our pain?

Over a series of emails I exchanged with Rabbi Y.Y. Jacobson about my life and the pain I have gone through, he told me, "*Ein chacham k'baal nisayon,* there is no person as wise as the one that has been tested." Thus, often the best empathizers—social workers, psychologists, rabbis—have experienced a profound sense of loss and despair in some way. This is the secret to Hashem's seeming abandonment of Esther. Hashem says to Esther, "I'll give you the gift of removing the Jewish people from their assimilation, but in order to do that, you need to have been in the same place willingly. You, the crème de la crème of the Jewish people, with such a lowlife gentile. And if you emerge from the situation with strength, imagine the courage you can give to the rest of the Jewish people! You need to go in there, and you must do so at your lowest, feeling My abandonment, because that's how everyone else falls into trouble. Don't be afraid; I am with you! You will fall, get up out of this mess, and you will inspire millions of Jews to do it too! You are the *ayelet hashachar*, the first ray of sun that rises after the blackness of night. Some people may not see it or recognize it, but the darkest hour is right before the dawn; and you, My daughter, Esther, have the opportunity to be the gift of dawn to so many." And so, Esther went from the highest levels of prophecy and being one with God to the lowest levels of divine desertion with Achashverosh. As we know, Esther's name is found in the Torah when it refers to Hashem hiding: "*Haster astir panai.*" Hashem makes her feel His abandonment to show that even when she doesn't feel His presence, He is still with her. This then becomes a shining example for the Jewish people, that even in the darkest and loneliest corners of life, Hashem is with us.

You know what else is beautiful about this story? The night Esther approached Achashverosh was the first night of Pesach. The Jews had fasted for three days, the last day of which was the first day of Pesach—the holiest night in the Jewish calendar; so much so, we don't even say the protective blessings in the bedtime Shema because we have such direct protection from Hashem! But you know what happens the next night, the second night of Pesach? We start counting the *omer*. In one moment, we go from the highest level to the lowest. But we immediately begin climbing back up. We count as a people, all of us together, leaning on one another and carrying each other.

In Parashat Vayeshev, in the book of *Bereshit*, the *pasuk* opens with the famous words "*Vayeshev Yaakov.*" Rashi comments that Yaakov requested to settle in tranquility, but then the whole ordeal with Yosef and his brothers happened. Rashi explains, "When the righteous wish to live at ease, Hashem says to them, 'Are not the righteous satisfied with what is stored up for them in the world to come that they wish to live at ease in this world too!'"

These words are puzzling! What was the problem with Yaakov's request that he was met with such an answer? What's the big deal? Don't we all want to sit in peace? Hadn't his life already been hard enough? Does he always have to be on the go? It's not like Yaakov's idea of sitting in peace is lying in a hammock with a piña colada in hand.

The first answer offered is that Yaakov believed that all this running away and having to work for his wives was preventing him from sitting and learning Torah. He was only asking that Hashem give him a little bit of peace and quiet so that he could be immersed in growth without constantly having to be on the move. Hashem's response comes to say, "Who decides what generates growth? Don't you see that you are meant for greatness? Once you settle physically, so too will you be settling spiritually!" In fact, the Torah says that in the future, Hashem is going to show the *tzaddikim* all the mountains they climbed, and they will be amazed. Who are we to know what bumps are needed on our path to growth? People choose comfort by default; we want to settle, we don't want to work hard, we would rather relax than work the muscles. But only Hashem knows our true potential, and He pushes us to get there, so we must hold on tight!

But it's more than that. Yaakov wanted to sit *"b'shalva,"* in tranquility. The Torah is telling us a big secret: If what you want is tranquility, let's see how you stand against the storms of life, against all the challenges and difficulties! It is the trials that really teach us tranquility. It is easy to be tranquil when nothing is triggering us. We might feel very calm hanging by the beach, but what happens when a shark attacks? What kind of panic takes over? If we can learn to stay calm when life gives us lemons, then we will have mastered the real secret to a happy life! We can take the lemons and make lemonade, and so much more! To remain connected with Hashem is to remain calm and collected through anything that comes your way.

I have been tested continually—as I like to say, a little bit of everything on the menu. I can't say I would have wanted it, but I also can't say I would choose to give it away because the pain is what makes me who I am. Like Mordechai said to Esther, *"u'mi yodeah im l'eit kazot, and who knows if for this time,"* who knows if for this moment you were created? Who knows? Only God knows! Your job is to use every moment of your life for your own sake and for the benefit of the Jewish people, but most importantly, for the sake of Hashem. I also know, even though I am no Queen Esther, in a way, I have been thrown into a pit of despair to help others climb out. I have the courage to share it and use it. And really, what is the point of any of this pain if I am not going to use it to my advantage? It will take me a lifetime to heal, but *Baruch* Hashem, I am on my journey, and I definitely hope you join me.

I've been in silent pain for so long, and while I am beginning to feel like a great weight has been lifted off my shoulders, there still remain so many questions: What if? Why didn't I? I could have… You fill in the blank. What I've come to learn is that, at the end of the day, the Master of the Universe runs our lives. The truth is we don't want to see it, but often, Hashem blinds us to many things so that we can go through the challenges our souls need to experience in order to achieve our purpose. This is the purpose of this book: to help you heal the past, prepare for the future, and fully live in the present. We can't choose most of what happens in our lives, and most of the time, we can't even choose how we feel about it at first. But we can definitely choose to gain control of our feelings, perception, and attitude. Everyone faces different God-given challenges in life. Many of us grapple endlessly with various forms of abuse, inner struggles, and toxicity. Yet, even if we don't share the same trials in life, everyone can find within themselves a pain that speaks to them, that speaks for them. We each suffer differently, but we share the human experience of pain and struggle.

These are the thoughts and inspirations that have helped me and continue to help me heal. This is what I have gained through experience, through good and bad choices in my journey. Like Queen Esther, I must choose to show up. So, come learn with me as I continue to grow and heal.

Quotable Emunahh

A famous Rebbe once said, "The greatest distance in the world is that from your head to your heart." This totally resonates with me. So often we have belief, but does it change anything in us? Does it affect our choices and behaviors? At the end of the day, what is belief and how do we get it? Is it a matter of saying it, like a magic word?

To believe is to "be living" with your faith, allowing your belief to guide your every move, to calm and soothe your heart, and to allow you to dance in the harmony of life. And though we may understand this on an intellectual level, oftentimes it's harder to accept on an emotional or spiritual level, so we pretend we don't get it intellectually either. We, as humans, have a tendency to turn emotional issues into intellectual issues. We allow the blockages in our hearts to become blockages in our minds. Our job is to allow our heads to rule over our hearts—to act according to what we understand and be smarter than our emotions. That is what it means to live a life of purpose.

The aspiration of this book is for you to learn, understand, and live by the principles and ideas of *emunah*, faith. Use these concepts on your journey toward healing and becoming a greater version of yourself. To do that, you must transport these ideas from your mind to your heart. The Rambam explains that the only way to get the heart to understand is for the brain to explain out loud, over and over again, until it penetrates and creates a crack in the stony heart—just as in the story of Rabbi Akiva, who watched as drops of water hollowed a cavity into a rock. Rav Israel Salanter used to repeat the phrase, "*ein od milevado,* there is no one else but God," for three hours a day! Recite these thoughts to yourself until they strike not one chord, but all of them; until they become an inseparable part of who you are!

For this purpose, at the end of every chapter, I will provide *Quotable Emunahh,* in which I will sum up the chapter with a short and sweet saying that pierced my heart, and hopefully yours too. Post them around your house, on your fridge, on the mirror. Read them daily, practice them, and allow them to become your mantras and the chorus playing in your head. Because the first time we say it, it's just lip-syncing. But as we chant our mantras over and over, we start to really listen until it's engraved in our hearts. Consider these quotes "post-its" for your heart: *"v'yadata hayom v'hasheivota el levavech,* and you shall know today and inscribe them in your heart." Read them, learn them, live by them.

PIN IT TO YOUR HEART!

"Like Moshe, sometimes we need to go down spiritually to help others rise up."

"There is no person as wise as one who has been tested."

"Who knows if for this moment you were created?"

CHAPTER ONE

HITTING ROCK BOTTOM

Sometimes we work hard to fix that which can't be fixed. We blame ourselves; we think if only we tried harder, were better, nicer, kinder, or tried something else. But we don't realize that sometimes we just need to get out of that situation and not keep trying to find solutions. My marriage was exactly like that; I prayed, I cried, I hoped, I toiled endlessly to make it better. But I was fooling myself; it was never going to happen. I didn't realize what was going on because so much had happened, and so much was still happening, that nothing made sense to me. But at one pivotal moment, the floodlights of truth opened up, and it came toppling over me like an avalanche, wiping out everything I had worked toward. Suddenly, all of it made sense. The truth is unforgiving, and I realized I was blaming myself for things that were beyond my control. I mean, obviously, all marriages have their problems... but this was something else, something beyond the run-of-the-mill marital issues. There was a unanimous voice as to where this marriage had to go; sometimes the right thing to do is the one that seems the hardest. I understand now why we say *mazal tov* when someone gets divorced. Because divorce is sometimes a mitzvah, a mitzvah no one wants to fulfill, but when you are doing it based on *daat* Torah, then you are making an incredible *kiddush Hashem* by making such a hard choice, which will obviously have so many extra challenges and repercussions. So a person deserves a *mazal tov* because they are choosing to do God's will, even at the hardest of times; just as someone who is facing starvation and is forced to eat pig, even though he has such a hard time bringing himself to do it, so too, you are choosing to follow God's will above all.

I remember going to one of the big therapists when everything came crashing down. I asked her, "What do I do? I have to get divorced, right?" and she said, "You are exchanging one garbage bag for another one. They are both going to be so difficult and challenging. Which one will you choose? What will you choose for your children?"

As I sit here on one more night alone, thinking about my life, crying, mourning, wondering, questioning...I think about how something's gotta give. I can't just be a victim of the world, of circumstances beyond my control, of God's will. I once saw an interview with an amazing woman whose child was lost; she had no idea where he was or what had happened to him. Interviewers kept asking her, "How do you move on? How do you live?" And she kept answering, "*lo bacharti elah nivcharti*, I did not choose, I was chosen." I too was chosen. I love the line, "With great power comes great responsibility." I realized that I can't just sit, night after night, wallowing in my pain and self-pity, crying to no purpose. I was chosen. Chosen for many things I wish I could give up, but chosen nonetheless. Therefore, I am choosing to take the high road, using the power of my pain, my voice, to give my suffering a purpose. I'm sick of playing defense; I want to be on the offense.

Yet, being chosen doesn't look pretty. We picture it as someone standing by a podium, accepting a medal, wearing a floral wreath, and being celebrated with a standing ovation. But that is certainly not how my life looks. Instead, I cry and cry and cry. Not even a pretty cry, but a profound weeping from within. And while I cry, I wonder if anyone can hear me, hoping that maybe if I cry loud enough, I can expel the pain from my life just as I expel it from my chest. But let's be honest: the pain is there, and it's not going away on its own. So, I may as well find a use for it.

So many times, questions overwhelmed my mind. My thoughts are flooded with doubt, complaints, defiance, and disappointment toward God. "Really, God?" I think to myself. "Me again? How? Why? What did I ever do to you? Can't you choose someone else? How come my life is such a tragedy? Couldn't there be any nice, enjoyable chapters? This isn't the life I dreamed of. This isn't what I signed up for. I could never even have imagined that these things could happen to me, to my children!" How often I have felt like Rivka when she said, "If this is for me, then take my life." But if I was chosen, I have no choice but to get up and keep going.

Two months before I sat down to write this book, I was in the gutter, wallowing in my own pain, ready to give up. But I'm doing better now. Today I got dressed nicely, taught, mentored, and gave to others. And slowly, slowly, I almost begin to forget. People forget; it's human nature. But I don't want to forget, at least not yet. Right now, while the wound is still open, I want to express my aching heart so that through my process of healing, you can heal with me. Our wounds can scar over together. I'm slowly settling into my new reality, even starting to get comfortable. But I want to hold on to the pain for a bit longer because pain helps you grow; it is a catalyst for the mind and soul to reach greater heights. I can't continue being the same person I've been until now. I've been hit so many times that I got used to it; I've come to expect it, and so I stay the same throughout. This time I don't want to get comfortable. This time I want to be like a phoenix: I want to rise from the ashes of my pain and be reborn with fresh detachment, awakened and inspired.

One of my favorite classes to teach—and if you were once my student, you definitely know it—is about vanilla and chocolate ice cream. Many of us are happy with chocolate ice cream, but that's only because we have never tasted vanilla. For example, even though I love chocolate candy bars, I prefer vanilla over chocolate when it comes to ice cream. I always tell my students that those who prefer chocolate ice cream are missing out by not tasting the vanilla. But then, every once in a while, there is no chocolate, and we are forced to try the vanilla. Suddenly it happens: Gan Eden, a heavenly flavor experience you never expected. In life, we often have these "Aha!" moments when we realize what we've been missing all along. But it doesn't matter what we do now; we can't ever compensate for all the lost time. I like to look my students in the eye as they realize, "Oh my gosh, I really am missing out!" Then I explain that that's our lives. No one is saying chocolate is bad, but you could also have vanilla. When you think about it, it's sad that we make peace with only ever having chocolate, that we become indifferent to vanilla. I then challenge my students by adding this thought: Isn't it sad that in the physical world, no one is ever satisfied with chocolate? We all want vanilla. Actually, forget about vanilla; we want French vanilla. We always want what we don't have; we want the best of the best. But when it comes to the spiritual and emotional world, where it really matters, we often choose to settle, to be satisfied with the chocolate that we are given. And there are even those of us who will settle for even less, for the really mediocre flavors that no one ever really wants, like pistachio or banana. Why? When did we get used to life being mediocre, to accepting less than what we truly want and letting go of our goals? I then ask my students to think about how often they've heard someone say, "I don't love my job, but it pays the bills," or, "I don't love my marriage, but at least I'm married."

All along, throughout those classes I taught, I was really just talking about myself without realizing it. I pride myself on being honest, but I was living the biggest lie. I was living in "at least mode." At least I'm married. At least he helps out. At least he celebrates my birthday. At least he buys me chocolate. Not only did I live in "at least mode," but I also convinced myself that it was actually good. I became indifferent to my own happiness, hopes, and dreams. Who needs to be happy anyway? Not all marriages are great. Even worse than that is the fact that I was in an extremely sad and difficult marriage, and I accepted it. How ashamed I am to write this, to openly admit that I had made peace with knowing I was going to be unhappy for the rest of my life. I knowingly gave up on any hope for change, choosing a marriage that was destroying me and my children. All for the sake of what? Seeming normal and fitting in? Worrying about what others would say if I gave it all up? What was I even so scared of losing? What was I trying to save? There was nothing to save. I might try to convince myself it was for the sake of my children, but it was bad for them too. They were living in a volatile environment where we were all nervous, panicked, and angry. Was I truly choosing to willingly give them the kind of childhood that I so badly wanted to escape as a child myself? Again, I am not saying that marriages need to be perfect or that someone with Mr. Banana should go and look for a Mr. Chocolate, but my personal situation was far worse. A marriage is worth fighting for; we need to look for help and go much more than the extra mile. But sometimes in life, you have to amputate a limb in order to save the whole body, and that's what the Torah teaches us: Your life comes first. And when the choice is either losing your whole self or staying alive, there is only one choice.

I needed to recognize that accepting my own tragic fate was sacrificing the happiness of my children. I was tired of living in "at least mode." But to be honest, I wasn't brave enough to do anything about it. I was too scared and too lonely. Then Hashem appeared, seemingly before me, and slapped me in the face with change. Oh boy, was it a hard slap! The pain and the trauma were overwhelming but definite; I was forced to figure out how to move on, where to go from here.

I had hit rock bottom. Actually, I had hit lower than that. I didn't want to live anymore. Not for anyone, not even for my kids. I thought that they might even be better off without me. But then

I realized, didn't God pick me to be their mother? So, who am I to decide not to be? And those beautiful, pure little souls, what did they do? How could I be responsible for adding even more pain to their lives? And they still wanted me, even though I didn't want myself. I had to be strong for them and happy. Then I thought of my students. They looked up to me. How could I disappoint them? How could I go down without a fight? But I argued with myself; I had been fighting all my life. My whole life had been a never-ending mountain climb! Well then, how could I give up before reaching the top? There would be no point to any of my suffering.

I felt like such a nebach—pathetic and weak and utterly unfit to be a role model for anyone. I had to push through to show my children and my students that I can and I will make it through the pain in my heart. And once they see my success, they will realize that they can too, and they will. I knew if I gave up, they might give up too—on God, on faith, on their lives… I didn't want them to give in to the idea that life's just not fair and to question God's treatment of their role model. I knew I had to show them differently; I had to choose life, choose God every day. I had to show them that my love of God and of life is unconditional, and that living with God in my heart means being committed to living. I thought I was a nebach, but I didn't know yet that I was going to become a source of inspiration for them.

If you have ever suffered loss, then you know that the hardest part is the sense of loss in yourself. You feel lost. Where do you go from here, and how do you move on? You weren't expecting this turn, and you don't know how to make your way back. There is nothing worse than feeling lost, insecure, and unstable. Being lost is hard. We like to know where we are, to have control of our movements in life; it gives us a sense of security. All we want is to find the place—our place—where we belong.

When a person dies, we comfort them by saying, "*HaMakom yenachem etchem,* the Place will comfort you." One of the names for Hashem is "the Place." Why? Why don't we use another name? What is so comforting about the word "Place?" Everything needs a place, even the world itself. Whenever you look for something, you can only find it if you know the place where it is kept, where it is supposed to be. Without a space in which to exist, the entire existence of the item itself is called into question. Therefore, the item may be, but the place must be. The place is a constant; it can't get lost; it needs to be permanent so that we know where we are going and where to find what we are looking for. When we refer to God, we often say, "He is in the world," but that's a misstatement. God is not in the world, our sages teach us; the world is in God. In other words, it's not that the world is the place of God, but that God is the place in which the world exists. If it were true that God is in the world, then it would make sense that we sometimes lose God because it would mean that the world is permanent and God is transient. But if God is the place, then He is permanent. We may get lost in Him, but we are always in Him, and we just need to open our eyes to find what we're looking for. So too, we comfort those in mourning by reminding them that they aren't lost; they are still within God.

See, many times life is like falling; we don't feel the bottom, so we don't realize we are being contained in space. But once you have finished falling, once you hit the base, you suddenly gain your bearings and can see where you were all along. You were in God the whole time; God is the space that contained you throughout. You just needed to land to feel His embrace. Wherever you are, whenever you fall, you are never falling into nothingness; you are simply falling into God. How comforting is that? No matter what, I'm not nowhere; I'm within Him, my all-loving, merciful Father.

Every day, we praise God in the *Pesukei D'zimra* prayers. In the opening of this praise, right in *Baruch She'amar*, we say "*baruch gozer u'mekayem*, blessed are You, God, Who decrees and sustains." Our sages ask, what kind of praise is this? I mean, it is great that God keeps His word and is strict in doing what needs to be done, but wouldn't we prefer Him to decree and not sustain? Forgive and forget, so to speak? Yet, the gift in this is huge: sometimes in life, you deserve certain difficulties; Heaven decrees particular obstacles, and you feel like you can't make it through. You don't think you'll be able to hold strong and remain standing. But "decrees and sustains" means He sustains you. Even though Hashem Himself is the author of the decree—which we need, deserve, and must experience—He is also the One Who sustains us, Who supports us through it all. He is the One who holds us up so that we are able to fight. This is why there is no letter *nun* in an opening verse of the *Ashrei* prayer. The Talmud implies that the missing *nun* stands for the word *noflim*, the fallen, and is therefore redundant because the fallen never stay fallen. As we see in the next verse, "*somech Hashem l'chol hanoflim*, Hashem supports all the fallen ones." He may decree the fall, but He also sustains the fallen.

So many times in my life, I thought I wouldn't make it through my struggles; I wanted to give up. But I have always felt His love, felt that He is sustaining me in my life, even when He was also the one hitting me. One of my favorite song lyrics goes, "If you're lost you can look and you will find me / time after time / if you fall I will catch you, I will be waiting / time after time." Many times in life we are lost—emotionally, physically, spiritually. All we need to do is look, and Hashem will allow you to find Him. He will be waiting, ready to exclaim, "I was here all along, waiting for you to reach. I'm sorry it had to be this way, but this was the only way for you to get here!" God will always catch you, so let go. I love the quote, "Sometimes you need to hit rock bottom to understand that God is the rock at the bottom." It helps me acknowledge to Hashem that, "Yes, it's painful to reach the point of rock bottom, but now I know that You, Hashem, are the rock at the bottom. Now I can trust and let go."

A few months ago, I shared a little bit of what was going on in my life with my students. One girl—it was plain on her face that she had come from a problematic home—approached me and said, "You've had such a hard life! I don't know everything, but from what you told us, I want to know…how do you not give up? How do you continue pushing ahead?" In that moment, I knew suddenly what it all was for. You. I'm pushing for you, reader. Because you cannot give up. You are going to make it. So much is waiting for you. The journey may look hard, the outlook may look bleak, and you may think you can't do it anymore, but you can. You have to, and you will. We will.

The first words Hashem ever said to Avraham were "*Lech lecha*, go for yourself." Go where? For how long? Why? As I heard from

Rabbi Jacobson, there are some destinations in life that you may only reach if you have no idea where you are going because if you knew where you were going, you might never want to get there. I feel that; it resonates with me. It is painful but empowering. How much would you resist if God was pointing you in a direction you didn't want to go, were afraid of going? It's better to just go. Go where? Well, that's the point. You don't need to know, because if you did, you wouldn't let Him take you there.

So, Hashem, I'm here. I am accepting Your command, *lech lecha,* and I'm going where You lead. You have shaken me up and spun me around so that I feel lost, alone, forgotten, and abandoned. But I've reached the edges of Your space, and I feel You more than ever. Everything is so crazy that, unless You are behind it, it just doesn't make any sense. I know now that I have hit this low, and the only way left is up. I'm ready to accept Hashem's sustenance, despite His harsh decree, and I invite you to come join me in reflecting, understanding, forgiving, healing, and becoming. I am ready to be lifted higher and higher and higher. I'm ready to lift others higher.

PIN IT TO YOUR HEART!

"Wherever you are, whenever you fall, you are simply falling within God."

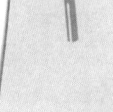

"I didn't choose; I was chosen."

"If you know where you are going, you might resist going there."

"Sometimes you need to hit rock bottom to realize God is the rock at the bottom."

CHAPTER TWO

THE DARKEST HOUR IS RIGHT BEFORE THE DAWN

There is a famous saying from our sages: "*Yeshuat Hashem k'eref ayin*, the salvation of God happens in the blink of an eye." This is generally interpreted to mean don't give up; everything can change for the good in a moment. In just one second, Hashem can turn your world around and bring salvation. But this also works the other way around: in one second, you can lose everything. In just one second, my whole life was turned upside down—like a bomb exploding next to me, taking the life I knew with it, and leaving me to suffer in the wreckage. And while the ashes of my life were smoldering and I was covered in burns and bruises, blinded by pain and losing all will to survive, I couldn't yet recognize that this was the salvation of God. I was at a low point in my life. I had been put on a break from my favorite job, my greatest source of pride and income, where I really felt I could get into the zone and put all of my heart and soul into the work. But Hashem had other plans. I was so hurt and lost. "Now what?" I asked God. "How will I carry the shame of this? Why would You take it away from me? You knew how much I loved that job." Intellectually, I understood, but emotionally it was hard. It was a huge personal blow, and I was struggling to understand. They say when it rains, it pours, and that is true for pain as well. Pain can be like an avalanche, obliterating everything that gets in its way. My avalanche had arrived, and in a short time, my life was completely and utterly obliterated. Or so I thought.

Back to my marriage: I was living in "at least mode." I also struggled with admitting there was a problem and thus struggled to emerge from my own tunnel. And whenever I thought of leaving, of starting over with someone new, I would tell myself that everyone has their issues and a different husband would just bring other problems to the table anyway. I was drowning in guilt and shame, and no matter what I did to try to make it work, nothing helped; it seemed that our marriage was destined to fail. And then what would people say? How can I fail in this too? Will I ever be able to remarry? What if I am making a huge mistake? What if, really, I'm the bad guy? What if it's all in my head? And my kids. What about them? How can they grow up without a father? Who will help me raise them? Will I raise them alone? These questions were impossible to answer, but impossible to shake off. So if you ever wonder why someone didn't get out of an irrecoverable marriage sooner, try answering all of those questions first, because that's what they were doing all that time.

While I lived in silent pain, people saw me carrying on as usual, full of high spirits and the life of the party—a giving, happy person whose goal was to inspire as many souls as she could. Yet through it all, I felt like a failure, like a fake, a hypocrite. As Rabbi Jacobson diagnosed, I felt like an impostor for not practicing what I preached. Who was I to teach others how to live if I wasn't doing it myself? I cried myself to sleep every night. Me! Happy-go-lucky Raquel. No one would've believed it if they knew. I had always been the life of the party, but the party had died down a long time ago. I had reached a point of giving up on ever being truly happy again. Every once in a while, I would try again to manifest the happiness I had surrendered. You should have seen me all of those Yom Kippurs, crying my heart out, striking out my sins as I hammered on my chest, begging Hashem to create me anew because I believed I was a defective product. I didn't know how to change on my own, so I would beg Him to take away my free will so that I could finally be good. I was tired of being what I perceived as a bad wife. I would make up my mind to work on myself again, to forgive and forget, let go and pretend. But again and again, my wishes were rejected—rejected by God and rejected by my marriage. How much can a person, especially a woman, with all of her sense and sensibility, handle? Then I would be overcome by fear of my bleak future, dreading that this is it and that I am destined to live like this forever. I couldn't live with myself anymore, not with the all-encompassing despair that threatened to take over my every will to live. What was I teaching my kids? My students?

It happens to many of us; the choices we make are not always in tune with our values and vision. If a person in our lives is trying to live their truth with no thought of the consequences to those around them, it can distort our vision of ourselves, and our reactions may go in unwanted and unexpected directions. When we don't know what is happening around us, we tend to fill in the blanks ourselves with ideas that are often so much worse than reality—second-guessing everyone, everything, and most importantly, our own selves. I had become someone I didn't want to be: angry and annoyed.

For eleven years, I kept asking Hashem how He could do this to me, how He could continue to add more and more bitterness to my life, and how He could keep making things worse. He had filled my life with so many difficult chapters that there were days I would wake up and wonder to myself, "What new disaster awaits me today?" I was blind to God's real intentions. Hashem kept setting the alarm, and I kept snoozing it. I kept choosing to photoshop my life, to portray a version of it that wasn't real, while all along Hashem was waiting for me to make the first move. I had turned a deaf ear to His wake-up calls until there was no more ignoring Him, no more denying the truth.

The wake-up call was certainly the yeshua, the salvation, I was waiting for all along. The Midrash says that when Bilaam, the most stubborn man to have ever existed, was on his way to curse the Jewish people, the angel of mercy appeared in front of him many times. But he couldn't see the angel; only his donkey could, and the donkey would stop to keep its distance from the fearful angel. Angry that his donkey suddenly refused to move, Bilaam hit the animal, unaware of the reason for his steed's disobedience. Until Hashem opened the mouth of the donkey, who cried, "Why are you hitting me? Aren't I your faithful donkey?" It was at that moment that Hashem opened Bilaam's eyes, and he saw the angel of mercy carrying a sword before him. The Midrash goes on to ask, was it really the angel of mercy, and if so, why was he carrying a sword? To all appearances, the angel would seem to be destructive, not merciful. The answer is that the angel tried to stop Bilaam many times, but Bilaam was too busy riding his donkey that he couldn't see what was in front of him.

In Judaism, the use of donkeys is a metaphor for physical matter. The Hebrew word for donkey, *chamor*, shares its root with the word *chomer*, matter. Bilaam was so comfortable on his donkey, in his physical existence, that his spirituality was suffering from lack of attention. So, to get his attention, Hashem sent an angel with a sword. You see, sometimes the mercy of God has to make its appearance in a cruel fashion. Sometimes, He needs to shake you, because if not, like the donkey, you won't move, won't budge for fear of what lies ahead. Like my mom always said, "There is no one more blind than the one who doesn't want to see, and no one more deaf than the one who doesn't want to hear." Hashem had sent me loud and vivid messages, but I was willfully deaf and blind. Until the merciful angel showed up at my door, brandishing that vicious sword.

As I mentioned in the prologue, there are many details that I am choosing not to share, but suffice it to say that suddenly, one morning in January, I found myself all alone, and the whole world fell on my shoulders. I was now completely alone, abandoned to the reality of my worst fears. Suddenly everything—and I mean everything—made sense; it had all come full circle. I remember coming home; my babies were there, and I couldn't even pack up a bag to take them out. I gave way to panic, shouting and weeping without control. I was utterly lost, frozen with pain. At that moment, and for the next few weeks, it was too much for me. The burden of the truth was now in front of me, and it was too heavy for me to carry on my own. I didn't think I could live anymore, and I didn't even want to. Yet, there was one quote from the Torah that kept crossing my mind: when Cain said to Hashem, "My sin is bigger than what I can carry!" I felt those words in the depths of my soul. "Hashem!" I cried. "What is this heavy load You have given me? I can't carry it; I will break from the weight of it!" I remember a song written in Israel about post-traumatic stress that goes, "Even if I didn't break it, I have to pay for it, let's go find someone to be mad at..."

I tried to find someone to be mad at, but not even my husband was there anymore. It was just me and my kids, and the whole world on my shoulders. To say I was experiencing trauma is an understatement. The battle was at its peak, and I was there in the firing zone, on my own, carrying four little kids. The house, the cleaning, the cooking, the childcare, the finances were all on me alone. And I had to fight through all of this while being completely broken on the inside. I felt like a widow. No, worse than a widow. At least a widow has compassion; she receives sympathy because she mourns a loving life lost through no fault other than sad circumstance. I was alone, with no help and little sympathy, and boy, was I mourning. I mourned the life I never had, mourned my own stupidity and blindness. I mourned my passivity, that I didn't get out sooner, that I worked so hard for nothing. Most of all, I mourned for my kids; I had selfishly brought children into this difficult life. I didn't want their lives to be ruined, to be forever marked by circumstances beyond their control. I mourned my husband; I was so angry at him but also so profoundly sad for him, so full of pity for him. I mourned my whole life, all of my choices, or lack thereof.

You know, when we experience trauma, we don't see much of what's in front of us. My children, my greatest joy and light in life, suddenly became an impossible weight on my heart. It's hard raising four little kids, two of whom are still babies, on your own. It began to affect my parenting; I found myself becoming more impatient and less compassionate. Minor accidents, small spills, and messes would make me react unreasonably, crying and yelling at them in response. I felt like this is how my life was going to be forever—constantly cleaning up messes. I would ask them to pick up after themselves, and my oldest daughter would yell at me with her Israeli attitude, "*Oof, ein li koach*, I have no strength." I would yell back even louder, "You have no strength? I have no strength! I didn't choose this! I didn't sign up to be a single mother!" I hadn't signed up to do it all myself—the cooking, the cleaning, paying the bills, doing pickup and drop-off—all by myself! I was supposed to have a partner; I was supposed to have help. It was too much for me; I wanted to throw in the towel and call it quits.

But I would pick myself up and keep on going because I had to. I had always taught my students that when you have to, you have to; but if you don't have to, you won't. I was annoyed with myself for ever teaching that saying in the first place. Why did I ever say those words out loud? So that I could be tested with them? But as another famed adage goes, "You have no idea how strong you are until you have no choice but to be strong." So, for weeks, I kept it all to myself. I was dying on the inside, and this time, not even smiling on the outside. It took me over a month to smile again. I thought the old me was gone forever, that I was never going to see light in my life again. But I did; and you will too.

To be honest, my kids… they saved me. The first therapist I shared my story with told me that it would be difficult with my children—very difficult—but in the long run, they would save me. She was so right; I don't even need to wait to see it in the long run. Their smiles, their mischief—it just keeps me feeling alive. Children are much more resilient than adults are; they live in the present; they aren't overwhelmed by the prospect of the future.

They feel what they feel and keep on going. My children rose to the occasion like I never could have thought or expected of them. They became little love-generating machines, as if they understood that I needed more hugs. They started to help me more, even the babies; the older ones took on responsibilities, becoming little mothers to the younger ones. They gave me hope and they gave me strength. I wanted them to have a good life, a normal life, to keep enjoying everything this world had to offer, to keep participating in anything they were part of. So, every morning I got up, put on my best face, and got them ready to go where they needed to go. Yes, there were some hard days, and many challenges presented themselves, but it was like magic: we became closer, we were there for each other, and I knew we were going to pull through no matter what, because we had to and because we wanted to.

In Parshat Shemot, Hashem sends Moshe to take the Jewish people out of Egypt. We all know how the story goes: Pharaoh gets angry and says, what? "If the Jewish slaves have time to think about freedom, let us increase their load and give them such a hard time that they won't have a moment to think of freedom." He then decrees that the Jewish slaves must do the same amount of work but without being given the materials to work with. Should they fail to do so, the Egyptians would get even more violent. Moshe felt so bad, so guilty and hopeless, that he innocently went to Hashem and asked, "*Lama har'uta,* why did You do this evil to this people?" He asked Hashem why he was sent just to give false hopes. Not only did he not accomplish any good for the Jews, but he actually caused even more distress. He wondered why he was chosen to be a messenger for such pain. Hashem was not happy with Moshe's audacity and answered, "*Atah ti'raeh,* now you will see…" Rashi interprets, "Now you will see how I take them out of Egypt, but you will not see how I bring them into Israel." There are commentaries that explain, "*Atah,* because of the now, you will see." Because it has gotten worse, you will see how it will get better, how this will be the birth of their salvation. You can't see it now, but it is precisely because of the now that it will happen. From here, our sages teach us the greatest lesson: that the darkest hour is right before the dawn. Sometimes in life, things have to get really bad before they can get good; we have to be in pain in order to heal. Like a seed, which is planted by being buried in the dark ground, it is exactly that darkness that allows it to flourish. So too, we need to go through extreme pain in order to grow. As Rabbi Zecharia Wallerstein would say on behalf of the seed, "You thought I was being buried, but I was being planted."

It's ironic, but the Jewish people were enslaved and oppressed for 210 years, and very little do we see them pray or cry out to God. Until this moment! When Pharaoh increases their workload, it is the first time during their years of slavery that they turn to God and pray. How could that be? And why did Hashem get mad at Moshe? Moshe wasn't asking for himself, but for the Jewish people; he was asking out of love and compassion for his fellow Jew. What was so wrong about his question? The answer is incredibly important to all of us. You see, in his phrasing, Moshe used the word *rah,* bad, as in, "Why did You do this evil to me?" However, what angers Hashem is Moshe's assumption that it is bad in the first place. Who is Moshe to call it bad? What gives him the right to categorize anything Hashem does as bad? Hashem responds, "I am God; nothing I do is bad. You will see now how this bad gives birth to the good. By you, Moshe, calling it bad, you are limiting your ability to grow, to understand. That is why you will not merit to enter Israel—not because I don't want you to, but because you failed to see the whole picture, thereby failing to achieve the necessary level of trust and oneness."

When we are in pain, there is only so much we can handle before we lose our positivity; only so much we can go through before we give up and become accustomed to it. Pain is supposed to wake us up and shake us up; otherwise, we get comfortable with our misfortune. It's like we sort of make peace with our pain and become indifferent to it. Take a woman struggling with infertility: for many years, she cries and prays to no end, but eventually, she becomes too numb to her pain and lives her life with no expectations of ever getting pregnant. She gives up; all of her hope has died away. A person whose family member is sick cries and prays, but as time moves on, they start picturing how life will look without their loved one. To feel the pain, over and over again, with no end, is just too much. Eventually, we just become numb to the pain and accept it.

If you were to read any book about the Holocaust, many survivors write about how, in the camps, they couldn't feel their own pain because when you're so caught up in your own survival, you don't notice pain or discomfort; you just focus on figuring out how to survive. So even life in a concentration camp becomes just another day of starving, another beating, another death march. I know it sounds crazy, but we all do this; it's human nature to adapt. The same is true for abuse victims: children beaten by their parents, people who were otherwise abused—at one point, it doesn't move them anymore; they've learned to expect it, and they are numb to it. We all disassociate from our pain; we live as passive observers of our circumstances rather than active agents.

I've been doing this all my life—growing up being bullied, struggling to find a husband, struggling to get pregnant, losing large amounts of money, losing my home to a fire, and obviously being in an impossible marriage. I just kind of got used to it all at some point. That's exactly what I call living in "at least mode," living a "one flavor" kind of life.

Nevertheless, God doesn't want us to become accustomed to our pain because then we stop hoping; we stop wanting, asking, aspiring. If we are numb to our pain, we are cut off from life. If you can't feel pain, you also can't feel pleasure, right? That is why Hashem commands us in the Torah to "choose life." To really live, you must choose to live; you must choose to be. And if we do become numb, Hashem will try to awaken us with fresh pain—pain that we are not used to. I had become numb to the pain in my life; therefore, God, in His infinite *chessed*, tried once more to wake me up and give me the opportunity to choose life by introducing pain that I'm not used to. Maybe, just maybe, this new pain will make us realize that our lives are in need of a spiritual makeover.

We open up the *selichot* prayers by saying, *"ben adam ma lecha nirdam."* The worst type of sleep is when you didn't know you were sleeping, when you are anesthetized, and suddenly you wake up and are utterly confused—what happened, where am I, and how did I get here? This happens constantly throughout the Tanach. Rachel grew accustomed to the fact that she couldn't conceive until she brought Bilhah to Yaakov. And then she cried out, "Maybe I will build myself from her!" to have Bilhah's kids be like her own. When Leah thought she was to marry Esav, she went out every day to ask her father how bad he was so that she wouldn't forget, wouldn't get used to her fate. So, we want the pain; we want to feel our sorrow. We don't like it, but we want it, we need it; our souls yearn for it. Yes, it hurts, but can we really say that it's bad? Of course not! It's the biggest gift; it allows us to recognize that we are stuck and need to get out.

It's like how statistics show that the Jews, as a people, have never existed in a country for more than sixty years without experiencing antisemitism. Why is that? Because Hashem doesn't want us to get used to the *galut*. He doesn't want us getting too comfortable, making ourselves too at home in the diaspora. God is showing us that there is something much better waiting for us. But we have to want it; we must choose it. I remember once reading that 80 percent of abused women stay in their abusive relationships. How crazy is that? In Spanish, we have a saying that goes, "Something known is better than something unknown." In other words, we settle for what we know, what we're used to. Who knows what terrible surprises the unknown may bring? But what if the unknown brings about good things? We'll never know if we don't try, if we don't embrace the pain and make it work for us.

The first commandment in the Torah says, "I am the Lord your God Who took you out of Egypt." But hold on a second—wasn't He the One Who put us in there to begin with? The answer is that we needed to have been in Egypt to understand what it is like to be taken out. That's the true meaning of "the darkest hour is right before the dawn." It needs to get really dark before we can recognize the emerging light. So don't give up, because sunrise is yet to come. When you are that low, the only way is up! As Sefaradim say in havdallah, "*Ki nafalti kamti, ki eshev bachoshech Hashem or li,* because I have fallen, I stood up; because I sat in the darkness, God was my light."

In Parashat Metzora, the Torah relates that when a person is hit with *tzora'at,* leprosy, it would strike the walls of their houses, and they would have to remove the stones and rebuild the walls to restore the home's purity. Rashi comments that it was actually a great blessing because the nations that had formerly lived in Eretz Yisrael hid their valuables inside the walls of their homes. Once B'nei Yisrael were living in those homes, a *tzora'at* infection on the walls would force them to break down the walls so that they may find and take possession of these valuables and become wealthy. Torah commentators ask that if Hashem wanted to make B'nei Yisrael wealthy, why did He do it in this fashion—by forcing them to break down the walls of their homes? Wouldn't it have been better for the Canaanite nations to hide their jewels under their beds, so that the Jews could find the hidden treasures without having to go through the trouble of knocking down their homes?

We can never fully understand Hashem's ways, but we can and must know that hidden within every difficult situation in life is a buried treasure. Sometimes in life you have to go through destruction in order to achieve reconstruction. Don't be afraid of the pain because you can't know what treasure is hidden within the struggle! One day, we will see how every bit of what appeared to be stress and aggravation was, in truth, hidden treasure from Hashem. Hopefully, we can recognize this before complete destruction occurs, but even if it does, recognize the opportunity and take it! Your dream renovation is now in your hands, so don't be stingy with your hopes and desires.

I constantly thank Hashem for saving me. He did it in a way that felt very harsh for me, but He did it nonetheless. To be honest, even though the whole experience embarrasses me to no end, I wouldn't have gotten out if He hadn't forced me out of my situation. I would have been like the Jews in the desert, who dreamed of eating simple onions in Egypt. How stupid, how pathetic that was! They literally had God-given *manna*, a perfect food that could taste like anything they wanted while providing all the nutrients they needed, and they wanted to go back to onions? Our sages teach that a prisoner cannot take himself out of prison; only the authorities can. This was God taking me out of the prison I had made for myself, my own Egypt. This year, my Pesach had a whole different meaning. I was sad and struggling, but I also knew that I was on my way to freedom. With my whole life in tatters, I see that I am being given the opportunity to do renovations on my existence, to rebuild myself, my home, and my children in ways I've always wanted but never thought I could. There was just always too much stuff to clean out, so instead, Hashem just knocked down the walls to expose the secret riches, and now I'm ready to build.

I have been listening to the song *"Idan Chadash* (A New Era)" by Duvie Shapiro on repeat for the last few months. Most days, I listen to it and smile, then burst into tears that come from deep within my soul. *Idan chadash*, a new era, a new chapter. I just want a new chapter, Hashem; a blank new page. I sing the words to the song with such hope, but then feel the pain aching in my heart. How am I still the same person? I want to be different; let me be different, Hashem. God, give me life, renew my strength and hope. Give me You!

As the song goes, "God, You can turn around the world in silence, without sounds and thunders, and if we were sleeping, we will wake up from our slumber because our Father calls us with love…" Hashem, I don't need any more big, scary noises and special effects. I know now that it is You calling me to awaken. I know You can turn my world around. Please don't let me continue in my stubbornness, like Bilaam; please humble me. I am broken, but that's the beauty: there is nothing more whole than a broken heart. "*Hinei idan chadash, ani adam chadash b'toch olam chadash. Hinei idan chadash*, behold a new era, I am a new person in a new world. Behold a new era." From now on, Hashem, I will turn to You with all my heart. From right now, and not tomorrow, I want to be connected to You. From this moment, nothing will be the same. Behold a new chapter!

PIN IT TO YOUR HEART!

"There is no one more blind than the one who doesn't want to see, and no one more deaf than the one who doesn't want to hear."

"It is not your fault, but it is your responsibility."

"When you have to, you have to; but if you don't have to, you won't."

"I thought I was being buried, but I was being planted."

"Sometimes in life, you have to go through destruction in order to achieve reconstruction."

"There is nothing more whole than a broken heart."

CHAPTER THREE

THE GIFT OF BROKENNESS

Often in my life, I have found myself asking God why He had to break me so much. This time was no different in that sense. But this time, any attempt at finding answers seemed beyond my comprehension. I was at a total loss. I felt like a failure in every aspect of my life. I'd lost the most prestigious of my jobs, and now my marriage. The pain and stress of the crisis were leading me to be a poor mother; I was constantly yelling and crying, my nerves were a wreck. I couldn't understand why Hashem was humbling me in such huge proportions. Was I that proud, that arrogant, that I needed to be taken down so many notches? Did I praise myself too much, was I too boastful of my achievements? What was He trying to tell me? Every single thing in my life just kept going wrong. I was broken and then I was broken again; brokenness led to more brokenness.

I remember having to go to the post office with my infant twins. I asked Hashem for a parking spot, thinking that my life was already so difficult that He could at least help me out with something as small as a parking spot. But that first week I got three parking tickets. I was furious. But I couldn't stop the hysterical laughter from bursting out of me. What else could go wrong? What else do You want to send me, God? But it was like God simply sneered at my frustration and said, "I'm not done with you." One day the next week, I was ready to drop-off my four kids at school, going crazy from their yelling and complaining, only to notice I had a flat tire. This couldn't be for real! And then I got sick, and I never get sick. There I was, struggling to cling to the remnants of any humanity left in me, overwhelmed emotionally, physically to unimaginable levels with four little kids and the whole world on my shoulders.. and now this? I thought! Hashem , couldn't you have picked different timing? I guess my body was protesting the exhaustion, I even had a high fever. What's more, is then my kids, who also never get sick, got sick! So there I was, stuck at home, sick as a dog, having to get up, and function, and nurse my children on my own because single mothers don't get sick days. I was so exasperated, so resentful to God for adding more and more to my plate. I was so angry that my struggles kept multiplying, with no signs of them easing any time soon. Why was He always adding more and more to my pain? Couldn't He at least make life a little easier now, or at least not make it any harder? So I started taking medication to calm my nerves. But, of course, the side effects were nausea and fatigue, making exercise an impossible task. I always prided myself on being a queen of the gym despite my hectic life, I was a star of my kickboxing class even though I was the oldest one there. Yet there I was, stopping every five minutes to catch my breath, thinking this weakness will be forever. I remember getting home one time and angrily writing in my journal, "Now this You have to take from me? Even in this area of my life You want to humble me? What do I have left, where can I have joy in my life?"

I was losing all of my motivation to live; I had no drive anymore. I couldn't even be bothered to eat chocolate anymore! I didn't care about eating at all, or studying, or teaching, and now, not even about getting to the gym. People would come up to me and ask, "Raquel, what's going on? We miss your vibe. The class is so quiet now. We miss your *simchat chaim*, your joy of life!" But my reaction was simply that they had to get used to it. This is the new Raquel. There was no going back, I had lost all desire to even try.

The first *mitzvah* ever given to the Jewish people as a whole was the *mitzvah* of *Rosh Chodesh*, sanctifying the new moon. Why was this *mitzvah* chosen to be the first? The first Rashi in the Torah famously asks, if the whole purpose of the Torah is to give us the *mitzvot*, wouldn't it make sense that the Torah opens with the first *mitzvah* of *Rosh Chodesh*? Rashi answers that Hashem wanted to start the Torah with the creation of the world so that when strangers come to claim ownership of the Land of Israel, we can testify that it belongs to God, and He can give it to whoever He wants.

Ok, we say, so why not begin the Torah with creation and then continue with *Rosh Chodesh*? We know God has perfect timing, and chronology is not a concept adhered to in the writing of the Torah, but rather the necessity of any lesson given at every single moment. So what was the need, what was the lesson? When Hashem gave us the *mitzvah* of *Rosh Chodesh*, the Torah says, "*hachodesh hazeh lachem rosh chodashim*, this month will be for you the first month." What is the significance of the words "for you?" Isn't it obvious that Hashem is talking to the Jewish people? Why does He feel the need to specify it is for them? But what if by "for you," He meant "as a gift for you, at this moment in time?"

We know that most of the Jews did not leave Egypt during the exodus. In fact, eighty percent of them didn't. They were too afraid; afraid of not living up to the expectations of God, afraid of messing up. Pharaoh may be bad, but he is still made of flesh; God is perfect, nothing skips His attention. They didn't want to risk failing in His eyes, risk losing divine inspiration. So God, in His immense kindness, said to those who did leave: look at the moon, admire it, learn from it. The moon has no light of its own; it reflects the light of the sun, it changes constantly, and once a month it even slips away into nothing. Yet, it will always return. We wait and we hope, and watch as it slowly grows from a sliver of light into its full roundness.

Hashem was showing us that in life, it is not a question of if we will fail, but rather when we will fail. You will fail; and not just once, but constantly. Don't give up, there is nothing to fear, because we are like the moon. The moon, which has no light of its own but reflects the light of the sun. The moon, which is sometimes half and sometimes whole, depending on the light. Yet the full moon is always there, hidden under shadow, you just need to look closer to see it. The potential to be all it can be is always there, it simply has its back to the sun, rejecting its source of light, thrusting itself into darkness. But if the moon turns toward the sun, it can go from nothingness to fullness in an instant. What a metaphor for our lives! All you have to do is turn toward God, the source of light in this world, to be able to reach completeness. We must let go of our limited sense of self, of our egos and our need for recognition and for control, because God is the source of everything. The more you turn your back to Him, the more that your light is diminished, but the more you turn toward Him, the more divine light is reflected on your life. We are created in the image of God, full of grace and merit, but only as long as we accept it and allow His image to reflect upon us.

The moon has to disappear in order to return as a complete image. So too, if I want to project my own light then that area is denied exposure to the infinite light of God. But when I remove my own mundane light, I open myself up to becoming a vessel for all of my potential. Sometimes in life we have to stop being in order to become. It is precisely our brokenness which gives birth to newness, to wholeness. All my life I was holding on to who I thought I was, preventing myself from becoming who I was meant to be. Therefore, I had to be broken, and not just partially, but fully broken. Let's start from zero, make ourselves as new vessels for divine light, not simply better versions of ourselves, but new versions entirely!

God gives us the gift of night when we go to sleep. Sleep is actually one-sixtieth of death. People are often scared to learn this.

Fair enough, being that close to death is scary. However, it is also empowering, because if I "died" last night, then today I am not who I was yesterday. I'm not Raquel anymore. You can call me Raquel, but I am a completely new person; I am reborn, a new creation born from death. There is no connection between who I am and who I was. It's like a fresh start! But we don't use this gift of metaphorical death correctly, therefore God gives us *Rosh Chodesh*, from the word *chadash*, newness. We must take advantage and learn from the moon; disappear and start from zero. Similarly, He gave us *Rosh Hashana*, from the word *l'shanot*, to change! Renew yourself, pick a new identity, a new existence!

The problem is that we don't want to let go of who we were the night before. We hold onto our past with all our might, too scared of moving on. The only thing keeping you from becoming who you want to become is you! You are the only obstacle getting in the way of your own achievement. So let go! Don't hold onto the past anymore, let yourself flow, take shape, and become something new. That's what I needed to do in my own life. Once humbled and shamed, my image completely lost, I now have the opportunity, the gift, to paint a new portrait of myself. I am not going to let go of that without a fight. That's what I'm doing now: rebuilding, redesigning, reimagining, recreating myself like the new moon, basking in Hashem's divine light.

The Torah teaches us that when Sarah couldn't conceive, the *pasuk* says, "Sarah was barren, she had no children." That's a bit redundant, don't you think? Of course, if a woman is barren, it means she doesn't have children. Rashi tells us that it's not simply that Sarah was temporarily barren, but that she didn't even have a womb! However, the *pasuk* says "*vaizkor*, and He remembered." This was on *Yom Hazikaron*, *Rosh Hashana*, the holy Day of Remembrance! The day the world was created. It was on that day when Hashem remembered Sarah, because just as God created the world, so too did God create Sarah. Rashi teaches that Sarah was given a womb. How is that possible? A woman can't simply grow a womb spontaneously. But Hashem can! Hashem, the Master of Creation, can perform wonders and grow a womb inside an old woman. Though Sarah may have looked the same, she wasn't the same; she had been recreated by God, with new abilities, new gifts, new possibilities. That, my friend, is the gift of the moon.

I want to share with you one of the greatest thoughts I ever had in my life. In the *berachot* of the *Shema*, we recite the words, "*hamechadesh b'tuvo b'chol yom tamid maaseh bereshit,*" He renews in His goodness, each day, continuously, the work of Creation. When we say that Hashem recreates this world every day, most of us look at this world and think that it is simply being sustained in its continuation. That's a mistake; the world is being recreated from zero. Every moment in time is completely independent, unattached to the moments that come before it or those that come after.

Have you ever seen the origins of animation? Those famous flip-books of Mickey Mouse? Mickey would be drawn on the first page and on every consecutive page the same drawing would be sketched with minimal changes. When flipping through the pages quickly, the images would seem to move, animating the drawing before the viewer's eyes. Our eyes want to believe in the fluid motion of animation, so we don't allow ourselves to notice that each of Mickey's movements belongs to its own independent page, every frame a frame of its own. You could have had Mickey saying hello on the first page, then scratching his nose in the second one. Or, you could have Mickey on the first page, and Minnie in the following. Or even Goofy, or Donald, or even a non-Disney character. The possibilities are endless because technically each and every frame is independent of the ones before and after it.

Every second is a gift, every day is an opportunity, every moment is its own individual frame. What came before this moment does not have to be continued; there is no need to dwell on whatever already happened in your life. You don't have to expand on it or feel attached to it, because the next moment is a blank page. Draw whatever you want, whatever you hope for. Draw a new life for yourself! A new opportunity! A new chapter! A new character! That's exactly what I'm going to do. I have been given the opportunity to create a new life, a new beginning. You know me as Raquel, but the only thing I'm keeping is my name, my talent, intelligence, and godliness. I'm letting go of my anger, resentment, pain, grudges, doubts, questions, and challenges. This is a new chapter, and I am a new person in a new world.

In the previous chapter, we mentioned that the salvation of God happens in the blink of an eye, that it happens when you least expect it. But I want to share another interpretation of this idea: You can never not blink. Literally, it is not humanly possible to prevent your eyes from instinctively blinking. So too the salvation of God will come. We don't know how or when, but it must come some time. We often say that Hashem provides the cure before He sends the ailment. Let that sink in for a moment. We never know what difficulty is headed our way, but we do know that we have already been given the tools to power through it. You can either blink voluntarily or you will blink by force, but you will blink. So too we can choose to bring Hashem into our lives and embrace Him, but even if we don't, God will not give up on us! He will provide the cure no matter how hard it is for us to receive it. It will come, it will happen. Hashem is described as "*Melech ozer u'moshea*, King, Helper, and Deliverer." He helps you when you help yourself by choosing to blink, and if you don't, He helps by forcing you.

Have you ever realized how many times a day we blink? We are generally unaware of it; it is simply a natural and constant bodily instinct. So too, God is constantly showering us with blessings, guiding us, and taking care of us. Like blinking, we may sometimes notice it, but most often we don't. Sometimes what we are waiting for is right in front of our eyes; we just never took notice of it! Sometimes the salvation we are waiting for is already in the process of happening, but we are blind to it. We may have decided how it should look and that image is not how God chooses to express Himself. You need to let go of your preconceived notions, let go of your decision, and allow yourself to blink. Who knows? Maybe the next time you open your eyes, you will be like Hagar, who opened her eyes and suddenly saw the spring of water before her. Like Rashi explains, "It was always there, she just couldn't see it."

My blessing for us all is that we choose to open our eyes and see what is already in front of us, waiting to be noticed. Let us open our eyes to God Who is standing right beside us, holding our hands and guiding our every step.

PIN IT TO YOUR HEART!

"It is because I have fallen, and not in spite of it, that I can become a righteous."

"Sometimes in life we have to stop being in order to become."

"It is precisely our brokenness which gives birth to newness, to wholeness."

"Salvation happens in the blink of an eye."

CHAPTER FOUR

DON'T BE AFRAID OF THE PAIN

Why do bad things happen to good people? It's a familiar question. At some point in our lives, we all wonder about it. Personally, I've asked myself that question many times. I once heard Rabbi Manis Friedman speak on the topic of the Holocaust. Often asked the question of why the Holocaust happened, Rabbi Friedman would regularly respond that he does not know. He explained that it is actually better to not have an answer because being able to provide an answer would mean being able to understand the Nazis. Answering the question would mean making sense of the Nazi mentality, and in a way, almost justifying their actions through a logical and sensible explanation. This thought struck me deeply. If I need to answer the "why" for my own pain, then in a way, I can feel that I deserve it, and then it hurts less because there is a practical explanation for it, like punishment or revenge, or whatever you want to call it. But that attitude is wrong.

We have all been conditioned to believe that everything that happens to us is directly connected to whether or not we deserve it. If we make a mistake or do something wrong, then we are horrible people who earned punishment for our actions. We even go so far as to project that state of mind onto others. How often do we meet an older single person and seek out the reasons for their still being unmarried, looking for the elements that would cause them to "deserve" their circumstances? Or, when someone loses money and our instinct is to assume it was because he was dishonest in his business dealings. I know I have certainly made similar assumptions about myself many times. When I couldn't have children for four years, I had made up my mind that it was because I was undeserving; I was being punished for something. Every month, when I realized that I was not pregnant, I would cry, thinking that my actions had made me lose a baby that was never there to begin with, simply because I had fought with my husband the night before. Not to mention the outside assumptions being tossed at me. How many times did I hear that there must be a reason that God was not giving me children? Is this really what someone could say to a woman struggling to have children? Is this how to treat a woman who was forced to resort to fertility treatments and IVF just to be able to have what comes so naturally to so many?

Who are we to assume anything about what God wants to give any individual person? Since when do we get to decide that when God gives us something "good," it's a reward, and when He gives us something "bad," it's a punishment? What a hopeless way of thinking! Like pouring salt on our own wounds. We have fallen into the trap of *kaparot*, absolution. In the back of our minds, we believe that when things go wrong it is because something in our lives needs to be atoned for. Even worse, we tell ourselves that our lives are conditional, that we will only deserve something positive if we behave in a positive manner, and vice versa. What, then, happens to those who go through the motions accordingly, only to be met with a different outcome? By that definition, they will live their lives feeling unworthy of the good yet deserving of the bad. That's quite a heavy load for a person to carry.

Let me ask you this: Do you think Sarah was barren because she didn't deserve to have children? Or because she didn't have *shalom bayit* in her marriage to Avraham? Of course not. We assume it was all part of Hashem's divine plan. So why don't we give ourselves the advantage of that mindset? We, as a people, as a society, need to change our approach and start thinking differently about our own lives. We have been trained to think that everything in this world is conditional, even God's love for us, that we get what we deserve. This is certainly not a Jewish concept. Judaism believes in the idea of unconditional love, which means it doesn't matter what you do or don't do, God will love you regardless. Like a parent who may be happy or unsatisfied with their child's behavior, but can never love them any less. Unconditional love means wanting what is best for the loved one, deriving happiness simply through making them happy, and wanting to give to them. For example, I have a bit of a penchant for shopping on AliExpress. I like to get my kids little gifts and crafting activities for when they deserve a small prize. However, I often end up giving it to them randomly, regardless of their merit, simply because I love when my kids are happy and excited. It makes me happy and excited!

Let's take it a step further. We already established that we are made in the image of God. So that means His infinite divinity and mercy are interlaced with our very existence. Can God, in His greatness and perfection, love only some parts of Himself and not others? This is why the first words we say in the morning are "*elokai neshama she'natata bi tehora hi,* God, the soul You gave me is pure." And so even if I yelled at my husband and kids yesterday, or cheated my client, or spoke *lashon hara*, my soul, my infinite oneness with Hashem, can never be affected; it remains pure and good. You cannot add to or detract from godliness; it is what it is, always perfect and complete. Next time you think you aren't good enough or not deserving of something, stop and ask yourself, who am I to decide what I don't deserve? I don't have to be deserving, because God is not giving to me. He is giving to the parts of Himself within me!

Many times, in my classes on prayer, my students ask me, "But what if I don't deserve it?" I always answer that, first of all, who are you to think you deserve anything to begin with? What a chutzpah to think you can ever deserve anything from God. As if, in some way, you have provided Hashem with something that would warrant any kind of compensation from Him. When will you ever be able to repay Him for the kindnesses that He has done for you? Try compensating Him for just one of your eyes—you would never be able to. So how can you think you will ever reach a place of deserving anything? That's the beauty of prayer. You will never deserve Hashem's gratification of your prayers, but you don't need to! God loves you and He wants you to be happy. Once you understand this element of divine love, everything in your life will change! Because if you think that God is out to get you and that every bad thing that happens to you is a punishment, then you are constantly waiting for your next obstacle. If behaving wrongfully deserves penance, and we are imperfect humans who mess up all the time, then obviously we are constantly one misstep away from another punishment. However, if I firmly believe that God wants me to be truly happy, then everything in my life is tailored to that end goal, and therefore even the challenges may be embraced with positivity and appreciation. When you think about it, every relationship is built on giving and taking. Yet, not so with God. With God, we can only take; we have nothing to offer Him. How then can we have a stable relationship with God if it is so unbalanced in this sense?

The great Rav Dessler teaches that we are all either givers or takers, and if sometimes we are forced to do the opposite, even then it is a reflection of our choices. The takers will give in order to continue taking—like giving a gift to get one in return, and the givers will take as a way of giving—like accepting a gift to make the gift-giver happy. The only way to give to God is by taking, specifically, to be happy with what He gives to us. And that means accepting the suffering He sends you, too. Although to be honest, if you are happy with everything that God gives you, good and bad, then is it even suffering? Your perspective changes its very essence.

I remember when I went to Rav Yaakov Hillel for a blessing to get married. I asked him if there was a *segula* I could perform. In response, he asked, "Have you done the greatest *segula* of all?" I looked at him with curiosity, and he explained, "Being happy." My immediate reaction was that of course I'm happy. But then I realized, no, not really, I'm not happy with my state of being. I'm not happy with what I have been given in my life. In a way, I realized, I was rejecting Hashem's gifts. The more we can understand God's absolute and infinite love for us, the more that we will be able to be happy with our lot in life. Only then can we transform the pain into an opportunity for joy.

Here's what we've established so far: we aren't deserving, we could never be deserving, but it doesn't really matter because God's love is unconditional. Maybe that's why Yitzchak loved Esav. Yitzchak wasn't blind to Esav's faults, he wasn't playing dumb, so how did he not notice his son's wickedness? The *Midrash* explains that during *Akeidat Yitzchak*, when Yitzchak was on the altar to be sacrificed by his father, an angel shed a tear that left him nearly blind. Not physically blind, but blind to the world as it appears to be in reality. In other words, Yitzchak saw the world for what it could be, not what it was. He only saw the potential, not the reality. Esav could have been great, his spirit was divine like anyone else's, and so Yitzchak was able to see his son's potential capacity for good. Imagine if we were to see ourselves in that way! We would undoubtedly feel considerably more love and compassion for ourselves and for others. More importantly, we would more easily recognize God's infinite love for us.

Let's go back and flip the script for a moment and say that bad things don't happen to good people. Nothing that happens to us is really bad because it all comes from love. Things don't happen to us; they happen for us. So now our question is: What does God want me to learn from this? How can I grow from this? Let's reframe our original question and focus on defining the word "bad." How do we categorize something as being less or more bad? To do that we need to think about what actually constitutes "bad" in our minds, and it is usually one ingredient: pain. The more pain something causes, the more we attribute to it a negative connotation. For example, when a young person dies, we consider it to be worse than when an old person dies, right? Because a young death is unexpected, it is sadder and more painful, so it is worse in our minds. What if the young person was sick, in terrible constant pain? Suddenly, it's not quite so bad, because they are no longer suffering; their pain has ended. We've trained ourselves to connect "pain" with "bad." If bad things happen to good people, and "bad" is synonymous with "pain," then the question is altogether irrelevant to our discussion because everyone experiences some kind of pain in their lives. So, it's not that bad things happen to specifically good people; they happen to everyone.

But if we go even deeper and really analyze this concept, then we need to address why we're asking in the first place. If we are asking, it is because we want answers, because we believe God is good and loves us, so we want to understand why He would make us suffer. So really, we are trying to make sense of it because we want to keep our positive image of God intact. So, what is good, what is bad, and why is there pain? Good and bad have nothing to do with our experience or feelings. If I came into this world to be godly, then by definition, "good" is everything that brings me closer to God, and "bad" is everything that distances me from Him. Therefore, it has nothing to do with the pain of our struggles, but rather their spiritual outcome and consequence. But is all pain bad? Isn't there any pain you want, you need, you appreciate? Giving birth is painful, but it results in good. Having a root canal is painful, but you wouldn't skip it because ultimately it is for your own good. Sometimes pain is simply an expression of positive things. Like when your body aches after a great workout. Pain can be a sign of the bigger picture. When you think about it, why is cancer such a terrible illness? Because the symptoms are delayed; a person suffering from cancer doesn't necessarily feel the initial stages of cancer. If it is detected early, maybe something can be done. But by the time it hurts, it's already too late. Wouldn't we prefer the discomfort of the symptoms to appear earlier so that we can know something is wrong in our body and treat it?

So maybe we could say that only unnecessary pain is bad. But how do we know if our pain is necessary or not? Maybe its role hasn't been revealed yet. Imagine you are watching a movie, and in the middle of it someone comes in and starts asking questions about the end. Wouldn't that be super annoying? They can't expect you to know the end if you haven't yet gotten that far. And aren't we all kind of like that with life? We are always in the middle of the movie. Each one of our lives is just a short chapter in the eternal book of the universe. How can we possibly expect to understand all the answers now when there is still so much more to be revealed? We live in the generation of Netflix, where you can binge-watch an entire show in a short time or even skip every episode and get straight to the finale. I remember when I was younger and used to watch actual television, I had to wait an entire week for the follow-up episode of my favorite shows, and I had to watch them in order. Now you can watch endless reruns in whatever order you choose. You can know who won without having even watched the game. But is it fair to do that to yourself? To get to the end of something without following the process? Would you even enjoy watching the game if you already knew who won? Yet that's how we expect to live our lives. We are so desperate for temporal pleasure that we reject the opportunity to embrace the completion. We want to skip to the end without watching the process and appreciating the outcome.

The problem is not the pain. Pain is actually a great gift, a great necessity in our lives. Pain is the mechanism that creates and offers us the gift of choice, because if all good is pleasurable and all bad is painful, then who would ever choose bad? Therefore, good also must be painful at times. In *Pirkei Avot*, it is written, "*l'fum tzara agra,* according to the pain is the reward." The more pain you have to overcome, the more pleasure you gain. Part of the reward is the pleasure of overcoming the pain. In that case, maybe "bad" means pain with no purpose. But we have no way of knowing if and when pain has no purpose because we have no way of knowing the end. Having *emunah* means understanding that God has a purpose in everything. Yet, even though everything God does is exact and for a reason, the fact that we don't know the reason doesn't mean we can't find our own purpose and use for it. If I understand that God is in control, and has a purpose in everything He does, then I too can choose to find a purpose for it. I can now create a purpose for my pain. It doesn't really matter why God is giving me what He is giving me or whether or not I can see His purpose; our job is to find purpose in everything. Knowing that everything has a purpose in this world means we can label it to fit a need, and therefore what matters most is how you choose to designate each label to its purpose. In other words, I don't need to understand the "why" at all, I simply need to accept that there is a "why" so that I can navigate the circumstances. And maybe the purpose will be revealed at the end.

Try to think about the last hardship you experienced in your life. Was it painful? When it was over, were you able to recognize the reason for it to begin with? If so, did that make you feel better about your experience? Or does the pain of the experience still linger? Of course, just because you gain an understanding of your pain doesn't make the pain disappear. It simply allows you to obtain enough perspective to strengthen you enough to overcome it. Now think about a challenge you are currently experiencing in your life. If you were to know the "why," would it make the process any less painful? Of course not, it will still hurt. You don't need to understand the "why" to know there is a "why." Believing in Hashem means knowing He is the "why." The beauty of *emunah* is knowing that God is running my life with love, that He has my best interests at heart, and the reasons for how He runs it are irrelevant to me.

By embracing this idea, I have become empowered to write my own story and to decide where my pain will guide me. Pain is a must, but suffering is self-inflicted. We all experience pain, but we can choose to suffer from the pain or choose to embrace it. We can decide to accept the magical empowerment of pain and welcome what it can generate within us.

One of my favorite stories was told by Rabbi Wallerstein:

One time, God appeared to a man in a dream and said, "Tomorrow when you go out into the woods you will see a huge stone, I want you to push it."

"Why?" asked the man.

"Don't worry," answered God. "There is no need to know the reason. Just go out every day and push it."

So, the next day the man went out to the woods, found the stone, and pushed it. He did this every day until one day the *satan* showed up and started laughing in his face.

"Don't you know that you are Heaven's entertainment?" the *satan* jeered at the man. "I mean, you must know how stupid you look pushing that stone every day. You're not accomplishing anything; you can't even move it!"

The man was saddened by the *satan's* words and offended by their implication.

"Is God really just making fun of me?" he wondered to himself.

So, the next day, instead of pushing the stone as God commanded, the man refused to do it.

"Go find someone else for your entertainment," he told God. "I'm not going to make a fool of myself anymore."

God asked him what he meant by that, what caused his change of heart. The man replied, "I know you only want to make fun of me. Why else would you ask me to go outside and push a stone I can't even move?"

God answered, "I didn't ask you to move the stone. I only told you to push it."

"What is the point of pushing a stone I can't move?" demanded the man.

God told him that the point doesn't matter, only to go out and do as he was asked. Confused, the man continued to go out and push the stone every day.

One day, the man went down to the village and found a woman shouting for help.

"My husband! My husband!" she cried. "Please, help him!"

The man ran to help and found her husband stuck under a car.

"We need more help!" she exclaimed. "We need more people to lift the car so we can get him out from underneath."

But the man told her not to worry, he has been training his strength and can help.

"I'm going to lift up the car on the count of three," he told her. "You just pull your husband out!"

DON'T BE AFRAID OF THE PAIN

And so, with a great effort, he managed to lift the car, and the woman was able to pull her husband out from underneath. Once all was calm, the woman came to thank him for saving her husband.

"How did you do it?" she marveled at the man. "How were you able to lift a car on your own? How are you so strong?"

The man humbly replied, "It seems that all of the time I was pushing that stone it was so that I could strengthen my muscles to be able to lift up this car."

Friends, we all push many stones in our lives, and we spend so much time asking what the point is. When really, it's simple: God is making us stronger, training us, so that one day we will be able to lift all the obstacles that come our way. I've been pushing stones my whole life. To be honest, at times it felt I was pushing mountains, not stones. I get it now. All these years of pushing that stone are so that I can help lift you up, pull you out from under the weight of your struggles. I've been training my whole life for this, learning to pick myself up after a fall, building resilience and strength, collecting inspiration so that I may inspire. After seemingly endless years of pushing that stone, I am finally strong enough.

It's incredible to me that I am writing this just five short months after the biggest tragedy of my life. But as it says, "*atem nitzavim hayom kulchem,* you are standing here today." And indeed, I am, all of me, stronger than ever, and working through my wounds; choosing to share some of what I've learned with you so that we can heal together.

In the next chapter, I will share some of the mountains I had to push, on the tops of which I am proudly standing today. Someone very wise once said, "Life is a climb but the view is amazing!" I may not know the "why" behind my stone, but I have chosen to create a lot of purpose from it. It's rough, recalling all of my pain, remembering the hardest moments of my life. But the Jewish people don't choose to remember for the sake of never letting go but rather for the sake of letting God in, for the sake of learning and growing. I'm not remembering so that I can hold tight to grudges or to have revenge. I remember so that I may let God in and learn and grow.

PIN IT TO YOUR HEART!

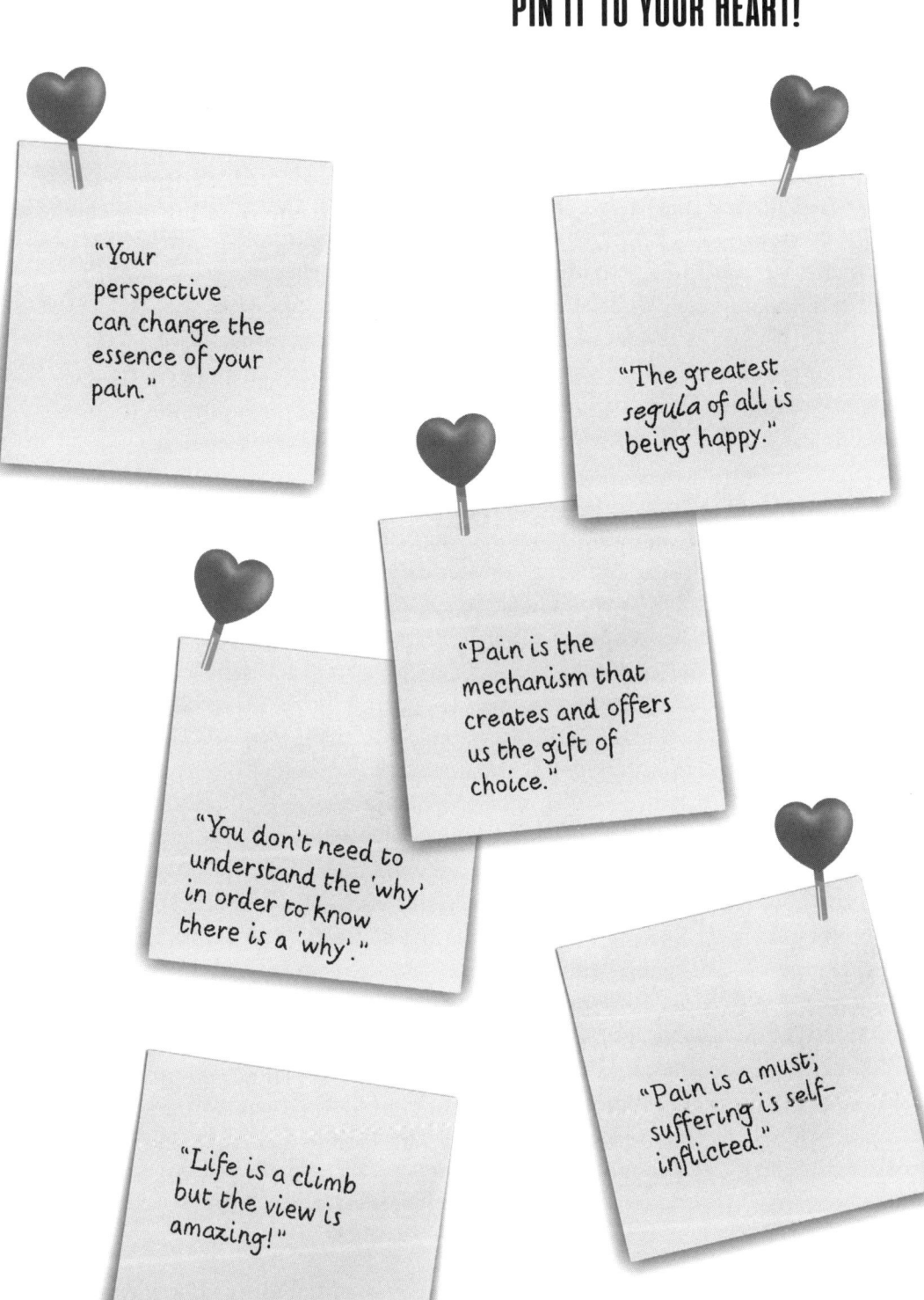

"Your perspective can change the essence of your pain."

"The greatest *segula* of all is being happy."

"Pain is the mechanism that creates and offers us the gift of choice."

"You don't need to understand the 'why' in order to know there is a 'why'."

"Pain is a must; suffering is self-inflicted."

"Life is a climb but the view is amazing!"

CHAPTER FIVE

MY INHERITANCE DOESN'T HAVE TO BE MY LEGACY

When Yaakov wanted to reveal the end of days to his children in *Parashat Vayechi*, Hashem took away his prophecy so that he couldn't. I always wondered why. Wouldn't it be easier to go through life if you knew there was a deadline coming up? As hard as it would be to reconcile the end of time, if you know there is an end to it then you are able to resist the pain, don't you think? Yet, I've come to realize, sometimes the pain is so great that you can't imagine pushing through it for even one more minute. All you can do is survive the moment as best as you can for that next minute, and that way you keep going. The Torah teaches us that we should wait for Moshiach every moment of our lives, that we need to live as if at any given moment it can all fade away and salvation will arrive. Why is this so important? Because sometimes in life it's the only thing that keeps you going, that gives you the faith to hold on.

I have always looked forward to these moments in my life because I understand that if I keep strong right here, right now, then maybe the next minute will be different, maybe it will be easier. I have often been disappointed in that sense, but I still look forward to the future, I still wait for my personal and our communal Moshiach and redemption at every turn. The problem is, that while I look forward, I am not looking backward to my pain. I choose not to dwell on it, but in doing so, I never realized that I was also choosing not to heal it. I thought that if I didn't give it any attention, it would just fade away. They say that time heals, but I don't think that's true. I believe we must confront our sufferings, accept them, and even embrace them, in order to resolve them. In Hebrew, the word for peace, *shalom*, is derived from the same root as the word *l'hashlim*, to complete. Only when we make peace with our struggles can we start to feel our lives are whole.

Picture a pilot flying a plane. Suddenly, the co-pilot sees a red light flashing and worriedly points it out to the pilot. The pilot, not knowing what the flashing light means but knowing that it can't be good, doesn't know what to do. So, he smashes the light until it breaks and the flashing stops. He turns proudly to his co-pilot and says, "Problem solved!" You can only imagine what the co-pilot would think in that moment—this guy must be crazy; he's certainly negligent. The plane is still malfunctioning in some way. He didn't actually solve anything. We all kind of do that, though. We turn off our emergency lights; we bury our feelings and just keep going, telling ourselves that if we aren't aware of the urgency, then it is not urgent, right? If we don't take notice of the problem, then there is no problem to fix. How careless of us to treat ourselves in such a way. And all for nothing, because the problems won't go away; they will always come back to haunt us.

I remember one time, there was severe water damage in my house, and we couldn't find the source of the leak. We kept on repainting and doing little spot treatments here and there. But the water kept leaking. Finally, we brought in an expert who explained that the water needs an outlet through which it can flow, and if we don't fix the root of the problem, the water will keep leaking into other areas and continue to cause serious damage. The same goes for our emotions. We can't just paint over the ugly parts of our lives; the problem will find other places to show up. We need to get to the root of it and fix it. Only once we have fixed the leak can we then start to fix the damaged walls of our lives.

The Torah teaches that you may not judge a person until you have been in their place. I'm sure many of us tell ourselves that we have been in a similar situation, or that the same thing happened to us, or that everyone's parents were like this, etc. But that's not what the Torah means to teach us. We've all journeyed across different routes to arrive where we are; we've all had to overcome different obstacles, and we were all shaped by different experiences. Our lives feel different from others' because we are formed emotionally, spiritually, and physically unique from one another. We can never truly understand what a person has been through, how it affected them, or the choices they made. Yet, we are still so quick to judge others! We aren't sensitive to the sensitivities of others, and we should be. At the end of the day, what makes a person who they are is the series of experiences they have lived and the choices they made based on those experiences.

Early on in my life, I decided that I wasn't good enough, that no one was there for me, that I would never keep up with everyone. I was convinced that I was selfish, ugly, unwanted... At the time, I had no clue how much that would affect me throughout my life and how it would affect future choices. And it did; it affected my work, my marriage, my motherhood. How often I felt like a failure, simply because I told myself I was a failure. I know better now. So why don't I just let go? But what am I letting go of anyway? Did I have the ability to understand what I was holding onto back then, what I was choosing to believe? These thoughts shaped my life. How can I just let go of thirty-seven years of trauma, of misunderstanding myself and the world? Is there a magic switch that I can flip; some fairy dust to make me forget? As an adult, do I have all of the tools? This isn't like Lego or a puzzle which takes so long to build and so little time to break down. It can only be done step by step. The first thing we need to do is find the leak, find the root of the problem, and then you can fix it.

Rabbi Jacobson often relates that science is finding evidence that trauma can be passed down through genetics. This creates a potentially damaging cycle through generations which needs to be broken. When I was young, as probably most children do, I often didn't think the nicest things about my parents. I resented them, felt very hurt by them and plenty of other thoughts which I'm sure crosses the minds of most kids now and then. I told myself I would never be like them. Yet, now that I am a parent, I have the ability to understand that we do many things we don't necessarily want to do as parents because we function on reflex and impulsivity. If I don't heal this generational trauma, then it will only get worse and eventually transfer down to yet another generation. I have decided to break the difficult cycle that I inherited because I have to be different for my kids. We have all been conditioned in some way, either by others or by our own selves, to respond and act in certain ways. I try not to judge because I have seen in myself how we can often act in ways so far from how we would like to act, of how we promised we would never become. Many times we feel disappointed and ashamed, and end up asking the questions where did this come from? How did I end up acting like that? Therefore, I try to remind myself to act with compassion and understanding, to be very patient with others and with myself. We need to go back and change the root of our impulses; it's up to each one of us to recognize the cycle and to break the pattern. But it's not easy work.

I would like to offer a small disclaimer before we continue. As I go deeper into the details of my own life experience, I want to make it very clear to my readers that it is not my purpose to hurt anyone through my sharing. I am not out to seek revenge or cause anyone pain. It is important that you understand the root of my internal wounds, how they spread and caused residual damage, but it is certainly not my goal to bring anyone down in the process.

For that reason, I am choosing not to give too detailed an account of what happened. My aim is to understand those who caused me pain, to have compassion for them so that I may have compassion for myself and change the narration of my past to generate a different present and future. I'm shaking as I write this. For the first time since I sat down to write, the words aren't flowing. I am frozen. How much do I share? What do I share? It's all so personal, so complicated. But here we go.

I used to blame others for many of the bad things that happened to me. Lately, I have come to the realization that the real problems in life don't necessarily stem from what happens to us, but rather the decisions that we make as a result. How does it affect our perception of the world around us? It's not the problem as such, but the problem we have with the problem. I am a big believer in the phrase "hurt people hurt people," not as a way of excusing such behavior, but rather as a way of understanding it. Those who have been hurt will often go on to hurt others. It's hard not to; your sense of self has been skewed. You want to feel the power that was taken from you even if it means it is misdirected. We do what we know; and if what you know is hurt, then that's what you are going to emulate. Many of us grow up thinking or hoping that we are going to be better, different, from what we see around us, but we never think about how much work it takes to break a pattern, to change years of reinforced behavior, even if we despise that behavior to begin with. For me the major lesson of "hurt people hurt people" is that the people we are hurting the most is ourselves! Whatever we don't heal comes back to haunt us. It works against us and sabotages any option and choice for happiness and healing.

Rav Yisrael Salanter said that it takes an entire lifetime to change a single character trait. It's easier to just stick to that which is known to us, where at least we find security and comfort, even if it's hurtful. Rabbi Dessler's book, *Strive for Truth*, discusses how a person can get to a point where he knowingly gives up his free will because he has chosen incorrectly so many times that his behavior has become automatic. It's easy to exercise free will when you decide to take up smoking cigarettes, but how hard is it to harness that free will when you decide to quit after smoking two packs a day for two decades? Sure, free will exists, but sometimes it is more of a theory than a practice. It takes incredible amounts of self-control, awareness, and introspection to stop this kind of behavior, to shift one's personality even a little bit. So much, in fact, that the Torah teaches us we can't cancel out a character trait entirely; we can redirect it to our benefit, but to get rid of it altogether is impossible.

Let me expand, as I said I've come to understand that "hurt people hurt people" often actually refers to the hurt people hurting themselves. No one can hurt a person more than he can hurt himself. After we are hurt by others, we start making poor choices, we no longer love ourselves, we lose our confidence and can't see that there is a way to be better. Nothing is more damaging to the self than hurting others simply because we were hurt. There is no pain like knowing you are guilty of doing to others the same harm that was done to you when you swore to yourself you would be different. Yet, here you are, repeating the same behavior that caused you so much hurt.

Both of my parents grew up in homes where they experienced incredible amounts of trauma and hardship, where they had to work really hard to get anything or anywhere in life. Homes where discipline was of utmost importance, and everything was fair game in showing who was boss. There were a lot of differences back then; people didn't have the skills we have now, life was harder, and people were tougher. But that also projected into how they behaved toward others, especially from the culture they were coming from. Back then, people confused respect with fear, consequences with punishment, and discipline with control. It is so interesting to realize that the way we teach Torah and try to pass it on to our children has changed tremendously. The definition of *yirat Shamayim* isn't perceived in the same way anymore. *Yirat Shamayim* that is taught as "God will punish you, He is out there to get you and He is always judging you" is not received well anymore; actually, it has brought about a huge "rebellion" among many of the Jewish people. We all want to hold onto the idea of an all-loving God; He is our Father who loves us, so where did that get lost in the way it was often passed on in *chinuch*? We understand better now and realize that real "fear of God" comes from a place of love and admiration! When I realize that a relationship is so valuable to me that I'm afraid of doing something that would jeopardize that relationship, this is true fear of God. This is what I have come to understand with all my children; it is all about building a relationship, and most important, building them up so that they will have respect and love for themselves. *Chinuch* has changed tremendously over the years because we have realized that our children need recognition, validation, and so much love; and that if we raise them to think they are great, wonderful, royal, able, and powerful, that's exactly what they will become. I recognize that both of my parents wanted to give us what they never had, that they worked extra hard to please us in any way they could, providing us with material things and experiences. A child bases all of his self-love and self-esteem on what his parents think of him; after all, they are his heroes! There is nothing more important for a child than to feel wanted, accepted, and loved in their eyes. To be honest, this has been one of the greatest desires of my life, to make my parents love me, to make them proud, to have them accept me. The challenge is that not always what we feel are we able to express, and many times there is a disconnect between the thought and intention and the action. As an adult, I know better now and understand better now, even though my inner child hasn't healed completely; maybe it is a lifelong effort and journey. But as a child, I couldn't see it, I couldn't feel it, and I couldn't understand it. When we don't get the love and value we need as children, specifically from our parents, we spend the rest of our lives looking for it anywhere we can. Obviously, we must build it from the inside. The challenge is that we don't know how; we weren't given the tools and directions, so how can we just practice self-love on our own without being sure how to love? And who can love you if those who were closest to you had such a "hard time" with you?

I've grown and they have grown; life always tries to guide us and educate us, and as long as "the candle of our soul is lit," there is still time to fix. What was doesn't need to be what is; we have choices, and we must believe we can change. If Hashem never gives up on us and there is always a door open for repentance, then we should never give up on each other.

So, going back, I see now that my parents worked hard to show us their love in any way they could. Looking back, I don't think they were ever taught any of the common love languages, and so, therefore, they just didn't know how to express their love. At least that is how I feel now. Part of their frustration toward their children, I'm sure, was that they didn't feel they received the recognition or gratitude that they thought they deserved or wanted. I mean, we were children; we didn't necessarily have the emotional ability to recognize or appreciate the complexities driving our parents' behaviors. Children can't always see the intention because they get lost in the action. Now we can try and hope to see and understand that everything they did was for our benefit, that it was all for the sake of building us up into responsible and strong individuals. At the time, however, it wasn't quite as obvious to us. My parents both had an understanding that life wasn't easy, and if you were going to face challenges in life, then you have to be prepared. That is what drove their parenting; they were raising soldiers to be prepared for battle at any moment. Their methods may not have been ideal, but I certainly owe them much of my strength and many of my achievements. My parents taught me the meaning of hard work, of not giving up, of pushing through no matter what circumstances come your way. I've survived everything that has come my way because I learned the skills of survival in my parents' home. The results of their parenting gave me the desire and the drive to push through life's trickier paths, to show up, keep fighting and not give up. My parents were very strict, and in our family, it meant we had to be the best at everything. If there is one similar trait that I see in all of my siblings, it is that we all push ourselves; we are not conformists, we yearn for greatness, and we model the resilience, discipline, and constancy that were ingrained in us growing up. Just as Hashem led the Jewish people into generations of terrible slavery in Egypt in order that they would be molded by the experience, so too my siblings and I were molded by our parents' training.

Recently, my therapist asked me to write about my parents, and I realized there was so much negativity built up inside of me.

But I also realized that just as they didn't see me, I didn't see them either. — I mentioned before how the more we lose respect for ourselves, the more we will continue to hurt ourselves and others around us. Sadly, that's exactly what happens when we hurt others. We feel bad on the inside and feel that we need to unload our emotional garbage somewhere. Sometimes, we dump it on ourselves, but many times, we dump it on others. Sadly, a favorite dumping ground for many of us is our kids. After all, they are right there and neither capable nor brave enough to confront us about it. We become critical, unforgiving, and unaccepting of the needs and feelings of others in the face of our own needs and feelings. We often think of life being like a seesaw, that in order to rise up, we must push others down. Understanding this is the key to compassion.

I can't explain how it felt to grow up feeling like I was hardly enough, hardly wanted, or understood, or even hardly ever really seen. It's an "if you know, you know" kind of experience. I remember how all throughout high school, I just wanted to get to my graduation so that my parents could see my successes and be proud. In my school in Panama, students were granted medals at graduation, and I knew I was going to receive many. In fact, as far as I know, I received the most medals of any one student in the school's history. I was smart, I won every contest I took part in, I was in the national math Olympics, the national Bible contest, you name it. But I didn't feel smart. I spent much of tenth and eleventh grade doing IQ tests to prove to myself that I was smart. I graduated with the highest honors but never even applied to college because I thought I would fail. Colleges sent me invitations to apply, but I wouldn't even let myself dream about it. I was such a failure in my eyes. I had such low self-esteem that I envisioned my future as a *paletero*, a street vendor, selling ice popsicles in the street. These feelings accompanied me throughout my life. Yet, if I had had more self-esteem in my youth, more confidence in myself, I would have never gotten to where I did.

I grew up in a great community in Panama; it was more like a huge family. Everyone knew everyone, everyone helped everyone; really, Panama is one of a kind in closeness, kindness, community, connection. But there were some things that back then, at least for many of us, felt like big no-nos. One of those taboos was being overweight, which was especially bad for my family as we were all chubby, even fat or obese. So much of my life I resented growing up there; it was beyond difficult. Today, I'm grateful and proud. No community is perfect—there will always be social norms and standards. Everyone wants the best of the best in every area of life, but to grow up in Panama for me has meant that I have a huge team cheering for me, caring for me. Literally, I wouldn't have survived so many of the difficulties I've had if it wasn't for the support and love that was given to me from my Panama family. Recently, through all of these challenges, so many reached out—my friends from high school whom I haven't spoken with in so many years since I left almost twenty years ago. I can't say how much it warmed my heart; the support, the help, my students from there—no words, thank you. Isn't that the definition of a family? We may have some internal issues, but we always have each other's back.

But growing up there for someone like me, really for all of my siblings, was incredibly difficult. We always felt like outsiders, we didn't belong, and sadly many times we didn't feel welcomed. I remember being bullied by kids on the bus, not having friends, not being picked for a sports team, not being invited to come over and play, so I barely had a social life. As time went on, the weight became a big issue in my house, since "obviously" you can't get married if you don't look good. I couldn't be seen eating, and I often had to hide. It was so bad that I used to hide close to the freezer and eat my feelings when no one was looking. Despite that, I tried hard to lose weight, but it didn't matter what I did; my weight wouldn't go down. I became addicted to exercising out of a compulsion to burn all the calories I ever consumed. But nothing would change, so it increasingly became a focal point in my life.

Ever since I can remember, I had been told that I'm too fat, too ugly, that no one will want to marry me. All that in addition to the fact that I had "bad character" and was a problematic child—so who would want me? I started believing it; I internalized it. At one point in my life, I was living in Mexico and was dating a religious guy who suffered from depression. He actually wanted to marry me, but I realized that I didn't want to marry him. I was told by someone very close to me at the time, "You know, Raquel, you aren't so pretty, so if someone wants you, you should take it. Who knows if someone else will ever come along." I didn't marry him, but the sentiment stayed in my heart. Throughout the many years that I wanted to get out of my marriage, I kept telling myself that no one else would want me anyway, so I may as well stay. I had grown up thinking I would never be deserving of love, that I should just take whatever comes my way and be satisfied with whatever I can get because I'm not good enough to aspire for anything better.

When I was thirteen years old, I had a major seizure. I was playing piano when I bit my tongue and woke up hours later in the hospital. The doctors said they didn't know why it happened, but chances were that I would continue to have them throughout my life. I remember that as a little kid I thought I was going to die. I lost all will to go on living, gained thirty pounds in six months, and it changed the way I looked forever. When I was fifteen years old, having won the national Bible contest, I got to go to Israel, and out of nowhere I became "Miss Popular" on that trip. I suddenly realized that I can be fun and liked and wanted by others. So, at 15, things started getting better for me. I had more friends, I was popular and fun…but inside I was still full of pain, easily built up, more easily broken down, and in desperate need of everyone's validation. Later, whenever I would go to a matchmaker, I would tell her to make sure she told the guy that I'm on the heavier side because if he says no to me after a date, I will know it was because of that, so I would rather he knew that I was heavy to begin with. I was so obsessed with my appearance that I wasn't actually living; this kind of life wasn't living. But that's how it was for many years, until I was able to finally let go and have a normal life.

Before I started dating my husband, I had this constant worry in my head: "Who else would want you? It's obvious that you are going to get someone with baggage, I mean look at all of the baggage you have…" We got married, and I didn't believe him when he told me I'm beautiful. It took me many years to realize that weight has nothing to do with beauty—I am healthy, built strong, I exercise, I am not the images I see in my mind; and there is so much more to me than my appearance. But for as long as I could remember, that's what defined me. Not my talents, or intelligence, or my great, funny personality. I was just fat, and fat and rejection go hand in hand. It was only when I began to become religious that I understood that I was made in the image of God. The healthier I got, the more my self-esteem grew, the more feminine I felt, and the happier I became with who I was.

Nowadays, I am often praised for how well I put myself together, for my respectable yet feminine appearance. But it took years to get here, and it only happened because I finally found that my beauty lies in my soul; it lies in the fact that I am made in the image of God and therefore must represent Him by dressing the part. Even today, this is an issue that I constantly have to work on; I have to focus on being balanced and healthy, knowing my worth, knowing my body's worth. I make sure to recognize the beauty of my daughters, reminding myself that beauty is all-encompassing and not just physical. I actively remind myself to see them as the beautiful souls they are, just as I am, made in the image of God. It's sad how we as a society reduce people to so little when we are really incredible, infinite, and divine beings. We don't see others as deserving the same respect that we would want. I'm sure my childhood bullies had no idea of the pain they caused me. And I think about all of the times I made fun of others, or made myself look good by making others look bad, all those times I put others down to feel better about myself.

Many people ask me why I became religious. There are so many reasons; it's hard to think where to even begin. First of all, I saw the marriages, the family dynamics in the religious community, and I wanted and craved that for myself. And then there was something I never knew in my life, which was the intrinsic value that Judaism places on each individual life. Religion allowed me to see that I am good as I am. Simply put, I am enough! It's funny, but even when I was little, I wanted to be a *rebbetzin*. I didn't even know what it meant to be a *rebbetzin*, but that's what I wanted to do. When I became religious, that was a new point of attack for others. I was bullied for being fake, always exaggerating, being a hypocrite since I didn't put into practice each thing I learned. As if we achieve perfection simply by choosing to work toward being better. That chapter in my life became a very bitter one for me. There were not many religious people in my community in Panama, for sure not my age. At 18, I was alone in my beliefs. I didn't party with my peers, didn't have my family's support, I was labeled the crazy one. But at least I found comfort in God, in the Torah. Who could have known that it would become my life's purpose and a source of inspiration for others?

When the Torah talks about Esav and Yaakov, the verse says, "Yitzchak loved Esav because he was hunting with his mouth, but Rivka loves Yaakov." In the Hebrew, we see that Yitzchak loved Esav, in the past tense. Because in the material world we value achievements and honor, and this is why the Torah gives a reason for the love. In this case, love is conditional; it goes according to what you do, who you are, and how you look. Most importantly, this kind of love is temporal—it only exists when it is deserved. Conversely, Rivka loves Yaakov, period. The love Rivka had for Yaakov wasn't earned; it simply existed, unconnected to any cause or conditions. Later, when the Torah describes Yaakov, there is no extravagant depiction or title of achievement. The Torah states in simple terms, "Yaakov was a simple man, he sat in his tent." And even then, mainly then, he was loved. We should not have to earn love; we should be loved simply because of our essence.

A few weeks ago, my therapist asked me to write down the reasons I should love myself. It was so hard for me, I couldn't come up with anything, and then, I felt a strong drive inside of me and the first thing I wrote was, "Why should I have reasons?" Aren't I made in the image of God, and isn't that enough? But that was the problem; it isn't enough, and I couldn't find reasons why I should love myself. I had to dig deeper and work harder. You see, even though I experienced what I did, those were all decisions that were made for me. I didn't need to live by those choices; I could and should have disposed of them long ago. So why didn't I? Why do we choose to stay in a place of hurt? Why don't we choose to change the voices in our heads, the way that we narrate our lives? Why do we let the choices of others define us? I don't want to live like that, a slave to someone else's negativity. I want a life of acceptance, understanding, tolerance, patience, and love for others, but mainly for myself. The Torah is wise in advising us to "love your neighbor like yourself," because if you can't find a way to accept yourself, you will never fully accept others. And for a long time, I struggled to accept others. I couldn't bear to see anyone else's light shine out of fear that it would cast a shadow over mine. After all, back then I felt that my light was so tiny that I was afraid it was going to be extinguished.

But I thank God for all of this hardship. It has allowed me to be sensitive, to embrace others, see their divine beauty no matter the rest of the package, to invite and guide others into looking at their own light. If I had only loved myself more, would I have ended up where I am? Would I have made better choices? It's too late to answer that, but it's not too late to change it. I blamed everything and everyone for all of my struggles when really the power to change my fate was in my own hands all along; I just had to do the work. I have to get rid of the negative voices in my head, tell them they are not welcome, and that they are wrong—just because I was told something about myself doesn't make it true. I need to stop nurturing those damaging thoughts and reject them entirely.

Like I said earlier, pain in life is inevitable, but suffering is self-inflicted. We don't have to be victims of our pain. Instead, we can use it like a trampoline, a base to jump higher, toward happiness. As I write, I realize that by holding tight to that which does not serve us allows it to control us, to define us, and follow us throughout our entire lives. Instead of dragging my pain with me wherever I go, I will finally address the emergency lights so that they no longer have control over me.

When Adam hid from God after eating from the forbidden tree, Hashem asks, "*Ayeka*, where are you?" The word *ayeka* is used to pose the question, "How did this happen, how did you get here?" So often in my life, I have stopped and asked the same question. When my marriage was failing and the distance between my husband and me kept growing, I kept asking myself how we could possibly bridge the gap, undo what has already been done. We become addicted to unhealthy thoughts. We may convince ourselves that we are in control, but really the negative thoughts are hijacking our minds. Life is like an avalanche; it starts with a few flakes of snow, but if you don't leave fast enough, you end up buried by the wave. You end up asking yourself, *"Ayeka,"* how did you get here? So, let's do ourselves a favor and confront the negativity, right here, right now. Let's write down all the negative feelings we have about ourselves and about our lives and ask ourselves if it is worth believing what we wrote. Is any of it worth keeping? What benefit do we gain from hoarding those thoughts?

The *Zohar* says that when a person gets angry, he is likened to a stupid dog. If you were to take a stick and hit a dog, what is the dog's immediate reaction? He bites the stick. He doesn't bite you, the one who guided the strike; he bites the object of attack. The dog's narrow vision doesn't allow him to see that there was someone holding the stick, directing it against him. So too, with us. Can anything happen to us if God doesn't will it? Of course not. Every one of life's challenges is just a stick in God's hands! Bad people, tough circumstances, all of it. So don't get stuck on the stick. Understand that there was a purpose for the strike and let go of the anger which will only hurt you more. And remember that while striking a dog is not always led by good intentions, when God hits you with difficulties, it is only for your benefit.

One thing I've come to understand is that even though people have choices and can choose to behave in hurtful ways, they are still just messengers of God. So, really, there is no point in being angry or holding grudges; they are just the messengers. It will only eat you up inside, as they say, holding a grudge is allowing someone to live in your head without paying rent. All this time, Hashem was helping me develop the strength I needed to get to this point; I just couldn't see it fully. I've been blaming the messengers instead of understanding the messages. But I'm ready to embrace them now.

PIN IT TO YOUR HEART!

"Don't ignore the emergency lights. Fix the problem before it spreads."

"We've all journeyed across different routes to arrive where we are."

"Holding a grudge is allowing someone to live in your head without paying rent."

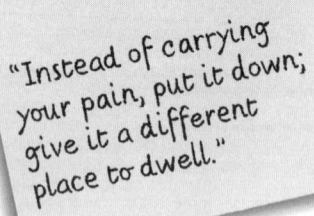

"Instead of carrying your pain, put it down; give it a different place to dwell."

"Don't get stuck on the stick that strikes."

CHAPTER SIX

TAILOR-MADE FOR YOU WITH LOVE

How many times have you heard the phrase, "If Hashem is giving you this test, it is because you have the strength to go through with it?" Or, "Only you can handle it, only you are strong enough to withstand it." I can't even tell you how many times I've said those same words in my classes. But now, every time I hear those words, they pierce deep within my heart and make me cringe. Only me? What's so great about me that I am the only one who can handle this? Is this what being me gets me? Is my greatness having a life of difficulty, being chosen for many challenges? Are you sure, Hashem, that this is all my baggage? It can't be; I can't carry it all. At least, I don't want to. It's just too heavy. Who is going to help me out? Can't You send someone else to carry the load? Not someone to give me inspiring speeches, but to actually bear the weight with me? It is too difficult, too lonely a task!

I'm not going to lie, I myself have given the *emunah* speech to many people. My main listener, though, has been me; I've had to say it to myself millions of times. But I so badly wish I hadn't, wish I didn't have to say it at all. I just wish I could just give it all away. Don't choose me, I want to say to Hashem. I don't want to be great; choose someone else, I'm perfectly fine with being *ploni almoni*, just an ordinary person. But unfortunately, we can't give up our challenges so easily. We can only choose to carry on with dignity or to be squashed and buried by the weight of our own misery. When people laud my personal strength, it only makes me wonder—was I ever given a choice in the matter? Did I ever have any other choice but to be strong? I mean, if I'm forced into it, then I will certainly give it my all, do my best to carry my struggles with poise. Like I said, my motto in life is "if you have to, you will, but if you don't have to, you won't." And God knows, I have to… for me, for my kids, for you, for the Jewish people. So, I keep pushing forward, and even though I know I will fall, I'll still get back up again as many times as I have to. Most importantly, you will not see me giving up without a fight.

The Torah relates the story of the righteous man Iyov, who was a known *tzaddik* in his time. The *satan* approached Hashem, belittling Iyov's goodness with the opinion that obviously Iyov would be righteous if everything in his life was smooth. The *satan* posed a challenge and asked Hashem's permission to test Iyov to see how strong he would be in the face of difficulty. Hashem agreed, and the *satan* began to slowly add strife to Iyov's life. Bit by bit, Iyov lost everything: his wealth, his children, and then his own health. In the beginning, he remained strong in his *emunah*, saying that if he thanks God for the good, he will also thank Him for the bad. "Naked I came from my mother's womb, naked I shall return," he said. Eventually, though, it became too much for him, and he started complaining, questioning the agonies he was forced to suffer. What's incredible is that Hashem didn't come to him and say, "I was betting on you; how could you disappoint me? I thought you were great." Instead, throughout the story, Hashem goes down to Iyov and comforts him, embraces him, sits next to him, empathizing with his pain.

Pain can consume us; it can wear us out and overwhelm us, making us lose ourselves entirely, making it hard to think straight and look at the world objectively. As Shlomo HaMelech said, "Pain makes the wise man into a fool." It's easy to be wise until your wisdom is tested. Then you realize you were never that wise to begin with. What would you do if you were? Would you still remain you? Would your response still be human? Even in matters of *mitzvot*, we are allowed to give up the Torah if we are being tortured. Because being tortured is more unbearable than simply giving up your life. There is no end to it, and the difficulty is beyond comprehension. Many times, we think we have *emunah*, a strong relationship with God, but maybe it's just because life is easy, it's flowing smoothly. But what if there were obstacles? Would you stay strong? They say that commitment starts when you want to quit; you aren't committed until all you want to do is get out, but you still choose to stay. Would you take the leap if you weren't certain that you would be caught? Can you have trust when you are blindly being pushed in different directions? Can you really let go? Pain blurs your vision and blocks your heart. How can you trust in God if it is God Who disappointed you? How can you have *emunah* when it is Hashem who is the source of your difficulty?

That's exactly how Iyov felt. He asked Hashem, "Are You sure You have the right person? Why are You doing this to me? Maybe there is a mistake, maybe a storm passed and You got a little confused and instead of thinking I was Iyov, you thought I was *oyev*, Your enemy." *Iyov* and *oyev* have the same spelling, except for the place swap of one letter, the *yud*. To which God answered, "Do you see the hair on your head? I made it so that no two hairs grow from the same follicle. Yet you think I confused your name and its letters and sent you something that isn't for you? You accuse Me of running this world like a storm, when in reality I run it with the precision of a hair." When we look at our hardships, we think that's exactly what happened—there was a misunderstanding; God's running of this world is not precise. But if He is so precise with your hair, which has no purpose and is only cosmetic, do you think He will make any mistakes with your life? Of course not! I get that sometimes our lives are just too heavy to accept, and it would be easier to think there was a mistake, but the thing is, just because we believe something, doesn't make it true. Therefore, not only are we denying our reality, we are also turning our backs to our own purpose and growth.

If we look at God's answer to Iyov, the verse says, "God answered from within the storm." Sometimes our lives look like a mess; there is no order, meaning, or purpose—it's all dark, cloudy, and muddy to us. But God is there in the midst of the chaos. He answers from within the storm. He is not behind the scenes; He is up front and center. Hashem is the cause of the storm and when you realize that, everything in your life changes. Suddenly, you realize that your life is in fact organized chaos; it may look messy to you but that's only because you can't see or understand the configuration. Because you are being affected by it, you are unable to appreciate the logic behind it. So many times, we turn emotional issues into logical issues. As we mentioned earlier, the greatest distance in the world is that from your head to your heart. We think that because our hearts don't understand, there is no logic to be found. If we were to try and follow the chaos, we would see there is a source for it, and therefore a method behind it. God is right there in the storm with you; He is leading the storm so that you are shaken up, so you can choose to wait it out or find refuge. Just remember that when it's over, the sun will come out.

Everything in our lives is tailor-made for us. I know, I know, you don't like to hear it. Me neither, but it's the truth. Perfection can only create perfection. Therefore, by definition, everything in our lives is perfect; it's just that our understanding of perfect is not the same as Hashem's meaning of perfect. We think perfect means that everything is the way we want it to be, and we want life to be comfortable and enjoyable. However, Hashem's definition of perfect is that everything is as it is in order for you to achieve your purpose. At the end of the day, what are we here for if not to grow? If we are here, it is because we must have a choice to make, a say in the matter of our existence, and therefore what we do matters. I can't be an observer in my life; I have to be a presenter. Just because I can't see God, doesn't mean that He isn't there. I may have an image in my mind of how things are supposed to look, but that's completely subjective, and who says I have any legitimate knowledge or understanding of what reality means? At the end of the day, I'm the character, not the writer. That's one of our biggest misunderstandings in life. That's what I needed to understand in my life; no event in my life was random, there was purpose to each moment of struggle, and suddenly, at the peak of the storm, I understood it all. One of my favorite quotes from Rabbi Nachman is, "Even in darkness within the darkness, that is also where Hashem is found." This doesn't just come to say that Hashem is there, but that He is intentionally there. He brings about the storm and waits for you to find Him there. Like we said earlier, sometimes you need to fall to feel Him at the edge.

When I was becoming religious, I thought everything would work out smoothly, but I realized very quickly that there would be many more obstacles coming my way. But then I realized something incredible, and I found the root of so many of our problems! We put our trust in God and ask Him to do what's best for us, but only as long as it works with the plan we made for ourselves. We pretend to give over the control of our lives to God, but we don't actually relinquish control. We hold onto our ideas as strongly as we always did and refuse to budge from what we think is best for us. We only agree to give God control as long as it matches our agenda, as long as He fulfills our wishes. So where are we really leaving room for God's control? Where are we really letting Him do what's best for us?

I realized something that has really affected the way I think, feel, and live my life. When I own my thoughts, everything changes, and I become empowered and inspired to live a life full of meaning and purpose. I may not always put it into practice, though. Sometimes I want to be a victim, complain, and cry about how miserable my life is. As a way of battling these thoughts, I have a collection of ideas that I call my "*Emunah* Savings Account," which, like a savings account at the bank, is to help keep me afloat when I'm drowning, so to speak. If you live paycheck to paycheck and you are struck with a sudden major financial burden, like car repairs or dental surgery, then that is really going to affect your bank balance and cause lots of stress. But if you have savings to withdraw when you are in the red, then it will hold you over until your next paycheck comes. I do this with *emunah*; I lock up little tidbits for a rainy day. Let me share with you my favorite thought from my *emunah* savings account. It's a bit of a life-shaker, a rough wake-up, but I find it to be incredibly empowering:

Imagine you were a kid at a birthday party; not the birthday kid, just a guest. What would be your favorite part of the birthday party? Some people prefer the cake, others say the piñata. But honestly, some of us don't like the piñata because you have to be feisty and fight your way in; and even though I love cake, I don't love all cake, only vanilla or *dulce de leche*. We all have our preferences. But there is one thing we all love at a birthday party. And that is the party favor, the goody bag! As a kid, you always loved the goody bag; you knew there was always one waiting for you. You didn't have to fight for it, it was already designated for you. And it was full of surprises; there were always things inside that you liked, and other things that you could share or exchange with others. Now imagine if, as a child, you went to a birthday party and there was no goody bag for you. How would you feel? Punished, left out, forgotten? You would have felt unloved and undeserving, right? You would wonder why you're the only one who didn't get one.

Isn't that how we go through life? Feeling like God is handing out goody bags full of treats to everyone but us? We wonder why we aren't getting one like everyone else. We deserve it, we expect it, we showed up! And when we don't get it, we are so disappointed; we feel excluded, unwanted, uniquely chosen to suffer. We see others getting married and having children while we wait for our turn. We see everyone being happy, and wonder to ourselves, what about me? So, you search for anyone else going through the same pain. And that's the only thing that makes you feel better, knowing that you are not the only one suffering. But wait, are we really so spiteful that seeing others' pain makes us feel better about our own? No, of course not. As children at the party, we feel forgotten and left out and are overwhelmed with the feeling of being the only one overlooked. We feel like we are being pointed out, made to feel there is something wrong with us. We feel like we are the problem. So, when we see someone else who feels the same way, suddenly we're not lonely in our pain; we realize that we are not the only ones being left out. To accept being rejected is hard, but to have someone else share the rejection means that at least we're not the only ones. It's not that we want other people to suffer, we just don't want to suffer alone. We take it personally when it's just us, but when it's others as well, we can understand that there is a bigger picture.

Now, let me ask you, all you want is that goody bag, right? Getting a goody bag will make you feel loved and wanted, give you a sense of belonging, of being noticed and remembered. But the truth of the goody bag is that no one made you a goody bag with your name on it. There is just a whole pile of them, being handed out at random. You are just one more recipient in a room of recipients, just one of a number. And if you hadn't gone to the birthday party, they would have found someone else to give it to. In other words, that which makes us feel so special is actually the reason why we shouldn't feel special at all. No one thought of us in particular; we're just one of many.

Let's take the metaphor a step further: What if my goody bag has cookies in it but I'm gluten-free? What if it has candy inside but I have diabetes? It wouldn't be good for me. I so badly want to get the same thing that everyone else has that I don't stop to wonder if it's even good for me. The fact is, it's not always good; it could be damaging to my life. Now here comes the painful but empowering and liberating truth—when Hashem gives you a goody bag, it is tailor-made for you. It has your name on it. It's not just one of many. If you don't get it, no one else will, because it is useless to anyone else. It also means that your goody bag is not going to have the cookies or candies that you can't digest; it will only have veggies that are good for you. It's a painful thought, of course, the cookies and candy look much better. But ultimately, you know it is not good for you, and the mature and responsible choice is to let go of wanting the things that can only cause damage. Focus instead on the heartwarming and comforting thought that your goody bag is tailor-made for you, with love, thought, and dedication, and full to the brim of good things for you.

Every morning, we thank God, *"she'asah li kol tsorki*, Who took care of my every need." You may not notice it, but this blessing is written in past tense. It's actually the only blessing of all the morning blessings in the past tense. In my opinion, it's the one that makes the least sense. What does it mean, He "took care" of all my needs? I mean, I'm glad if I had food and shelter yesterday; I'm very grateful. But to be honest, I'd like to have my needs met today as well, and tomorrow. Every other blessing is in present tense because we say it in the moment in which God opens our eyes, lets us stand straight, etc. So why doesn't this blessing follow the same pattern? There are two answers which are magnificent. Remember that time you lost your job? You were so sad, but then you got a better job. And remember when you broke off your engagement? But then you married the love of your life a year later. Well, those heartbreaks were your needs at the time, you just didn't know it back then. Sometimes you can only recognize your past needs in the present. It takes understanding that something is lacking in order to achieve fulfillment and pleasure.

I remember how devastated I was when the fertility treatment for my second child was unsuccessful, all the frozen embryos failed, and I was mad at Hashem. I thought about how, not only does He make fertility treatment necessary for me, He forces me to do them multiple times and suffer the pain of disappointment multiple times. During that time, I was dreaming about a couple of major things. One of them was to be invited to *Sinai Indaba* in South Africa—one of the greatest Torah gathering events in the world, an amazing initiative by the Chief Rabbi of South Africa. I dreamed about it, but always forced myself back to reality, reminding myself how far-fetched it would be. I was too young, not famous enough, and the event only features the greatest and most famous speakers in the Jewish world. There was no way I would ever make it. After all, who was I? You can imagine how shocked and excited I was a few weeks later when I received an invitation from the Chief Rabbi to come to South Africa and speak at the event. I was floored; I just couldn't believe it, didn't understand how it could possibly be real. Yet there I was, six months later, living one of my biggest dreams, the most wonderful opportunity and gift from Hashem. And not only that, but they even flew out my husband and toddler, so it was a family vacation as well. If that fertility treatment had been successful, I wouldn't have been able to achieve one of my biggest dreams. I would have been eight months pregnant and missed out on one of the biggest honors and privileges of my life. I didn't know it at the time, but not getting pregnant was my need at that moment.

But I have another explanation for the wording of the blessing. When we think of this blessing, there are two main ideas that we generally have in mind: a) Whatever I have is what I need b) Whatever I don't have, I don't need. But there is a third option we don't think about: it's not just that whatever I have I need and whatever I don't have I don't need, but also: I need to not have whatever I don't have. In other words, it is necessary for me not to have it; it is in my best interest for whatever reason. Perhaps it will distract me from what I need to achieve, or perhaps it will ultimately have a negative impact on my life. It might just be the candies in my goody bag that are bad for my diabetes.

It is difficult for us to accept that God handles our lives with such precision and love. We would rather believe that we have a much better understanding of what we should or should not have in our lives. But let me ask you this: how many times have you met someone who wanted something so badly, only to have that thing turn into a source of hardship? We think that if only we won the lottery, our troubles would end. But do you know who doesn't want to win the lottery? Those who won it. So many lottery winners have come out and admitted that winning the lottery simply ruined their lives. One of the earliest examples of this kind of behavior is in the Torah, when we are told Adam asked God for a companion, so God made Eve, and just a few *pesukim* later Adam was already complaining about her. What do we know about what we really need? We want what we think will give us comfort and pleasure, but our vision and understanding are limited and temporal. Hashem wants to give us something that will fulfill us in the long run, not simply fulfill a superficial desire! There's a big difference between eating chips when you're hungry or having an actual meal. Sure, one is immediate, yummy, and available, but the other one is nutritious and satisfying. God wants us to have lives that are like the full meals, but if you fill yourself up on the snacks, you won't have room for the real food.

When Hashem wanted to eradicate the Jewish people after the sin of the golden calf, Moshe *davens*, asking for mercy. After some time, God agrees to forgive them, and an interesting exchange of words happens. Moshe asks, "*Hareni nah et kevodecha,* Can I see Your face?" and Hashem answers, "You cannot see My face, but you can see My back. No person can see Me and live." What is relevant about seeing the face or the back? Every face is distinct; like a fingerprint, no two faces are exactly alike. But a back can be indistinguishable; it can trick you, mislead you. Moshe essentially asks God the same question we often ask ourselves, why do bad things happen to good people? He wanted to understand the answer for it with the precision of seeing someone face-to-face. But God said he can't—not because He didn't want to show Moshe, but because Moshe is a human, limited by his human understanding. It is only when a person dies and their soul passes to the next world that they can grasp the true concept. The Chatam Sofer offers a beautiful insight on this: When something happens, we want to know why, right then and there. We wish to gain clarity as easily as recognizing a face. But humans are limited; they cannot understand everything that happens in the world. But we can see the "back," when we look back on our lives, then we may finally understand. Sometimes you just need to wait to look back a few days or months or years, or even a lifetime. One day you may come to understand it, and then you will see how Hashem was really taking care of you the whole time, from within the storm, whether you saw Him or not.

The Rambam says, "If I were to know everything that God knows, I would have to be God," and I'm guessing none of us can play that role. I don't think I would want to be God, to be honest; it's a hard job. No one is ever satisfied with what You give them, it doesn't matter how much good You do for them. No one accepts how You run the world; everyone thinks they could do it better. This is why one of my favorite quotes is, "For someone that believes, there are no questions. For someone that doesn't believe, there are no answers." Meaning, if you believe in God, then you have no questions; but if you don't, then there are no answers which will satisfy you. At the end of the day, it all comes down to one word—acceptance.

The Jewish day to question our pain is Tisha b'Av, when we read *Megillat Eicha*. *Eicha* means "how could this be?" When we are in pain, that's all we do: ask questions—why, how, when… everything is a confused blur. I believe it is the questions themselves that cause us pain and deny us the ability to make peace with reality. Because, let's be honest with ourselves, we know the questions stem from our egos, our desire for control. We believe that God owes us an explanation, and if it doesn't make sense to me, then it doesn't make sense at all. How funny we are as people, don't you think? And maybe a bit pathetic. Do we really think that our limited human minds are going to get it? Who am I? Who are you? Where do we even think we fit into the picture when it comes to the motions of life and the world? The more we demand to understand why, the more we are setting ourselves up for failure because, as Hashem tells Moshe, "No man can see Me and live." We cannot understand; we do not have the ability to understand God's thoughts. So, we need to let go of the questions; we need to stop demanding answers.

The *haftara* we read the Shabbat after Tisha b'Av is called *Nachamu*, which means to be comforted, but our sages also teach us it means "to regret." As it says in *Parshat Noach* when Hashem regretted the flood, "*nichamti ki asiti*, I regretted that I did this." What is the connection between comforting and regretting? The Torah relates that when Yosef revealed himself to his estranged brothers, they were shocked. Imagine what was going on through their minds—they must have had so many questions throughout their interactions with him up until that point. Who is this viceroy? Why does he care so much about our lives? Why is he trying to keep us here? Why does he want to meet our brother, Binyamin? I always imagined that if there was a visual for this scene, when Yosef says the powerful words, *"ani Yosef,* I am Yosef," his brothers' jaws would just drop in absolute astonishment. Suddenly it all makes sense to them; two words answered all of their questions. Here, our sages comment on this moment, "Oy, the day of rebuke!" No one is actually being rebuked here, so to what are the sages referring? As if to say the greatest rebuke we can experience is to be confronted with the truth we should have known all along. That is precisely what happens at our final judgment. We get to Heaven with so many questions, complaints, demands; and then suddenly the mask comes down and God reveals Himself. Just like that, everything is made clear and our jaws hit the floor with understanding. No explanations are needed, there's nothing to say, nothing to add; it's obvious, it made sense all along. We are just so bogged down with our own ideas that it prevents us from seeing what is always there—Hashem.

There are commentaries on *Megillat Esther* which pose the question: why doesn't the name of God appear in the text at all? The answer they offer is that while Hashem may be moving the pieces around the board, He does so in hiding. We don't see Him in action, but by the time the credits are rolling, we can see that He was the director all along. There is another answer I like, that when a work of art is a pure representation of the artist, he need not sign his name; the artwork itself is already imbued with his signature in the form of his artistic style. All of *Megillat Esther* is in God's signature style. Everything works out perfectly, it all makes sense, and the randomness is so exact that it can only be from God.

When we get up to *Shamayim* with all our questions, everything will be made clear to us; every puzzle, every enigma, every question will be solved. We will feel comforted, knowing there was a reason, a need, there was meaning and purpose behind everything we went through in life. God doesn't just sit with a deck of cards thinking, "Let me see how I can hit her next." Nothing in life is random. But at the same time you feel that comfort, you will also feel regret. You will regret questioning God, and you will regret doubting Him and yourself. Because when we look deep inside ourselves, we can recognize that we had the ability to see it all along, we were just too afraid to face the truth and therefore we chose to look the other way.

Throughout my life, I have often doubted God. I questioned His reasons and methods for certain occurrences in my life. As if I knew better and could have done it better. But then, it's as if I get slapped in the face; suddenly it all makes sense, God is standing behind everything, looking at me with compassion. "My child," He says, "I wish you could have trusted Me, had patience and understanding. You would have saved yourself so much pain and trouble. Pain and trouble that you generated because you didn't wait, you didn't trust Me." I don't know why my life has to be the way it is, but what I do know is that I could have been playing a bigger role in it all along, not just waiting to see how it turns out like any other audience member. I could have searched and created purpose if only I would have accepted my limited understanding earlier. The question now is how I choose to move on with this knowledge. A quote that is always close to my heart is, "*Kol hazman shehaner dolek tamid efshar l'taken,* as long as the candle is lit, there is time to repair." Don't give up, lean into your troubles; accept and be present. When Hashem calls to you through hardship, answer "*hineni,* here I am!" Hashem, I am at Your disposal, ready for You to take control, ready to own my choices and embrace what You have to give me.

PIN IT TO YOUR HEART!

"Pain makes the wise man into a fool."

"God answers from within the storm."

"Whatever I have I need, whatever I don't have I don't need; but most importantly, I need to not have whatever I don't have."

"When Hashem gives you a goody bag it is tailor-made for you."

"If you were to know everything that God knows, you would have to be God."

CHAPTER SEVEN

GOD DOESN'T GIVE YOU MORE THAN YOU CAN CARRY

I once saw an educational cartoon where men and women are running the same race. The women's track was filled with obstacles: children, laundry, cooking; while the men's track was clear. The point being that we demand the same results from those who have obstacles as we do from those who don't. With such a disparity between the two courses, how can we possibly expect those who are at such a disadvantage to compete with those whose paths are clear? I started my own personal racecourse at a disadvantage only to find it riddled with obstacles, some of them normal, but most of them extreme and complicated. So, the question now is how am I supposed to make it in life? Is it that some people are destined to fall behind and fail? How can we remove ourselves from our struggles and still aspire for more in life?

There is a famous question asked about Moshe: Why wasn't he enslaved like the rest of the Jewish people? Wouldn't he have related to them more if he had the same experiences as them? Our sages teach us that if Moshe had been a slave, he would have been limited in his mindset; he wouldn't have been able to confront Pharaoh as an equal. He would have felt too lowly, too limited by his position as a slave to have any influence over the ruler. So, is the Torah teaching us that it is true, that some of us are indeed at a disadvantage? No, because even if someone seems to have been given more of an advantage, it doesn't necessarily make them more worthy in the eyes of God. Hashem doesn't measure success according to where we are but rather by how much we have climbed to reach that place. Let's look at it this way: The Torah teaches us that we are never allowed to choose between two people's lives, because we don't know who is more righteous in the eyes of God.

Imagine you discovered the cure for cancer, but in order to confirm its effectiveness, you must try it on a person. There are two candidates for the experiment: a rabbi and a thief. You'd think the choice is obvious, right? Clearly, one's life is worth more than the other. However, the Torah instructs against this way of thinking because it is impossible to know which life is more worthy in God's eyes. We can never know someone's personal journey; what obstacles they had to overcome to reach the finish line. How can you be rewarded for something you didn't achieve, for inheriting a state of being? Sometimes, Hashem puts us in easy and comfortable situations. He may give us beautiful families with fantastic, easy interpersonal dynamics, but that isn't something we achieved. It could simply be the nature of the family as God gifted it. It is something for which we must feel grateful and fortunate, but it's not necessarily an outcome we accomplished through our own actions; it is not the result of growth or accomplishment. However, sometimes God tests us in every aspect of our lives, and it feels like we have been doomed for big time failure. This is where we are given a choice; here we can rise to the occasion and succeed. It may be that in the eyes of others we did not do a good job, but we can still look at how far we've come, what we have achieved.

Everything in life is about the direction that we take and the steps we climb on the ladder called life. Staying in the same place is no good at all. God didn't bring us into the world to have a passive role in life. He brought us to the world so that we may propel ourselves to greatness. At the end of the day, all we get to keep are our choices, nothing else. Our choices belong to us; the outcome belongs to God. We are only expected to do the best we can with what we have been given, even if it doesn't generate the applause of others. It's between me and God, and no one else. I love to teach the credo that "greatness is measured by how much light you generate in a dark place." Your merit depends on how much darkness you were able to expel by shining your own light, externally and internally. Your merit is measured according to what you have had to overcome, what you have achieved to be who you are today, and who you want to be tomorrow. So yes, we all have our baggage; some are fifty kilos and some are ten. Yet some of us break under the pressure of the ten while others thrive under the pressure of fifty. What matters most is not which struggles are harder, but how we respond to the struggles themselves. The objective levels of difficulty mean nothing when life is about the subjectivity of the struggle. Our job in life is to learn how to carry our struggles with acceptance and grace, not to be bowed by the heaviness of our baggage. We must see the waves as an invitation to ride them so that we may master them.

Renowned psychiatrist and Holocaust survivor Victor Frankl said, "Everything can be taken from a man but one thing: the last of the human freedoms—*to choose one's attitude in any given set of circumstances, to choose one's own way.*" Put more simply, life is not about what you carry, but how you carry it. What you carry is up to God; like we said, He decides what goes into your goody bag. But how you carry it is entirely up to you. Life can be hard, but it doesn't need to feel that way. When Pharaoh asked Yaakov his age, the *Midrash* explains that Yaakov lost a year of life for every word of his answer. Why? Our sages teach us Yaakov looked old, tired, depleted; his challenges had taken a toll on him, and even though it makes sense and is logical, it showed in a sense that he was challenged by his challenges, he didn't accept them fully. Because in answering the question, stating, "The days of the years of my life have been few and miserable...", he was inadvertently criticizing God for how difficult his life was. Because Yaakov didn't carry his years well, because he seemed old and harried, Pharaoh was confused as to his real age. By justifying the question with an answer, Yaakov was basically complaining. Therefore, he had an evident consequence of what he felt and how he lived. We can carry our struggles with dignity, or we can carry them with shame and regret; it's up to us.

I remember when I had been married for three years with still no baby on the horizon, I met with one of my students. She told me she was depressed because she was married six months and still wasn't pregnant. She asked me how I managed to still have *emunah*, to not give up or get depressed. I answered that I had been learning how to surf the waves of struggle all my life. I have been pushing stones all along, so I've developed some muscles. I don't know why we have to carry what we do, and the more you ask yourself these questions, the more you are setting yourself up for failure. We ask "why" as if we have a say in the matter, as if we can do anything to change reality, but we can't. God runs the world, not us.

I once read something that moved me; something so simple, yet so profound: When God gives something to a person, He does so from the standpoint of a Creator, not from the perspective of a created being. In other words, it doesn't matter how much you try to understand, you will never be able to have the same viewpoint as Hashem. Not only is it not within the realm of your understanding, but you will never be able to view it with complete objectivity. I mean, how could you, when you are obviously biased? Asking why is like giving yourself false hope for control. God doesn't give us more than we can carry, but He also doesn't give us any less than what we can carry. In other words, the more spiritual muscles we have, the heavier the spiritual weight we are given. When kids ask to bring something to the table, do we give them each the same item or weight to carry out? Of course not. The bigger kids get the heavier items because the small kids would drop them. At the same time, we don't give the bigger kids the tiny items because they can handle much heavier things.

We see this often in the Torah. The Ramban asks, what was the point of Hashem testing Avraham? Doesn't He know what Avraham is capable of achieving? The Ramban provides a powerful answer—Hashem is not a potter who needs to sound out His vessels to see which are strong and which are weak. God doesn't need to test anyone because He knows what the outcome will be. Says the Ramban, since a man always has complete freedom of choice, if he wishes to act, he acts; if not, then he doesn't act. Therefore, it may be a test for Avraham, but Hashem provides the test in order to invite the choice to act. He provides the opportunity to activate potential so that Avraham may be well rewarded not just for a good heart, but for a good deed. Until Avraham experiences his trials, his capacity for faith and loyalty exists only as potential. His qualities of goodness and devotion are not yet forged into the very essence of his character, like an inexperienced actor waiting for his breakthrough role.

Pirkei Avot writes, "With ten *nisyonot* Avraham was tested." Avraham sees them as tests, but Hashem presents them as goals to be achieved in this world. We see struggles in life as trials because we don't want to move out of our comfort zone, but the truth is that they are opportunities to achieve our full potential. There is a famous *Midrash* on *Tehillim* 11:5 where the psalm mentions Hashem testing *tzaddikim*. On the objective behind divine tests, Rav Yonasan comments: "When one makes linen out of flax, if the flax is broken, he doesn't beat it too hard because it can break. But when it is fine, he beats it hard because that way it becomes finer and finer. So too with the *tzaddikim*." Rav Yochanan says: "When the potter tests his pottery, he doesn't hit the weak pots because if he hits it even once it might break; therefore he tests the strong pitchers because they can endure many knocks and not break." Rabbi Elazar says: "It is like the farmer who has two cows, one strong and one weak. He puts the yoke on the strong one because he can handle it. So too, Hashem only tests the *tzaddikim*."

This *Midrash* presents three different ideas to understand and appreciate why we are tested:

1. **To refine a person**
The one that's hitting the flax does it only for the sake of refining the linen. So too, Hashem only hits those that have the potential for refinement and can withstand the process. The trial exists for the sole benefit of the person experiencing the test; something had to change, there had to be introspection, reflection, growth, and commitment which lead to a refinement of character.

2. **To bring out our hidden qualities**
The potter tests his wares to show his buyers the quality of his goods. So too, Hashem tests the *tzaddikim* to show others their potential, their less obvious qualities. When *tzaddikim* are tested, there is a huge opportunity for *kiddush* Hashem. They become role models for how to accept hardship with happiness. That is the beauty in Aharon HaCohen's reaction to the death of his sons. By remaining quiet, he provided a lesson to the world on accepting God's will, even when it seems most difficult.

3. **To protect the world**
Hashem only puts the yoke on those who can carry it in order to protect the rest of the world. How does that work? Our *chachamim* teach us, "*Kol Yisrael areivim zeh la'zeh,*" all of Israel are responsible for one another. Therefore, when one Jew suffers, it atones for everyone else. Hashem makes the *tzaddik* suffer in order to help others of his generation. Sometimes, Hashem will cause a *tzaddik* to suffer in order to bring the Moshiach closer. The *tzaddik* carries the yoke of the whole world because what defines him as a *tzaddik* is his commitment to the Jewish people. It's like when we see someone struggling to carry their grocery bags, and we offer to help, even if it means adding to the weight of our own load, because we have the ability to carry more than that other person.

I don't know if Hashem is making fine linen out of us or showing off His pottery-ware through us, but I do know that life is not random. Hashem has His reasons; your baggage in life was chosen for you because Hashem recognizes your potential. The Torah teaches that when a person had *tzora'at*, leprosy, he was removed from the camp until he did *teshuva*. As long as the *tzora'at* spread across his body, it was a sign that he hadn't fully repented. The Torah asks, what if the *tzora'at* spread all over the person's body and he is still outside of the camp? It's pretty ironic, but he would be returned to the camp. The purpose of the *tzora'at* is to awaken him to repentance. If he refuses to do the work, then there is no purpose to the test. This means that when God tests us, it is not only that He believes in our potential, but that He believes in our willingness to work on ourselves, to grow and live our potential. If a person is never tested it is because he has no desire to grow, no willingness to change, so Hashem doesn't bother helping him achieve growth or change. The more you are tested, the more potential Hashem sees in you, the more He believes in your desire to become great. Like a used tube of toothpaste that you squeeze from the bottom to get every last drop, more and more comes out.

I want you to think about the people you admire. Why do you admire them? What do all the people that you admire have in common? I can guarantee you that it is because of their strength and resilience, their willingness to keep going. You admire their choice to overcome and become better. It's not that you want their lives or their challenges; you'd much rather relax on a cruise, sipping a piña colada. But that's what you consider greatness, and that's who you would want to be and how you would like to be seen—through the eyes of admiration. So next time you are being tested, give a wink and a smile and say it out loud: "God, I'm ready! You believe in me so I will give it my best and make both of us proud!" Once your mindset has changed, you can choose to do what needs to be done; you will be able to carry anything.

When I moved to Israel, there was some slang that I found really annoying. In the Western world, there exists the concept of politeness. Well, we all know that doesn't work as well in Israel. Here, people are real. As we would say in Spanish, they have no hair on their tongue, which means they say whatever they feel, even though it may come out as rude or aggressive. One of the common speech patterns in Israel is that when you ask "*lama*, why," people will often answer "*kacha*, because." Why? Because. As in, that's just the way it is, so deal with it. At first, I was really annoyed by this. Where is the empathy? I mean, people should respond with compassion, but in Israel, people are tough; they just keep going. Suddenly I understood. Why? Because that's the way it is! It's not that people don't care, but rather it is what it is; that's just reality. Therefore, stop asking why. If the Jewish people just kept asking why, we would still be slaves in Egypt. Instead, the Jewish people don't have time to ask why; we're too busy moving forward.

A week after my house burned down (literally while I was giving birth to my second child) I was in the park, taking my daughter for fresh air. People would stop and ask me how I was able to be out and about. Most women stay in bed for a month after giving birth, but there I was, as if nothing had happened. As if I hadn't just had a baby, wasn't homeless, wasn't spending my days and nights cleaning the few belongings we managed to salvage from the fire. What strikes me most about these interactions is the beauty of the recognition and awareness of others. Everyone wants to be great, but no one wants to experience the challenges that make them great. You can't just go to sleep and wake up great; you have to do the work.

When I suddenly became a single mother to four little kids, I told myself that there was no way I could possibly make it through. I mean, I know I'm strong and capable, but people don't realize how single mothers never get a break, and I was dealing with trauma, mine and theirs; the weight of our world was on my shoulders alone. It doesn't matter if I was sick, hurt, or just couldn't get myself out of bed—I had to show up. On top of it all, Pesach was coming. With the help of God, I managed to make a beautiful Pesach. I remember how people would say, "You aren't going out with your kids, right? You can't possibly go on trips with two kids and two babies and no one else to help you." But I wasn't willing to let my kids miss out on an amazing Pesach, so I took them on trips anyway. I carried the babies, the bikes, the stroller, all in the rain. We even went to a water nature reserve, me and four little kids in the water. Yes, it's crazy, but we did it. Everyone was happy, everyone had fun.

"*Why*" is not a question. "*Why*" allows you to be a victim, and even though victimhood is not a happy place, it is a comfortable place for many of us. Victimhood allows us to blame the world for everything that's wrong with our lives and let go of the need for any effort on our side. After all, if the world is out to get me, then no matter what I do, it will go all wrong, so what's the point of trying? People love being victims; it gives us room to be passive observers of life instead of active characters. But these so-called victims are doomed to stay in the same place; they wallow in their misery and lose hope in a better life. They get used to their situation because they are too afraid of thinking differently, of opening themselves up to opportunities for change, opportunities for greatness, in case it fails. They sit idly and watch their lives quickly fade in front of their eyes because they weren't strong or brave enough to change any of it. *Kacha*, it is what it is. It's not that I don't care about your pain—I can help you carry it, I can cry with you and hug you, but I can't take it away or change it for you. All I can do is stand by you, cheering you on, trying to transmit the strength to change your outlook.

Psychology says we only use 70 percent of our brainpower. I don't want to disagree with science, but that statistic seems very limiting to me. It's like saying there is a limit to what we can achieve, and there isn't; you can do anything. However, you won't do it on your own, you're too comfortable to mess with what you have. Yet, God loves you too much to let you waste your potential, so He helps you grow into your abilities instead. It may not be in the form you want it, but it is the only way to breed the greatness within you.

One of my favorite movies is *Soul Surfer*, based on the inspiring true story of Bethany Hamilton, a professional surfer who lost her arm to a shark bite. Bethany wanted to give up surfing entirely, but she was inspired by the endless love and support she received from the people around her. It gave her the strength to learn to surf with one arm and take part in a major competition. Even though she doesn't win the competition, reporters swarm around her, full of questions. One reporter asks her if she could, would she go back and prevent losing her arm. She firmly answers no because she never would have been able to embrace as much with two arms as she has with one. At the end of the day, the question is, are we put on Earth to live for our bodies or our souls? The most important part of life is to let our souls soar higher and higher, closer to God. Do we all have the potential to become great people? Yes, of course. But it is difficult to choose greatness over going to the mall, or to the movies, or over any other earthly distraction.

When people ask me how I deal with my challenges in life, I echo the woman who said, "I was chosen, I didn't choose." Because the One who chose me sees my ability to not only overcome the hardship but actually glorify it. Just the other week, I thought to myself how people see me now—totally functional, nicely put together, teaching—and they have no idea that a little less than five months ago, my world literally crumbled in front of me. When I think about it, it amazes even me. But it also irritates me. How do I hold it together; why do I do it? Can't I just break down and allow others to pick up the pieces for me? I mean, it would be totally understandable; wouldn't it be better to stay in bed, wallowing? And that's all I want to do, to be honest. But instead, here I am. I thought my life was over, but now I am really living, changing, learning to thrive—writing a book that I hope will help others do the same! Fight! Heal! Live! Why? Because. I have finally come to understand that it just is what it is. It may be ugly, but it's what we got, and it's what we're going to have to work with. And I'm so proud that at the lowest point in my life, I am able to maintain a stable home for my kids, I am able to get up and daven every day, I am able to give to others even when I have almost nothing left to give to myself. I may criticize myself a lot, hold myself to impossible standards, but I am amazed at what I have accomplished in these past few months.

Once you stop asking *"why,"* you can get to the next question, the one that sounds the same but has a completely different meaning and dimension to its greatness: *l'ma*, for what? For what is this pain? What is its purpose? What can I do with it, how can I grow, where will this take me, how can it lead me? These are the questions I ask myself every day. I can't change the reality of what I'm living, but I can change the way I'm living it. Asking yourself "for what?" will give you back your power. Because when all is lost and you feel helpless, nothing will give you greater pride or happiness than mastering your pain and once again regaining control of your life. While I may not have control over my circumstances, I can always have control over myself and the way I choose to see things. By asking yourself "for what?" you can transform everything into an opportunity, and even into a blessing. It doesn't matter what comes your way, your happiness and sense of self will remain intact because you will be the narrator of your own story. Hashem gives us pain, and sometimes the pain is so great we wish we could just cut off whatever hurts, but He doesn't give us suffering. Suffering is chosen; suffering happens when you choose to be a victim of your pain, to allow it to go through you, but not inspire you.

After Yaakov fought with the angel on the eve of his meeting with Esav, he demanded the angel give him a blessing. Yaakov's request implies that while the angel tried to destroy him and failed, he is still left with residual pain and trauma. He insists the angel bless him so as to give a positive reason for the suffering he was caused; he won't let the angel go until he turns the pain into a gift. In other words, it is the painful things in life that generate the good. It's interesting to consider how, when the Jewish people left Egypt, a census found that the Tribe of Levi was the smallest tribe by far, with less than half of the population of the tribe just above it. How could that be? Our sages teach us that every Israelite birth in Egypt was sextuplets, specifically because the Israelites were in pain. As the *pasuk* says, "As they made them suffer, so they would grow." Since the Tribe of Levi wasn't enslaved, they didn't experience the suffering of their brethren. Therefore, they didn't benefit from the abundance and blessing of their numbers.

I'd like to take this concept to the next level: We said that divine tests are an expression of your potential, but the truth is that this statement is incomplete. It is not only that divine tests are an expression of your potential, but that you have no idea of your potential until you are tested. You can't know what you can become until you are pushed to become it. God is constantly coaching us into greatness, inspiring us to keep going so that we may level up. Look back to your life—how many times were you ready to give up? Yet here you are; stronger, more resilient. How did you manage it? You managed because you had to, because you were being pushed in that direction and you embraced it. I remember the first time I realized this concept. I was twenty-eight years old, planning my first international speaking tour, and I thought to myself, "Wow! How did you get here? You, little Raquel? Didn't you think you were just going to sell popsicles on the street?" I couldn't stop smiling to myself because I realized that all this time God was training me. He pushed and pulled me in many directions, all to bring me to this moment. We think potential is something innate within us that lays dormant until it's activated. But that's a mistaken idea. Potential is something we create within ourselves as we go. Like I always say, when you have to, you have to, but if you don't, you won't. When you are being called on, you will rise to the occasion. But how can you rise to the occasion if none exist?

Humans have a tendency to survive the impossible. Like the thirty-three miners who were stuck in a mine with enough food to last three people one week. Yet, all of the miners survived for more than two months underground. How? And how did people survive the Holocaust? We all know people who managed to survive impossible situations, and we know that if it had been us, we would have given up much sooner. So how did they do it? If God only gives you that which you can carry, then it means that before He gave it to you, He gave you the ability to carry it! Listen to the beauty of this: Each test comes with new tools, new ways to expand on oneself. These gifts are given to you alone, and only you can use them because they are needed for your specific journey. Because others haven't been given the tools, they can't possibly understand how you can come out the other end. It's like reaching a new level in *Mario Brothers*. You have to confront new obstacles; you aren't facing the same little mushrooms from the first level. Now you are given the snow gear, the helicopter, the flowers to shoot at oncoming enemies. This new level is more challenging, so you need the right equipment to beat it.

I saw an amazing TED Talk by Amy Purdy, who at eighteen years old was very sick and lost both of her legs. As if losing her legs wasn't bad enough, she was a professional snowboarder; she depended on her legs. With her legs gone, she questioned what her life was about, what could she possibly do now that she lost it all? What she didn't know is that by losing it all, she really gained it all. She went on to become a Paralympian and traveled around the world teaching and inspiring. At the end of her presentation, she said some of the most powerful words I've ever heard: "Our borders and our obstacles can only do two things, stop us in our tracks or force us to get creative."

When I visited Taglit's Center for Israeli Innovation, I was amazed by the sheer number of startups, ideas, and inventions being created and nurtured in Israel. How do you explain how such a small country can have so many impressive achievements? The answer blew my mind. Israel is plagued with difficulties: we are literally surrounded by enemies, 60 percent of the land is desert, and we have limited natural resources. However, we are rich in brainpower. Therefore, instead of being stuck and asking why, we generate creative solutions. It is precisely our challenges that produce extraordinary outcomes, allowing us to transform what seemed impossible into the possible. Even though today we approach innovation as a concept without borders, I know that in my life, innovation has only been possible because of my borders. Borders may represent existing limits, but they also represent where imagination and creativity begin. Maybe instead of looking at our challenges negatively, we can look at them as gifts through which we may ignite our imagination, helping us to reach places we never thought we could go. Life is not about breaking down our borders; it's about expanding them to see how far they go.

PIN IT TO YOUR HEART!

"It is precisely our challenges which produce extraordinary outcomes, allowing us to transform the impossible into the possible."

"Life is not about what you carry, but how you carry it."

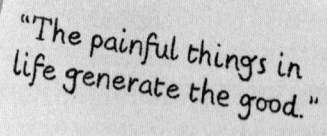

"The painful things in life generate the good."

"Divine tests are an expression of your potential, but you can't know your potential until you are tested."

"Life is not about breaking down our borders, it's about expanding them to see how far they go."

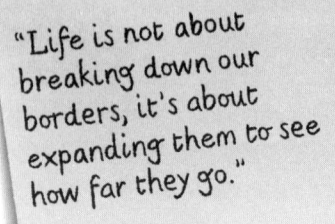

CHAPTER EIGHT

FEAR AND CONTROL

The most difficult state of life to be in is that of the unknown, where you have no control over the situation, no idea what is going on, or how long it will last. We were created in the image of God and therefore often fall into the trap of thinking we are godly in our ability to create and destroy. While this is true to a certain degree, and though we can make certain choices and control the outcome to an extent, the world is far more complicated than that. The unknown generates a lot of confusion, instability, despair, and doubt. Therefore, people love control; when we know what to expect, we can plan accordingly. But when we don't know what comes next, we are constantly wondering what we are going to do next and how we can prepare for whatever it is. When you don't know what comes next, you are stuck in a kind of holding pattern. Life becomes hard to manage, like preparing for a battle without knowing where or when the battle will take place, or even who the enemy is. What kind of planning could you possibly do?

And then there is the fear of the unknown. What if you plan a vacation and then you can't make it? What if you choose a career without considering the possible changes that may occur in your life? When you are single and you start dating someone, it's terrifying because you know everything can change in a minute. The fear of putting yourself out there and nothing happening. How long will you be single? How many more times will you have to go out on a first date and have the same conversations? What if you get married but don't get pregnant? There are no guarantees, no promises of what's to come. But there is always that one question hanging over you, generating fear, doubt, and panic: What if? What if I never get married? What if I never have children? What if I never find a job? Fear can be too much to handle; it can freeze you in your tracks, preventing you from reaching your goals. Even more so, fear can transform you, take over who you are. Living in fear means you are constantly in fight-or-flight mode; all you think about is surviving.

Of course, the unknown can also be the greatest gift, forcing you to grow and draw strength from within. It can push us to cultivate our *emunah*. Yet, the process of reaching that *emunah* can sometimes be full of hopelessness. *Emunah* means existing in a place of not knowing; like closing your eyes and jumping, with no idea who will catch you, like a trust fall. A trust fall depends on two things: trusting that you will be caught and trusting that the one who catches you has the ability and strength to do so. The funny thing about trust falls is that, despite understanding that the point of the exercise is to trust that the person behind you will catch you, you are still worried that you will not be caught. Your only job is to trust that someone will be there and that they will catch you. Think about it, you would never perform a trust fall if you didn't know that someone is standing behind you, ready to catch you, right? It's too much of a risk. But when you know someone is there, it's easier to let yourself fall. The same applies to life—it's about taking the plunge. We may be falling with no direction, but we trust that we will be caught regardless. That's precisely how it works with faith as well. Do you trust God? Are you willing to be led to a destination that you don't know? Will you just stand still until situations are resolved on their own, or will you trust yourself and God and take the necessary actions?

The *Midrash* tells us that when Nachshon ben Aminadav jumped into the Yam Suf, the waters only separated once it reached his nose. Not because he couldn't breathe at that point, but rather because the nose is the seat of pride. If his nose was higher, the water would have split later. We need to lower our noses, bow our heads in humility, and accept that even if it doesn't make sense, doesn't look like it will work out, we need to trust in Hashem and jump in. That's all God wants from us, trust.

We see in *Pirkei Avot* that Avraham was tested with ten trials, but as usual, the rabbis don't agree on exactly what the tests were. When I was studying, I found it interesting that the Rambam considers *"lech lecha"* to be the first test, and not "Ur Kasdim." In other words, as far as the Rambam is concerned, Avraham being thrown into the fire for his beliefs is not a test, but being commanded by God to travel to an unknown destination is. Both experiences are hard, but in the first one Avraham was willing to give up his life while in the other he was just sent to travel. The Rambam explains that in order for a test to be considered a test, it must defy logic. Avraham knew he was going to be thrown into the fire and willingly chose to accept it as his fate because he believed in God and was willing to sacrifice his life for his faith. It was Avraham's choice to give up his life; he was in control of his fate. But when he was commanded *"lech lecha,"* Avraham was forced to relinquish independence. The choice he made was to give up control, to be guided to a nameless location simply because he trusted in God. It's almost incomprehensible to think about, but that's exactly the point. That kind of trust goes against all logic and reason, and is therefore a true manifestation of *emunah*.

People often ask me how I manage to have so much *emunah*, and the answer is that I had to develop it; otherwise, I would have given up a long time ago. The thing about *emunah* is that it's not all or nothing; it is made up of complex layers that we can't always understand. At the same time, having *emunah* doesn't mean we see the world through rose-colored lenses; we still anticipate the pitfalls of life. But the degree to which we develop *emunah* is directly related to our ability to overcome our falls. The truth is, it's easier to be in an unknown state when you know God is running the show. As painful as it is, if we work on our *emunah*, then we have the ability to trust that God only wants what's good for us and ultimately there will be a positive outcome. Obviously, it's easier said than done, but at least we have that.

In my classes on prayer, I teach that often we will pray but not receive what we prayed for. We think God said no to our request and we accept it; we even feel good about it because we feel we are accepting God's will. The reality is that many times, this isn't the work of the *yetzer hatov*, but rather of the *yetzer hara*. The *yetzer hara* disguises himself and makes you feel comfortable with the rejection so that you won't want more, you won't want better, and you accept your life as is. Sometimes accepting "no" is easier than accepting the possibility that there is a "yes"; it just isn't the right time for the "yes." That's because we don't know how much more we can try, how much more rejection we can take until we get what we so badly desire. How many more tests can we pass before we get our reward? Accepting the "no" is easier because at least it gives us a false sense of control. It might sound crazy, but we do it all the time. Our minds play tricks on us, disguising our difficult reality in nicer colors so we will stop pushing. We revert to the "at least mode" mindset and become accustomed to our difficulty, so much so that at some point it doesn't even move us anymore; it barely hurts us.

When I was struggling to conceive for almost four years, it was one of the hardest things I had to deal with up to that point in my life. There was a part of me that thought, "Well, maybe I just won't have kids, maybe it's part of my mission in life, what God wants for me. And if it is, am I willing to accept it? Am I willing to live my life devoid of the happiness I crave? How will I be able to walk on the street, seeing all of the families around me, wondering what happened that I was left out?" You see, my fears were so strong that at some point, I made a kind of peace with the idea of not having kids. Most of us don't realize it, but to feel the same pain over and over again, to relive it in every scenario, makes it so that eventually we accept the possibility as a probability. That's exactly what the *yetzer hara* wants; he wants us to lose all excitement for the future and accept reality as it is, to make peace with our rejection. This way, our lives will remain static and we won't be actively trying to grow. We can be so bogged down with fear that we can't take the first small steps because the "what ifs" get in the way—What if it doesn't get better? What if I don't make it through? But... what if you do?

The thing about fear is that when you don't know what is going on, you become consumed by possibilities. When you don't know what is, then suddenly everything can be. During my marriage, I suffered from panic attacks and constant nightmares where I imagined all sorts of terrible things that could happen to me with no one around to protect me. The worst part was that, in these dreams, the people hurting me were those who should have been the ones protecting me. I had nightmares in which the roof and walls around me seemed to be contracting, closing in on me, and I would wake up, yelling that we have to hold them off or we will be crushed. My dreams were reflecting my subconscious fears about being crushed by the weight of my reality. So I convinced myself I was doing the right thing by leaving things as they were. I told myself that the Torah doesn't want couples to get divorced, that I'm doing it for my children. I chose to sacrifice my own life for a greater good, but was there really a greater good, or any good at all?

What many of us don't understand about fear is that we will do anything to have a hold on that fear, and many times that means we become control freaks as a result. When you're living in survival mode, your animalistic instincts kick in. But what kind of mother can you be when your survival instincts take over? What kind of wife? How can someone in survival mode build strong relationships when the definition of survival is taking care of oneself? I had become a controlling person, holding on to everything I could so that

I could feel in charge of my life in any way. But the problem with seeking control is that the more you seek it, the more you express a lack of control. People who suffer from eating disorders, self-harm, and addictions generally do so as a way of taking control of their own lives. Of course, eventually their so-called instruments of control take over, and they lose control of themselves entirely. And that's how I felt. My need for control was affecting every aspect of my life, especially my relationships with God and with my children. I couldn't keep living like that; I had become angry, bitter, and resentful. I was disappointed with my lot in life, and I couldn't see the beauty of life anymore. I felt like my life was rolling downhill at high speed and I couldn't do anything to stop it.

When Yaakov fought with the angel, the *pasuk* says "*vaye'avek ish imo,* and a man fought with him." One interpretation is that sometimes we have to fight to keep our humanity because with everything going on around us, we may not always be aware of who we are anymore, of who we want to be. To be honest, I didn't like myself. I was so afraid of imitating the behavior I saw as a child, yet there I was, mimicking and reflecting so many of those behaviors, constantly triggered and acting on my triggers. I never had much compassion for myself; throughout my life, I was ashamed of who I had become and allowed myself to be overcome by that shame. I kept oscillating between, "Why would Hashem allow me to be a vessel to teach His Torah?" and "Why don't I practice what I teach?" I couldn't understand who I was, where I was holding in life. I felt so lost, so embarrassed, so guilty. It seemed that everyone was seeing something I didn't. How can the world love me? I'm not being a hypocrite; I've always been open about my personal failures and my struggles. Many have said that the reason people connect to my classes so much is because of my rawness, my open vulnerability, and authenticity. But I felt like a fake; I felt that if anyone saw who I really was, they would be disgusted by me. I treated myself so poorly when, really, I should have given myself more credit. I was giving and giving—to my children, to my spouse, to my students—but I wasn't giving to myself.

I'm crying as I write this, thinking of how much I misunderstood myself. I didn't think I could share; I was so embarrassed, scared for people to see the real me, scared of being rejected again. I was so critical and judgmental of my behavior while using all I had left just to survive. I should have been more compassionate and understanding; I should have believed in myself more. The guilt was consuming me. I was so harsh on myself. Couldn't I find some room for forgiveness for myself? "Raquel," I should have told myself then, "you tried all you could. You were still giving, hoping, praying, despite it all. Your whole life, you've been struggling. You never had a day off, not one day where you were on safe ground. Do you even realize that you never got to be you because you were always in fight-or-flight mode?" I just wish I could go back and give myself a hug for all the times I was so critical of myself and there was no one there to hold me and comfort me. Now I can understand that all this self-loathing and negative thinking was the inner voice of my childhood self speaking. If only I could have recognized it earlier, heard and validated it sooner.

When my divorce became public, I slowly began to feel trapped in something I couldn't escape. My personal fears began to get the better of me—the fear of being a failure, of what people would say, of how it would reflect on my religiosity. When I finally publicized my divorce and people reached out to me in support, I still felt the need to provide excuses. "I hope I didn't disappoint you," I would say. "I didn't mean to fail you. Please don't think this has anything to do with religion..." Where was my self-worth, my self-respect? There were so many years where I didn't put myself as a priority; I was losing my livelihood because of the fear of moving on. But these were legitimate fears. What will happen to me, to my teaching, to everything I've built? How can I live with a scarlet letter on my forehead? How can my kids grow up without a father? Who will help me? How will I manage? How will I keep up with all of the housework? How will I manage as an immigrant who doesn't even know the language here? Will I ever get remarried? Will anyone ever love me? How can I start again? What's going to happen when I publicize this? How will people look at me? How will I pay the bills? I don't know how to do anything!

STOP!

Why are you sabotaging your happiness? Why are you putting yourself into self-destruct mode? You have to let go. Since when are you inadequate? You are one of the smartest people you know. Why do we make such erroneous assumptions about ourselves? Through what foggy lenses are we looking at our lives? At the end of the day, who am I living for?

I've been asked many times by therapists and rabbis how I survive, how I manage to stay normal, and how I manage to continue to give to others. What's incredible is that when I did pour my heart out and finally shared the difficult trials of my life, I wasn't met with disdain, rejection, or shame; I was met with applause! Praise for my bravery and courage, for my honesty and vulnerability. All those years, I was terrified of what was going to happen, and once it did, I was okay after all. In fact, I was more than okay. When you carry your shame alone, you convince yourself that it is humiliating and too heavy a burden to let go, but when you set it free, you also let go of that heavy weight.

One of my rabbis, Ari Winter, always taught me that fear stands for three things:

Forget Everything and Run

False Expectations Appear Real

Face Everything and Recover

I spent most of my life relying on the first two options, but now it is time to take control, to face everything and recover. I am certainly on my way to recovery; I've never been this self-aware, this vulnerable. Even as I write this book, I'm still thinking, "Will you really do it? Will you let people see all of you?" The answer is yes. We need to learn to see all of ourselves, acknowledge that every part of us is part of who we are. We can't exile the parts of ourselves we don't like because, as we said before, they will only come back and haunt us. When we welcome our least favorite parts of ourselves, embrace them, and choose to understand and have compassion for them, then they can start acting for us and not against us. We need to tell ourselves: This is me! I don't want to be afraid anymore; I am not living my life for the approval of others. The only approval I need is from The One Above. At the end of the day, when I have made my bed and sleep in it, will I like my bedfellow? Or will I make myself uncomfortable? What kind of sleep can we have when we can't sleep with who we are? It's all about the self-acceptance. I'm gaining acceptance, self-love, understanding.

I remember hearing Rabbanit Rachelle Sprecher Fraenkel, the mother of Naftali Fraenkel H"yd, speak at one of the programs I was leading. She told the story about how after her son and the two other boys went missing and the IDF spent two weeks looking for them with no luck, they thought it was time to show her evidence of what they believed may have happened. They had a recording of the last call one of the boys had made, in which a gunshot was heard in the background. The soldier asked her if she wanted to listen to the recording. She panicked and said, "No, I can't."

The soldier, lacking tact but making up for it with earnestness, asked her what was the worst that could happen.

She answered, "I'll fall, I'll break!"

"So what if you fall?" he asked, "So what if you break?"

"What do you mean?" she cried. "I'll fall!"

But the soldier pushed, "And then what?" he asked.

"And then..." she said, slowly, "and then I will get up and keep going."

We will all fall at some point; we will all break. It's inevitable in life. There were dozens of times my own falls and breaks were so brutal that I doubted my ability to get up. But I did, with the help of God and the angels He sent. I got up, and then what? I kept going. I always kept going, stronger than before. I'm proud; I will applaud myself shamelessly. I will applaud my own ability to never give up, I will applaud myself for conquering my fears and facing them head-on, and staying true to myself through it all. There is a *pasuk* in *Tehillim* that says, "*Kol Hashem ba'koach,* the voice of God is in our strength." I had no idea how strong I could be; I was too afraid of having to find out. Thank you, Hashem, for giving me no other choice but to do it. It's been difficult, but I have paid the bills, taken care of the children, made sure everyone is happy and moving on, and most importantly, I have taken care of myself. Despite all the pressure of what's going on, with all its added stresses, I feel freer and lighter now than I ever have before.

When the Jewish people stood in front of the Red Sea and Hashem told them to walk into the water, they froze. They were too afraid; they felt like there was no way out and they were closed in from all directions. On one side were wild animals, on another side was the desert, the Egyptians were closing in from a third side, and in front of them was the vast sea. They were hopeless; they couldn't simply walk into the water, they would drown. Bitterly and despairingly, they cried out to Hashem. And then, Hashem spoke some of the most powerful words in the whole Torah: "Moshe, why are you crying out to Me? Speak to the Children of Israel and tell them to go." It's an odd question that Hashem has for Moshe—why are you crying out to Me? What do you mean, isn't that what the Jewish people do? We pray. Is Hashem telling us not to pray? No, we just misunderstand what prayer really is. Prayer is an affirmation of our belief that Hashem runs the world; prayer evokes a command for action. Do you believe? Then why are you standing there? Act, jump in. Yes, it is scary. Yes, it seems illogical. But it will get you to the other side. You just need to jump.

We are often so afraid of what will be that we allow fear to take over, allow it to freeze us in place. But, as we've said, the fear of what will be is greater than the thing itself. Your fear makes expectations appear real when they are not necessarily as you may imagine them. We must face our fears, get up, and believe in ourselves and in God. Once we reach the other side, we'll realize... was that really it? Is that all it took? We did it. Don't wait anymore; you are only waiting for yourself on the other side.

PIN IT TO YOUR HEART!

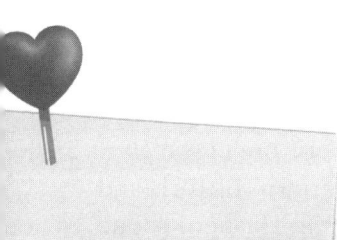

"It is a great challenge to exist in a state of not knowing, but it is a gift."

"*Emunah* means jumping in with your eyes closed but your heart open."

"*Emunah* is like a trust fall; it depends on two things: trusting you will be caught, and trusting that the one catching you has the ability and strength to catch you."

"Fear stands for Face Everything and Recover."

"The only approval that matters is the approval of God."

"The fear of what will be is greater than the thing itself."

CHAPTER NINE

DANCING IN THE RAIN, SINGING THROUGH DARKNESS

There is a beautiful *Midrash* that tells us what happened when the three Jewish advisers, Mishael, Hananiah, and Azariah, were thrown into the fire for not bowing down to Nebuchadnezzar's idol. Miraculously, they were saved from the fire, and when Nebuchadnezzar saw this, he was so inspired that the *Midrash* tells us he sang praises that were more beautiful than *Tehillim*. But God saw this and said, "Do you think you can sing better praises than my son, David?" He immediately sent an angel to hit Nebuchadnezzar and make him stop singing. This

Midrash is certainly confusing. Why would Hashem want David HaMelech to remain undefeated, with no competition at all? Why can't Nebuchadnezzar express himself? If he felt like singing in praise, let him sing. So what if it is greater than *Tehillim*? His praise is an honest reflection of what he feels in his mind and his heart. Can no one else sing praise to God just so that David HaMelech may remain the king of praise?

There is no power like the power of *Tehillim*. These are prayers that, for generations, we have connected to as a people; prayers that we turn to whenever we feel lost or hopeless, crying out to Hashem through the holy words of King David. But why is *Tehillim* so powerful? When we think about it, there is no one who suffered a more difficult life yet still sang out in praise to Hashem the way that David did. Throughout his life, David HaMelech suffered constant persecution; he wasn't treated as his father's legitimate child, he had to flee King Shaul's wrath, and one of his sons tried to kill him. Even when he became old, he couldn't find comfort or warmth in his body. When we look at his life, when we see how he was tested, we could easily say that he should have given up, thrown in the towel, and doubted the benefit of doing what's right if this is how Hashem rewards him. But he didn't do that. He did the exact opposite when he wrote *Tehillim*, which means "praise." King David found a way of praising God, not in spite of his difficulties, but amid his difficulties. He saw God in everything and in every situation.

It's interesting to note that the word *Tehillim* is in plural form. Perhaps this is because the wisdom and greatness of life is to sing continually, to add in praise, to add in song. Maybe the reason David HaMelech became who he was is because he made a song of praise out of everything in his life. He found rhyme and reason to everything that he was doing and everything that happened to him; he found purpose, connection, and opportunity. King David didn't reject his struggles in life; rather, he welcomed even the most difficult moments with an open heart. That's why he writes in *Tehillim* 23, "Even if I walk through the valley of death, I shall fear no evil, your cane and your stick will comfort me." David HaMelech found comfort in the cane and in the stick—in that which supports you as well as in that which hits you and rebukes you. Why? Because when you live with God, that's exactly how you feel; it is all the same, all coming from the same source, and therefore our perception and understanding of it is what's lacking. In its essence, it is always perfect, always good.

Maybe that was the whole point of the *Midrash* on Nebuchadnezzar. Everyone wants to sing when they feel inspired, when they are surrounded by miracles and God opens their eyes to His greatness and majesty. But do they still want to sing when they are being beaten, when things aren't going well, when they are in pain? It's not that God minds if Nebuchadnezzar's praise is more beautiful than *Tehillim*, but the beauty of *Tehillim* is not in its words or rhymes; it is in its meaning and emotion. The beauty of *Tehillim* is that David sang through the dark times. Hashem is essentially saying, "Let Me hit you, and if you still want to sing after that, then I will receive it fully, but if not, then you are not singing from a place of truth but rather from spiritual infatuation and temporal inspiration." We only sing when we are inspired, connected, but what about during challenging times? During times of darkness?

In *Tehillim* 92, David writes, "*L'hagid ba'boker chasdecha, v'emunatcha ba'leilot,* to speak of His kindness in the morning and of His faithfulness at night." When we thank and praise God, we do so in the morning, when we can easily recognize His kindness and can testify to His goodness. But what about the night? In the night, we don't have much to say except for, "I trust you, Hashem. I don't see you, but I trust you!" It's interesting to note that in the verse, the word "morning" is in singular form, while "night" is in plural. Why? Because that's how limited our *emunah* and relationship with God is. When life is good, and everything is rosy, we know within ourselves that God loves us and cares for us. In those moments, it is easy to acknowledge Him as the source of good. But at night, when it is dark and we start to reflect on the negativities of life and feel like we are being attacked from so many directions, it is harder to see God's goodness. What's going on, Hashem, did You get confused? Is someone else running this show now? Yet it is always God; we just don't always have the clarity to perceive Him as the source of everything, good and bad. Maybe we don't want to.

When we speak about *emunah,* we know on an intellectual level that *emunah* means belief in God, trusting in His ability to run the world. Emotionally, however, we tend to think that *emunah* means that everything will be the way we want it to be; that is the only way it can be good. When we say we have *emunah,* it's often conditional—it only applies if things turn out for the good in a way in which we define what good is. We don't always accept whatever God sends us, only whatever we want to receive. Yet, *emunah* really means knowing and accepting that everything God does is good. Whether or not we see it doesn't affect the essence of the matter. So, how do we get to that place of accepting and understanding? "*L'hagid ba'boker chasdecha,*" speak of the kindness of the morning, remind yourself about the good things, when you did have clarity. Make yourself an active seeker of truth, of kindness, and then you will have enough emotional fuel to keep you going through the difficulties of the night. We can't stay connected to God when we are running low on gas. We need to access our emotional savings accounts, to make a withdrawal from our stores of knowledge and awareness of God from previous situations. Only then can you have true faith at night. *Emunah* means loyalty to and faith in God, so even though circumstances may make us want to let go, we trust in God's ability to do what is best for us.

The inspiration of David HaMelech is that he learned how to dance in the rain, how to sing out to God even from the lowest of places. He wrote *Tehillim* in the middle of the night, during a period of so much confusion and darkness, because he understood that difficult circumstances are also part of life. It is especially those moments of struggle in which Hashem guides and sustains us. That is precisely why David's instrument was the harp—because the stronger you pull on the strings, the more it allows for beautiful and clear sound. So too with our lives. Hashem may pull hard, but look at the music that results; look at the symphony that is created by finding harmony in it all. That's our job in life; we must learn how to sing through the difficulty and understand that it is all one song.

Often, when a woman goes through fertility treatments, she will be plagued with questions and doubt. Will I ever be a mother?

Will I ever get to nurse a baby? Not having children is not easy, especially in the religious world where we often value a woman based on how many children she has. As women, we are often hard on ourselves, often questioning our place in life. Why am I a woman if I can't fulfill my role as a mother? Will I be lonely forever? How will I be able to be a part of the Jewish community, which revolves around family, when I don't have a family? All of this is in addition to the physical and mental intricacies of the medical treatments themselves. The emotional and spiritual weight of the treatment is overwhelming and extremely painful. We go through so much, and more often than not, we are disappointed. We put all of our hopes, dreams, and yearning into these attempts, all for nothing. Failed fertility therapies can create so much strain in a marriage, in relationships with others, with yourself, and with God. Of course, you can come out of it stronger—my best *emunah* and prayer classes are given as a result of these experiences—but often the emotional rollercoaster may be too much to handle.

As a society, we teach our children to have as many children as possible. But what happens with those who can't? Do we use the same energies to teach tact, compassion, and understanding? Sadly, no. The reason why most couples experiencing infertility don't share their struggles is because it's a taboo in our community. It is still seen as a disability, a sickness. That's how I felt for all those years I struggled to conceive: disabled and incomplete. I couldn't understand why even this had to be difficult; couldn't I catch a break? The worst was that some people just wouldn't stop offering their two cents on the matter. Maybe you should be skinnier... maybe you exercise too much... maybe you are too stressed... maybe God doesn't want to give you children... I understand that people want to help—we Jewish people love to give advice even when it is not asked for or welcomed—but many times it is just hurtful. Why do many people always assume it is the woman's fault and blame her without foundations of guilt? After two years of trying to have *emunah* and give God space to act at the right time, we began the process of fertility treatments and quickly found out what the issue was. It was hard to accept, but I pulled myself together and thanked God for creating the option of fertility treatments so that we could welcome a child.

Apart from the usual difficulties of the treatments, my experience was amplified. Even though my husband came with me to all of the appointments and supported me throughout, this brought many more challenges to our relationship. I cried and cried because I felt that even if Hashem had wanted to perform a miracle for us and give us a baby naturally, maybe we didn't give Him enough time or space to do it. I worried I would be a stranger to my children, like I wasn't the mother of my babies through natural means. I felt I wouldn't be able to raise them with happiness and security if they had come to this world through so much pain and difficulty. Nowadays, I understand that my children have elevated souls, the kind of soul David HaMelech had, and therefore they had to come to the world just like he did, hidden so that the *satan* couldn't stop them from coming. My children are God's greatest gift to me; regardless of how they came, they are full of light, love, giving, and just pure, innocent joy.

When I was blessed with my first daughter Batsheva, beautiful Shevy, I was overwhelmed with gratitude, overjoyed by my beautiful miracle. I had waited for her for four years and she couldn't have been more precious to me. She was born on the 13th of Elul, the month of mercy, and I felt all of Hashem's thirteen attributes of mercy in my life. The pregnancy itself was smooth; I felt so good and healthy. But that year brought immense challenges in my marriage and much loneliness. I kept questioning what I should do, maybe I should have gotten divorced at that point, but I was pregnant. Then I had a baby, and how could I forgive myself for bringing a baby into such a situation and starting her off in the world with such an obstacle? Instead, I found comfort and shelter in her; she was the light of my life, the only reason for joy in my life. People used to laugh at me; I was so obsessed with her. In class, we would have "the Shevy minute" where I would just boast and admire how special she was and share one beautiful thing about her. Yet, even though I was so grateful and so happy, it was all quickly hijacked by obtrusive negative thoughts and emotions.

So, I was finally a mother, overwhelmed with feelings of gratitude, but also anxious, worried, sad, and disappointed. Isn't this supposed to bring a couple together? What happened to us? Are we going to have a real family, a real home? Because it felt like we were strangers living together. Instead, I gave all of what I had to my daughter, to my students, and just kept going. Later, when we started treatments for another child, many attempts failed but my teaching career was flourishing. I was able to fulfill so many of my dreams and it felt like God was pushing me away in one way, but also pulling me closer in another. It might not make sense that I wanted to bring another life into such a house, such a family, but is there any greater expression of love and godliness than giving life? I so badly wanted the joy of being a mother again, of carrying and cuddling a baby. And to be honest, I wanted the baby more for Shevy than for myself; I wanted her to have a friend, a companion. So I begged and begged Hashem; I couldn't wait for her to be a big sister. I wanted it for her more than I wanted it for anyone else. So we started the process again.

During the first round of fertility treatment for Shevy, they gave me so many hormones that I almost ended up in the hospital; I was too sick to function. For the second round, they decided to give me almost no hormones. I went in for the egg retrieval procedure and there was only one egg. This is terrible news to receive during the IVF process. You place all of your hopes in that one egg, and who even knows if it will develop, if it will become an embryo? And if it does, who knows if the pregnancy will even be viable? And sadly, there won't be any spare frozen eggs for backup. I was devastated; why did I go through such a difficult procedure only to have just one egg? I was crying when the non-religious nurse came in and reminded me that, "God only needs one egg." That's when I knew I was going to get pregnant. Because God only needs one egg, and I have one egg.

But the pregnancy was not a calm one. I caught a virus which has a high percentage of causing birth defects in fetuses. The doctors tried to get me to consider my "options" several times, but I refused to pay any mind to their hints. What's crazy is that testing for this particular virus is required before treatment, and it seems that I tested positive at the time but that the doctor had missed it. Again, I knew this baby was going to be an elevated soul. Throughout the pregnancy, doctors would ask me to do tests to check that everything was alright with the baby, and I would give them all an *emunah* shiur. "Hashem doesn't function on statistics," I would say. "I don't care what anyone says, Hashem can do anything. If there is a problem, He can take care of it; and if there isn't, I'm not going to look for one." The doctors were shocked by my approach; so many of them told me how my attitude was a point of strength for them, that they were in awe of my *emunah*. But, as we know, by then I had learned how to surf the really tough waves in my life, and I had spoken so much about God's kindness, that I had faith even at that moment of nighttime in my life.

At the time, we were living in a tiny apartment full of mold and no windows. We couldn't afford anything better, but we had made it our home and decided to stay there until we had two children, when there really wouldn't be enough space. But in Israel, housing prices are so high, so we calculated that we could stay in the apartment until the baby started crawling before it would really be too cramped for a family of four. I kept dreaming of having a house, but no option seemed feasible. But Hashem doesn't need options; He creates His own. And boy, was I being prepared for a surprise. Erev Pesach, the night of *biur chametz*, I went to the hospital to give birth to my gorgeous second daughter—a child who is pure sunshine, full of joy and laughter, and really adorable. What I didn't know was that, while I was giving birth, God had other plans, and our little apartment went up in flames. Like a *biur chametz l'mehadrin*, everything was burned. I was newly post-birth, with a toddler, and completely homeless. It was Pesach and there was nowhere for us to go. I didn't have much family here, and even what family I did have couldn't take me in. And then, one of the greatest parts of my life's journey took place.

I can't continue without sharing what was going on in my mind and my heart at that point. I had waited so long for a baby and this is what happened? I mean, you've got to be joking. People have babies without difficulty all the time, and by the time I'm finally blessed with another baby, it has to come hand in hand with such disaster? I felt disconnected, angry, resentful, sad, overwhelmed, and panicked. What now? I felt Hashem was demanding I pay a price for having my baby. After all, people did say that maybe I didn't deserve to have children. I was homeless and confused, questions flooding my mind. Where will I go from here? How will I do it? Everything I'd built for thirty-one years was now lost—our home, our memories. People think the greatest loss was the financial loss, but it wasn't. After losing your home, you are unstable and insecure; a nomad with no direction and zero control over anything. I had a newborn baby to care for, and no home in which to care for her. I felt like I had been abandoned, like I was being punished. We mentioned the profound loss of self that accompanies all loss, but this scenario felt even worse than that. I not only lost myself, but it felt like I lost my past and my future. I didn't know how I could possibly move on from this. I couldn't understand what God wanted from me, what my purpose was in life. I quickly gathered my thoughts, reminded myself that I had wanted a baby with all my heart, so if this was the price I had to pay, then so be it. "I don't know why You did this, Hashem," I said to Him, "but I will give in to You. I'm now homeless, but You are my Father, so take care of me!"

It was *Erev Pesach* and I thought about how when the Jews left Egypt, they were so scared that many of them actually chose not to leave. They were too afraid of the unknown, afraid of where they might end up, what the final destination might be. Yet those who trusted in Hashem very quickly received the reward for their trust. I asked Hashem to help me accept His kindness, I asked that I may grow from this new challenge, and I prayed that He may open my eyes to the blessing so that one day I could sing out my *emunah* and understanding of His ways, thanking and praising Him for all His kindness. And that's how my beautiful Shira Bracha came into the world. Shira refers to a song of praise and Bracha means blessing. I chose that name as a form of praise, but also as a request for better days: May we merit to sing Your praises by seeing the hidden and the revealed blessings that will come to us.

I remember that as I lay in my hospital bed, someone sent me a *chizzuk shiur* broadcast. The speaker related a famous story about a man who was told by his neighbors that his house was on fire and that he had lost everything. Every time they tried to tell him the news, he fainted. They went to the rabbi and asked him what to do since the man couldn't accept the news. The rabbi said that there must be a mistake; it must not be his house. The villagers asked how he could know that. The rabbi explained that if the man can't handle the news, it means he hasn't been given the strength to overcome this obstacle. Therefore, it must not be his house. I remember hearing this and thinking, "Wow, I must be stronger than that guy. I can overcome this; I will overcome this! I will rise from this struggle too, and my daughter will be a testimony to all of the praise and prayers I will sing to Hashem."

The Torah writes, "*Mehamar yatzah matok,* from the bitter came the sweet," and that is exactly what happened to me. What happened next was mind-blowing. Mere hours after the fire, my students had set up a GoFundMe campaign and they managed to raise money from people all around the world just for us. My phone was exploding with kind messages, people were cheering us on. The sheer amount of *chessed* and kindness that I experienced from Am Yisrael is priceless. The months following the fire were some of the hardest in my life. We moved houses six times in six months, dragging with us whatever belongings we were able to save from the wreckage of our apartment. You can hardly imagine what it was like. Imagine having everything you own, every piece of clothing, all your home goods, toiletries, shoes, games, books, reduced to carbon. Everything was strewn across the sooty floor, and we were forever cleaning, organizing, carrying, moving… there was no day or night, everything was just black ash with no end. I gave myself permission to cry twice a day; otherwise, I just wouldn't have stopped. On top of it all, I was finding it hard to connect to my baby, I could barely even feed her; by some miracle, she gained weight. Shevy was all over the place; she was suffering from behavioral regressions and tantrums. Our life was a mess; I felt like a mess.

I remember the first night out of the hospital, my students came to visit me, and I said, "Don't expect me not to cry." They reminded me that I had taught them that all is for the good, and that we must accept pain with joy, but I didn't think I could live up to those words. If there is one thing that is too difficult for me to accept, it is being a *nebach*, a sad and pathetic person dependent on the kindness of others. I always prided myself on being capable of pushing forward, of being strong and independent. And now here I was, unable to do anything on my own—I had no house, no clothing, and a newborn baby! My biggest challenge was learning how to receive and accept help from others, and receive I did—whoever wanted to help or give anything was welcome with profound gratitude.

The experience opened my eyes not only to the beauty of the Jewish people but also to my own beauty in the eyes of others. I thought no one loved me, no one cared, and yet here were thousands of people taking care of me. I needed to see that I wasn't alone, that I was cared for and loved. I finally understood that for all those years I wasn't giving in vain; I was building connections, sympathies, and relationships. And they came through at my moment of need. I guess, in a sense, I was asking for it to happen. I wanted to know people cared, to finally realize I was good enough, I was loved. That Hannukah, I made a *chanukat habayit* for my new home, a *kiddush* for my daughter, and *seudat hodaya* for the miracles we had experienced, and I marveled at how God did all of this. It took a couple of months, but I was able to look back and understand how this sweetness stemmed from bitterness. I should have trusted You from the beginning, Hashem, but I'm glad I finally did, that I was able to let go.

This challenge came to humble me, to help me understand that I am not superwoman, that it is okay to need help and to ask for help; it's okay to depend on others and it's okay to allow others to give to you. It's a mitzvah to give to others; there are no favors in this world, just the merit to be able to help others. I had to learn so many lessons, but not all of them were fully absorbed, and in my guts, I knew it was a matter of time until my next test. Speaking about dancing in the rain, about singing through the hardships, I learned it all the hard way. But I'm so blessed and grateful I was able to learn it after all.

Every day, as part of the *Pesukei D'zimra* prayer, we say "*baruch ata... yotzer or u'boreh choshech,* blessed are You... who forms light and creates darkness." Notice that the prayer differentiates between the "formation" of light and the "creation" of darkness. What is the difference? There are philosophical teachings that tell us that "to form" means to give shape to pre-existent material, but "to create" means making something out of nothing. God is pure light; but when we look at light directly, it is blinding, it impairs your vision momentarily. As Hashem told Moshe, no one can see Him and remain alive. However, light refracts in many colors so that we are able to grasp the images through individual colors instead of the blinding brightness. That's what a rainbow is—the refraction of light into isolated colors. Even though we see each color individually, all of them come from the same source. But being that light is infinite, it can't actually be divided; we may perceive the colors separately, but they are simply a categorized manifestation of the greater whole. So too with God. Sometimes you may perceive God as yellow in your mind, or sometimes as pink, but it's all the same because all of these colors stem from the same source. What color is light? It's not yellow or white; it's kind of transparent, right? But what does transparent mean? People think it means a lack of color, but the real definition means that every color is being reflected. That's how God's goodness works—we can't recognize His greatness all in one go; it would be too much for us to handle. Therefore, He divides the abundance into more easily digestible parts, giving us the opportunity to put the pieces together so that we may see the whole.

So then what does it mean that God creates darkness? First of all, if darkness is created it means it doesn't actually exist in perpetuity. Everything that's created needs to constantly be supported and sustained for it to continuously exist. If the Creator decides to stop sustaining it for even a moment, it fades away. Darkness is an illusion; its existence is relative, not absolute. It is the absorption of light. It is all-consuming and selfish, eating up the light that came before it. Light is giving, darkness is taking. Once we understand the difference between the two, then we can understand that the outcome of our circumstances depends on us. Consider it as if God is trying to shine His light into the world through a projector but we keep walking in front of the lens, blocking the light and obscuring the image.

If darkness is the absorption of light, then even though it may look pitch black, there is really more light in the darkness than there is in light itself. What I mean is that while the darkness contains the light in its embrace, the light is just waiting to explode outward, escape the dark; imagine the amount of light that may burst forth all at once compared to the light that already shines evenly. So too in our lives, there is more potential for light, for greatness, for growth in our moments of darkness than in our moments of light. That's what Yaakov meant when he demanded a blessing from the angel. He sought purpose in the fight, wanted a blessing to come from what seemed like a curse. We may not be able to see the blessings in our moments of darkness because our egos get in the way, blocking out the light. Only once we step outside ourselves, put down our egos, can we see God's light and understand there was a reason. Then we can begin to learn and grow and be blessed. Just as darkness is the absence of light, so too wickedness is a lack of godliness in the hearts of men. If we understand this, then everything changes, because we get to choose what ray of light we want to see, what color we want to reflect! Do we want to be givers or takers? But even more than that, we can understand that if everything comes from God, then everything is good in its essence—it is us who are limited in our vision, not Him!

The Torah teaches that a person must bless God for the bad just as he blesses God for the good. How can the Torah expect this from us? Pain is pain and pleasure is pleasure; the two are not comparable, so how can we be expected to respond equally to both? The *Gemara* teaches that in this world, we have different blessings for the bad and for the good. When something bad happens to us, we say, "*baruch dayan ha'emet*, blessed is the Judge of truth." It's like we are telling God that, even though we may not like it, we may not agree, we trust Your judgment. When something good happens, we say "*hatov u'metiv*, the One that is good and does good." We say this specifically because we can only perceive God's goodness when we ourselves feel we are surrounded by good. When *Moshiach* comes, God willing very soon, we will realize that all of the good and the bad in the world has always been one and the same. All of it was good; it was all light, because there is only one source of light and it is infinite. That's the secret of the *Shema* prayer, which we will discuss in later chapters. If we understand this, then what difference does it make if our lives are hard or easy, painful or pleasurable? It's all the same, it's all God.

There was a question about *Purim* that always bothered me: On *Purim*, it is said that we should get drunk to the point where we can no longer recognize the difference between blessing Haman and cursing Mordechai. What's the deal with that? Are we really meant to forget who's the bad guy? And why do we have to get drunk in order to do that? When we are completely conscious and aware of the world around us, we are limited by our logic; we perceive the world through a subjective lens and not an objective point of view. But when a person is drunk, he can connect to something greater than himself; his mind lets go of logic, thereby removing his limited understanding, and he is able to rise above himself. When you get to a place of no worldly limitations, with nothing holding you back from reaching more open ideas, then you can suddenly see what you couldn't before. You can suddenly see the whole picture. We are here to develop ourselves, develop our souls, and become godly. Who cares what the path is and which journey we take, the main thing is to reach our destinations. Yes, we can say Haman is bad, remind ourselves that there is pain in life; but if it brings us into greater consciousness and awareness, then is it not also the greatest gift? Some people get closer to God through the Hamans in their lives, some people get closer to Him through the Mordechais. Most of us choose the Hamans as our wake-up calls; it's a much louder alarm, much harder to ignore.

This is why on *Purim* we sing, "*mishenichnas Adar marbim b'simcha*, whoever enters the month of Adar increases in happiness." The Torah commands us to be in a constant state of *simcha*. How can we do that? More specifically, how do we do that when we are experiencing pain and struggle? The word *simcha*, happiness, shares many letters with the word *machshava*, thought, because happiness is dependent on one thing—how we choose to perceive our lives. If your perception of God is that He is the source of the light and the dark, the blessings and the curses, then it is all the same to you. This is why the *Shulchan Aruch* opens with the phrase "*shiviti Hashem l'negdi tamid*, I put Hashem in front of me always," to remind us that we should always remember there is a camera rolling every second, recording your every move, your every thought, and every emotion. But I like to read this *pasuk* in a different way: *shiviti*, meaning *shava li*, it is equal to me. The joy, the pain, the bitterness, the pleasure… everything is equal in my eyes because Hashem is in front of me always. So really, it's all a question of how you choose to live with God, how close you feel to Him, how you accept His running of the world and how He takes care of you.

I have had to learn how to sing through the darkness, and that has forced me to look for the light. People say to be grateful for everything in life, and it kind of just makes us want to quiet them. But I've come to understand that by being grateful, by forcing myself to see the beauty in everything, I am doing myself a favor. We must be able to recognize at least one positive element in our lives in order to be thankful. And when we do that, we often find many more.

PIN IT TO YOUR HEART!

"Life is like a harp, because the stronger you pull on the strings, the more of an opportunity for beautiful and clear sound."

"Make yourself an active seeker of truth, and then you will have enough emotional fuel to keep you going through the difficulties of the night."

"The wisdom and greatness of life is to sing continually, to add in praise, to add in song."

"Mehamar yatzah matok, from the bitter came the sweet."

"We must be able to recognize at least one positive element in our lives in order to be thankful. And when we do that, we often find many more."

"There is more light in darkness than in light itself."

"A person must bless God for the bad just as he blesses God for the good."

CHAPTER TEN

CHOOSING TO LIVE

In his famous book, *If You Were God*, Rav Aryeh Kaplan asks his readers to consider what they would do differently if they were God. Don't we do that all the time? We think God did a poor job with the way He runs the world or how He handles our lives. I mean, I love God, I have so much *emunah*, but I, as Iyov did, have asked myself plenty of times if He has gotten confused at some point, and if this is really how my life should look. It seems impossible not to ask myself this question at times. Even when I accept the pain and the challenges, there are still times where I can't help but wonder why certain things had to be presented as challenges, why they couldn't have come to me in another way. Like when people tell me to be grateful for the house fire because I got a new house out of it, or to be thankful for the fertility treatments because I got to have children. I am thankful, I thank Hashem constantly. But… there are plenty of people who get new houses without experiencing a fire, and plenty of couples who can conceive naturally without help, people who receive blessings unaccompanied by struggle. Sure, maybe they appreciate it less, and maybe I should stop looking at what others have, but it›s only human to have those thoughts. We want things to be good for us, we want our lives to be smooth, with fewer bumps in our paths.

Everyone reminds me that God saved me. "Look what He did for you," they say. "If He hadn't, you wouldn't have gotten out of that marriage. Be thankful, see His kindness." But don't they understand that I've had dozens if not hundreds of thoughts to counter that? Like, why did I have to get married at all? Why didn't He get me out before? I mean, I know Hashem has His *cheshbonot*, accounts, but some of them are hard to swallow. Sometimes we think that Hashem wants us to experience pain as a form of reparations for some wrongdoing. People have suggested to me that perhaps the reason for my struggles has been because I needed to cleanse my soul in some way. For real? How many sins must I have committed in this life, or in a past life, or in any life? Am I cleansing for the whole of the Jewish people? Is that really something to tell a person, that they are bad and need a whipping to repent? How is that helpful? Why would anyone want to carry on if they feel the load will only get heavier and more difficult with every wrong step? We must have it all wrong.

We know that when Nadav and Avihu died, Moshe felt a lack in himself; Rashi explains that he said to Aharon that God had told him that He would be sanctified through those that are close to Him, thinking through himself or Aharon, but was proven to be incorrect. His tears were not only for obvious reasons, but because he feared for his own fate. Hashem had promised that He would sanctify His name through those closest to Him. Nadav and Avihu were chosen by God as priests; they were among the holiest men of their time, as close to God as men could be. Yet they met with such terrible deaths. Moshe felt that he wasn't as elevated or holy as they had been and therefore worried what his own destiny might be. Is that the reward for holiness? Why did Nadav and Avihu meet with such deaths? We find the same idea with Rabbi Akiva! There is a famous *Midrash* which tells us how Moshe sat in the audience of this holy *gadol* and asked Hashem to see his reward, and God shows him Rabbi Akiva experiencing the most painful of deaths where his skin was being shredded by a copper comb. Moshe, confused, humbly asks, "Is this the Torah and is this the reward?" Allow me to paraphrase for a moment—"Hashem, are You kidding? Is this for real? Is what I'm seeing right now true? Shouldn't Rabbi Akiva be given a lavish banquet and a crown on his head?" And Hashem tells him to be quiet, it is beyond his capabilities as a human to understand. Hashem explains that Moshe sees and judges the world according to his limited human understanding. He is incapable of reaching God's level of understanding, and therefore incapable of understanding God's motives. And that's why Hashem tells him to be quiet, because he can't put God's ways into words, he can't understand. Hashem tells Moshe, "I know it hurts, I know you want to fight it, I know you want justice, but this is the greatest gift and the greatest reward Rabbi Akiva could have ever asked for." There is a famous *Gemara* which tells of a student who dies and appears to his rabbi in a dream, saying, "I can't tell you what I see here, but '*olam hafuch ra'iti*, it is an upside-down world.'" Trying to understand God's motives is like trying to calculate how life works with the wrong units of measurement.

Rav Moshe Shapiro offers a comforting answer to the question of Nadav and Avihu's deaths. He explains that when God created this world, He wanted to govern with Judgment, but He saw that the world couldn't be sustained in that way because with such high standards, none of us would be judged favorably or found to be deserving. So instead, Hashem chose to rule the world with Mercy. However, there are some special souls—elevated, holy souls—like those of Nadav and Avihu, and of Rabbi Akiva, and maybe even yours and mine, that stepped forward and offered Hashem the opportunity to do things how He had originally planned; souls that accepted *din*, judgment, so that they may receive their true rewards in the world to come, instead of the brownie points in this world. These are holy souls which, in a sense, gave God permission to run the world in the way He wanted, but it also means their actions are taken seriously. Nothing is forgotten or swept under the rug.

Think about it, we say that there was discourse between Hillel and Shamai, but we go according to Hillel because he represents mercy. Yet when Moshiach comes, we will follow Shamai who represents judgment. Does that mean, then, that really Shamai's way is preferred? It is certainly the more difficult way; how would we manage if all of our actions were under constant examination and we had to provide an account of everything we ever do? Yet that is the way it is really meant to be. You see, judgment is where the relationship really is. Judgment is like a synchronized dance, whenever you take a step, your partner takes a corresponding step in return. When there is judgment, everything is balanced out; every action has a reaction. That's what it means to be godly and to exist in the image of God. Mercy is a delayed reaction, like a dance partner who is offbeat by just a few seconds; it ruins the flow of the dance, the movement is not smooth, not even.

We like mercy, we need mercy, but mercy equals leniency, rendering one unfit to be judged at such high standards. Mercy is like a favor, like rounding up your grade so you don't get left behind—you didn't earn the grade, so you don't feel the same satisfaction from it. This is why even though God ends up running the world through mercy, He intended to run it through *din*, and He goes so far as to tell us that it was His original plan! In the very first chapter of the Torah, Hashem is referred to only by the name that represents His quality of Judgment, *Elokim*, whereas in later chapters, He is referred to by the name that represents Mercy, YKVK. The point being that though Hashem runs the world on mercy, we should live as if He ran the world by judgment. Assuming that God only ever exercises mercy would probably result in our always assuming that God will clean up our messes, that He'll brush them under the rug and let everything slide. But that's not how Hashem wants us to live our lives. He wants us to believe that every single thing we do matters, that our actions are important and valuable. Each one of us is individually responsible for this world. Why was the world created with only one human, Adam? It comes to teach us the precept, "Whoever saves a life is as if they saved the whole entire world." Because one person can be a whole entire world to God. When we live our lives the right way, we give purpose and meaning to the existence of the whole world.

Tractate Bava Kama says, "Whoever says that Hashem is indifferent to his actions, then let Hashem be indifferent to his life." Meaning, if you were to sometimes wish that some of your actions were to go unnoticed, then you will end up with a relationship to God in which all of your actions, your whole life, will go unnoticed by God. Kind of harsh, no? It's not that we want Him to ignore us completely, it's just we wish He couldn't see some of the bad things we do. It's more like we want to photoshop our lives in a way, retouch some of our weaker moments and only show God the good moments. Why is it, then, that if we ask for that, then God just ignores us completely? The answer is difficult, but when you get it, you will understand and appreciate yourself more.

There is a famous *pasuk* in *Tehillim* that asks, "Who is man that we should remember him, and a person that we should mention him?" Every *Rosh Hashana*, I stop for a minute and think, "God, who am I that You care so much about what I do? Why would an omniscient and almighty God care about little Raquel and her actions?" I mean, we all get to *Rosh Hashana* and know that we are going to be judged, but how does that make sense? Does the king mingle with the paupers and the villagers? Of course not! He has servants who do that for him. But on *Rosh Hashana*, Hashem Himself judges us, one by one and all together from every single angle. The question is why? Is it because He wants us to fail? Is He out to get us?

Growing up in a family of eight children, I noticed some cute and funny family dynamics. For example, the firstborn has tons of photos taken of her. Every day, with every outfit, every single move. The next ones have fewer and fewer photos taken of them over time until by the time the fourth or fifth kid comes around, there are hardly any solo photos, just group photos of the whole band together. As a younger sibling, you can forget about a photo of you in a cute outfit; it's a miracle you were even dressed that day at all!

CHOOSING TO LIVE

When a parent has their firstborn, God forbid should they miss out on any of their milestones, their first word, their first step... First-time parents will never leave their child for fear of missing something, of not having every moment recorded. Eventually, however, the child will talk so much that the parent will wish they were deaf for a bit, and they will run around wreaking havoc on the house and the parent won't be able to keep up with them. By the time the fifth kid comes around, the parents are content watching some of those milestones over video chat from their much-needed vacation. So, what happens between the first and the fifth child? What changes?

There's truly nothing like the firstborn; it comes with a lot of exciting first experiences for the parents and lots of emotions: excitement, curiosity, and anticipation. Parents will document every moment of the firstborn's life out of love—pure, intense, abundant love that they have never before experienced. We are all like God's firstborn; there will never ever be anyone else like any one of us. We are all unique; our lives are not copies of others, so God can't bear to miss a single, glorious moment. There is no sweeping things under the rug or photoshopping imperfections because we are perfect, loved creations. He wants to revisit and relive every moment of our lives because that's how much He loves us, like an adoring parent who can't stop taking photos of their child. Asking God to turn a blind eye on certain things, to retouch certain moments, is asking Him to let go of who we are, of what makes us special to Him. It's like denying that loving relationship, denying the value He places on our lives. A Jew doesn't get that compromise, doesn't have the luxury of separating himself from a relationship with God. We are chosen, we are loved, and therefore we have to live with God lovingly watching us at every moment. And the more He loves you, the more you are going to take center place.

That's what Moshe understood from the death of Nadav and Avihu. They were being judged in such a strict way because they were up to the highest standards in God's eyes. Because their potential was so great, He had to squeeze every ounce out of them. But did they really need to experience such a terrible death in order to make a *kiddush Hashem*? When holy people die for a *kiddush Hashem*, like victims of terror, for example, don't we say they are *kadosh*, holy and elevated? In other words, they are what we should aspire to be; that is the ultimate level. But obviously, we don't actually want that for ourselves or our loved ones. So instead, we choose to believe they didn't deserve such fates, or that they were being cleansed for misdeeds. It's easier for us to understand such fates in terms of punishment rather than reward. It may be soul cleansing, but maybe they are really the biggest *kiddush Hashem*.

A person experiencing hardship yet who remains connected to Hashem is like the metaphor of the potter who shows off his best wares by testing their strength. It is easier to die *al kiddush Hashem* than it is to live *al kiddush Hashem*. Dying, even by choice, is over and done; living is constant, it's an ongoing effort every day. So, what about choosing to live when you don't want to live? Like waking up when you are in so much pain you wish you could just hide in your bed all day instead? What about when you not only wake up, but you get up and go out, you daven, take care of your family, go to work with a happy manner, still keep to your standards, and don't give up? Wouldn't you think that's a *kiddush Hashem*, wouldn't you think that person is *kadosh*?

It is said that Rabbi Akiva was happy when he saw his rabbi, Rabbi Eliezer, sick and suffering on his deathbed. Everyone was crying, but he was laughing. Appalled, they asked him how he could laugh, and in return he asked how they could cry. "All of the times his wine never went sour and he never had pain, I thought that he might have received all his reward in this world, leaving nothing for the next; now that I see suffering, I rejoice, knowing that his reward will be given to him in the world to come." Life is not always peachy; we all mess up. But when you are a *tzaddik*, God wants you to "pay upfront" in this world, not in the next. In Judaism, there is a concept of "*sheva yipol tzaddik, v'kam*, seven times the righteous man falls and gets up." Most people interpret it to mean that a *tzaddik* is not someone who doesn't fall, but rather someone who gets up after falling. However, my take on it is to move the seven so that it reads, "If you have fallen seven times, you will be a *tzaddik* and arise!" The number seven in Judaism represents a cycle. A *tzaddik* doesn't fall once, but rather is constantly falling. The greatness of the *tzaddik* is not the fact that he falls, rather that he uses his fall to help him get up, to reach even greater heights! It is because he has fallen, and not in spite of it. He must complete the cycle to become righteous.

The Torah tells us that if someone goes forty days without any suffering in his life, he should worry because perhaps Hashem is giving him his reward of *Olam Haba* in *Olam Hazeh*. Just as *tzaddikim* suffer their punishments in this world, so too *reshaim* earn their rewards in this world instead of the world to come. No one is fully bad; everyone does some good in their lives, but do we want full *reshaim* to get *Olam Haba*? Of course not, so what does God do? He is fair; He gives them the rewards coming to them, but He gives it to them here instead of there. Like we said before, this is an upside-down world. What do we know? If a person doesn't have suffering in his life, maybe God gave up on him, maybe he doesn't need growth anymore. Maybe he is like the person who was welcomed back into the camp with leprosy spread all over his body, because God tried and tried to get him to repent but he just wouldn't accept the wake-up call.

There is a famous *d'var* Torah about the snake's punishment in the Garden of Eden. After the snake convinced Chava to sin by eating the forbidden fruit, God punished him by forcing him to eat dirt for the rest of eternity. How is it a punishment to eat the dust when there is dust everywhere? It seems like the greatest blessing. The snake is the only creation in this world that doesn't need to put in any effort whatsoever in order to get its sustenance. Even the lion has to go out and hunt, and humans must work extremely hard to earn our keep. Our sages answer that it is indeed the worst punishment of all because it is Hashem saying to the snake, "There you go, I gave you everything you need, don't come knocking. I don't want anything to do with you at all."

This relates to one of the central concepts of prayer. Hashem doesn't give you problems and so therefore you *daven*; He gives you problems so that you will *daven*. Specifically, because He wants to hear from you! Some of us get calls more often, I guess. Sometimes He misses our voices more often than others, and so He messages us to come *daven*. Makes sense, doesn't it? The sages teach us, "*Hashem mitaveh letefilot shel tzaddikim*, God desires the prayers of the righteous." What do you do when you have a desire, a craving? Imagine a pregnant woman who experiences a craving for ice cream in the middle of the night. She would send someone to get her some real quick, right? It's the same with God. He craves our prayers. It's not that He is punishing us; that is a concept which was introduced by a world concerned with jealousy and competition, that's not the world of God. Everything He does is for you, and by definition, when someone does so much for you it is because they can't get you off their mind, they think about you constantly. He isn't indifferent to your life, He has you right there, front and center, but it feels like the opposite because this is an upside-down world.

I'm not going to lie, there have been many times I've wished I had another person's life, times where I've wondered why they have this or that, and why my life couldn't be as easy and light as theirs. Some people seem to get the best of both worlds. Their lives are filled with Torah, yet they also get to benefit from material things, all while I'm here struggling endlessly. But I take comfort in reminding myself that this is an upside-down world. We don't know the *cheshbonot* of God. Who knows how our efforts are valued, how the points are counted? Who knows what makes God truly proud of us? Who He looks at with pride, who He sees fighting and never giving up? Who knows? I certainly don't. I believe that Hashem, "*roeh kol chadrei baten*, He sees all the compartments of the belly." You might not really see you, and others probably see you even less. It doesn't matter how much they do or don't care; they aren't you; they aren't living in your shoes. But God sees you, even when you think you are invisible.

I'm sitting here, after a tough conversation with those close to me, those who are meant to be my support system, and trying to digest what just came out of their mouths. They said, "What you are doing is not a big deal, it is your obligation." And, "Until when will you be in pain? When will you accept the will of God?" It's only been five months. Five months of trauma, insanity, disaster. Five months since my world turned upside down, since my kids' worlds turned upside down. In one short moment, I was given more work and obligations, more emotional baggage and pain, than I had ever had before. The pain was so intense that I wanted to rip my soul from my body just so that I can have a moment where it didn't hurt. And this is the response I get from others? Hurting doesn't mean you don't accept; it simply means you are aware of what you have accepted, it means you have integrated it and it is calling on you from the inside to heal. We don't lose someone and accept it and move on in one day. We sit *shiva*, we mourn, we cry, then we have the *shloshim*, and then the *yahrzeit*. Accepting is not escaping, it is integrating, it is sealing the wound, and allowing it to scar over.

Why should I be made to feel guilty because I'm hurting? If someone broke a bone, wouldn't they put it in a cast for an extended period of time until it heals? How long do we need a cast for a broken heart or a broken soul? Some cuts need band-aids, others need stitches. But to heal an open wound, you have to clean it from the inside or it will get infected. Everyone needs to take the time they need in order to heal, not to reject what they are feeling; those are the symptoms that lead to the diagnosis. So why should I be criticized and questioned for being human? I stopped and I said, I am so proud of myself! Yes, it is my obligation, but not everyone follows through on their obligations. Some people just throw up their hands and say they're done, they didn't ask for this, they don't have to do this. And even if they do, you don't come to their house and see it being taken care of, see the kids happy, fed, and doing better than before, and judge them for it. Not everyone gets up and goes about their day with happiness, giving to others, making others happy, shining a light they don't even have. Because I've been teaching about *emunah* all this time, all these years while I myself could have thrown in the towel so many times. Yet, I did get up to pray, and I did tell my kids how much God loves us.

We were in the car one day during *Pesach* break; everyone around us was on family outings, and we felt the absence, we felt the brokenness, and my kids said, "We're the only ones without a father." I answered them, "Do you know who is the father of the people that have no father?" and they answered, "Hashem!" And we all started singing, because we have the best father and know He will take care of us. Recently, my daughter innocently said to me, "Mommy, people must really love us; look at everything they are sending!" I wanted to answer that really it is because they pity us, but I didn't. That is what choosing to live looks like! Choosing to live is hard, and at times not very rewarding. It's like choosing to love again, and to trust again; you may feel rewarded, but you also feel like if you break one more time, there will be too many pieces to be put back together.

Once, I was leading a Momentum trip and one of the women in the group, an amazing Israeli lady, got up to tell her story: She had pretty much had it all at one point; she was happily married and had a beautiful baby daughter. One day, they traveled to her parents' Chanukah party in an Israeli settlement. This was during the intifada—I'm sure just reading that word has shaken you, and yes, what you fear happened did indeed happen—and a terrorist blew himself up right next to her, her mother, and baby. She was badly injured, but she lost her mom and baby. We were all in tears as she told us this story, but then she gave the greatest life lesson! She told us about how she sat in the hospital bed wondering what she would do next, not wanting to live anymore, when she realized she had two options. She could either live, or not. But if she were going to live, then she was going to want to live. She wasn't going to live in order to survive; she was going to survive in order to live. She looked at our group and said, "I chose to live. I've had a beautiful life, I sing, I dance, I travel, and I fill my life with all kinds of beautiful things!" I am also choosing to live, and that choice is never-ending; it is a choice you must make every day of your life.

On *Lag Ba'omer*, I was standing by the fire, watching it slowly die out, but every once in a while, someone would come and start it up again with more wood. What a beautiful metaphor for life. Sometimes we all need that extra fuel to keep the fire going, more inspiration to keep believing. But you can only revive a flame that still burns, so don't let go of your flame. We tend to think that Judaism should feel like butterflies in our bellies, fresh and exciting. I have so often heard people say they are not inspired anymore, they don't feel like praying anymore, they feel so disconnected from God. But what do you think real life looks like? Real life is putting in the effort, looking for inspiration, reigniting the fire. Real life means doing the work when you don't feel like it because you are committed. When you stand there, talking to God in the midst of your pain, you are affirming that you believe in Him, that you trust Him, that you won't budge in your confidence in Him no matter what.

Rabbi Akiva's terrible death was his real reward. His love and belief in Hashem were so strong that even during the most torturous death, he stood fast in his *emunah*. Rabbi Akiva, in his suffering, cried out to Hashem, "Even if You push me away, I will not leave You, Hashem. You can never do anything that will make me not love you! Because I'm with you, not only when compliant but also when defiant!" He had reached that ultimate level of confidence in Hashem. I will say it now, too: I am here God, I'm not going anywhere, we might have little fights every once in a while, sometimes big fights. Sometimes I don't want to talk to You, and I want to yell at You. I'm sorry to admit it, but I do. But even then, all I want is for You to hold me, to tell me You see me and You are not going anywhere. I'm choosing to be here, I'm all in, every piece of me.

I asked you at the beginning of this chapter, what would you do if you were God? You probably came up with a bunch of revisions for the world, right? I've done it many times, too. In my mind, I think, God, can I advise You a bit? Wouldn't it be nicer this way? One of the thirteen principles of faith is to believe with absolute conviction that the world was created out of nothingness, that God created it from scratch. Why is this such an elementary principle? We understand that nothing can exist without God, and contrary to what science says, matter can be created or destroyed by God. But what is really the big deal, apart from the obvious? Why does it affect my faith so much? Isn't it just a logical statement? Let's say God did create the world out of something, it wouldn't diminish His master abilities. The world is so beautiful, designed with precision, it all but screams the talent and creativity of God. The pre-existence of materials notwithstanding, He still had to do this on His own. Think about it this way, if I'm not good at building with *Lego*, it doesn't matter how many pieces of *Lego* you give me, I will still only be able to build a simple building. A *Lego* master, however, can take those same pieces and build a rollercoaster, a dragon, and all those incredible, advanced sets on display in the *Lego* store. Having the building materials in no way diminished the sheer talent of a master *Lego* builder, right?

Imagine you are in *Master Chef*. I give you ten ingredients and tell you to cook your favorite dish, whatever your heart desires, according to your ability and talent. Would you be able to make exactly that specific food with the random ingredients I gave you? Even the most talented, hardworking, creative chef in the world would find it an impossible task to achieve without the exact ingredients for that recipe. If you want to make a chicken dish, but weren't given chicken, or if you needed a key spice that you weren't given, you couldn't possibly prepare the dish correctly. All the ability in the world means nothing without the correct ingredients. Limited ingredients mean limited outcomes. Limits only generate more limitation.

When we moved into our new house after the fire, everyone asked if it was the house of my dreams. I don't want to seem ungrateful, because I'm very grateful, but how could I ever have the house of my dreams? To really have the house of my dreams, I would need to have an unlimited budget for materials and designers and time to do it. Saying that the world was created out of pre-existent materials would be saying that the world is beautiful, but it's just that God did the best He could, given the circumstances. Even if you are the master creator, once you are limited by your materials, there is only so much you can do. And yes, the world looks amazing because Hashem is creative and works with what He has, but would this have been His first choice? Would this have been the full expression of His will?

Once you understand that the world was created out of nothingness, it also means that God Himself created the materials, which means the world is exactly as He wants it to be, if only because He could have made it any other way. God wasn't limited in His ingredients; He could have chosen any spice He wanted, any element from His unlimited pantry, yet this is what He chose. Because the world is perfect, because God's idea of perfection isn't the same as our idea of perfection. God's definition of perfect means perfectible, having the potential to be perfect. We are perfectible;

we have the opportunity to become our perfect selves, and our lives are made perfectly to give us the opportunity to achieve that task.

It's easier said than done, but then again this is an upside-down world, and we have no idea what our task even is, we have no idea where to set our goals. But Hashem didn't leave us unsupervised; He guides us with His footprints, so don't be afraid to step on them. They might be big and scary, but they will guide you. Take your ingredients, the ones chosen for you specifically, and go make the most beautiful dish you can. Remember, we must choose to live and not just survive.

Ultimately, I guess, if I were God, I wouldn't change anything at all. Because if I were God, I would see what He sees and I would know what He knows and I wouldn't have any questions.

PIN IT TO YOUR HEART!

"Hurting doesn't mean you don't accept; it simply means you are aware of what you have accepted."

"Holy souls are judged to the highest standards because their potential is so great it must to be squeezed out to the last drop."

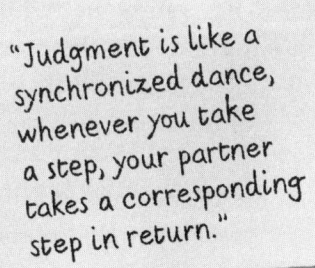

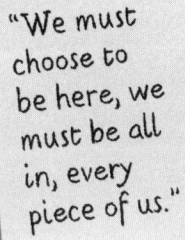

"Judgment is like a synchronized dance, whenever you take a step, your partner takes a corresponding step in return."

"We must choose to be here, we must be all in, every piece of us."

"Accepting is not escaping, it is integrating, it is sealing the wound, and allowing it to scar over."

"Real life is putting in the effort, looking for inspiration, reigniting the fire."

"Sometimes we need that extra fuel to keep the fire going, more inspiration to keep believing. But you can only revive a flame that still burns, so never let your flame go out."

CHAPTER ELEVEN

SELF AWARENESS IN THE IMAGE OF GOD

People often ask me, what made you want to do *teshuva*, what is it that inspired you? To be honest, the first thing that moved me was the beauty of relationships in the religious world: the respect and honor between husband and wife, parents and children. I know, ironic, right? After all, it's exactly what went wrong with me. You'd think I would be totally disappointed and start doubting my choice to become religious. But just because it didn't work for me it doesn't mean that there aren't people who are in a beautiful marriage, working on themselves; and what gives them the ability to do that? The values that the Torah gives us, the emphasis on self-work. Some people have had an easier path than others in that area, but marriage always needs work, and the Torah is a beautiful guide for wholesome relationships. The truth is, I know that we can't judge the Torah based on those who keep it. The Torah is perfect, God-like in its creation, and the Jewish people are just mere mortals trying to do their best and failing many times along the way. Every morning, when we wake up, we testify to the holiness and purity of our souls. "*Elokai neshama shenatata bi tehora hi*, God, the soul You gave me is pure." It doesn't matter what I did yesterday, what my past choices were, my soul is and will always remain pure. I just have to polish off the dirt that has collected on it during all these years. These impurities don't become our essence, they simply stick to it and dull the shine. It's just that we don't really look closely enough to recognize the difference.

When I think about it, it fills me with hope, yet also with pain. How do pure souls end up trapped? How do we forget who we really are so easily, forget who we are meant to be? I am surrounded by so many beautiful people who have forgotten their true essence, their purity, their innocence. I myself have been there many times, done things that are below me, behaved in an undignified manner. The same is true of all those around me. It's true of all of us. How did we get here? And more importantly, how do we get out? When the Torah teaches us that a person is made in the image of God, we may not pay attention to the beauty and depth of this idea, but what it really means is that when God metaphorically sees Himself in the mirror, we are the image shown in the reflection. When we see ourselves, we should be able to see the godliness within us, and that should reflect how we behave. Yet maybe that is exactly what is lacking, that's what we have lost.

In its description of all kosher and non-kosher beasts, the Torah never gives a reason for why we may or may not consume certain animals. Sure, many commentaries on these *pesukim* exist, but the written Torah only ever provides the conditions for an animal's kosher status, never the reasoning behind it. Except when we get to the creepy-crawlers, the insects. In this case, the Torah actually spells out why it is forbidden to eat these creatures: "Creatures that crawl on the ground are detestable and not to be eaten… Do not make yourselves unclean or be defiled by them." What does this even mean? What is the connection between eating something that looks disgusting and becoming disgusting myself?

When I was younger, I used to watch a popular show called *I Bet You Will*. The premise of the show was to persuade people to do extreme stunts in exchange for money. One episode, I remember vividly, took place at The Promenade in LA. The host chose a woman who seemed rather upper-class in her high heels and expensive purse and challenged her to eat a cockroach for twenty dollars. Obviously, she was disgusted by the idea and said no. The host then upped the ante, offering thirty, then forty, then fifty dollars, until finally offering her "double or nothing." So what do you think happened? The woman actually agreed to eat the roach for one hundred dollars. After all, what's a moment of disgust if you leave with a hundred dollars in your pocket? But the episode didn't end there. The host then offered the same woman another fifty dollars to eat another roach, right then and there. What do you think she did? Yup, she ate it! She already knew what to expect from eating the first roach, and who would give up a free $150? But there was still one last offer from the host—eat five more cockroaches for a total of $300. Would you believe she took the bet? She kept vomiting and drinking water, but she did it and left proudly with $300 cash for eating all of those cockroaches. But how much was the first roach really worth? And the second? Each one of the next five? Did she notice that even though she would never have eaten a cockroach for a mere sixty dollars, she ended up eating five of them for that amount each? How does that happen?

The Torah in its wisdom teaches self-respect 101. The more we respect ourselves and behave in a way that is dignified in our own eyes, the more we will preserve that dignity and respect in the eyes of others. But if we lose it, if we are lowered in our own esteem, then it's all downhill from there. Like it says in the Torah, when we repeat a sin three times, it becomes as if it is permitted. Well, is it actually permitted? No, of course not. It simply means that in our minds it seems to become permitted. The Torah is teaching us a profound lesson in human psychology here. In the beginning, we feel guilt and shame for having committed the sin, but as we continue to repeat the sin, we rationalize our actions, literally creating rational lies, which convince us that we are correct in our actions. We lie to ourselves to such a degree that we convert the prohibition into a *mitzvah* in our own eyes. Ask yourself, how many things did you promise yourself you would never do when you were young? How many of those promises did you keep? How many did you give up entirely? We did something that we're not proud of, but instead of reminding ourselves how beautiful and powerful we are so that we may correct our actions, we allow our negativity and guilt to take over instead. We allow ourselves to be misled by our own shame and convince ourselves we are not good enough to fix the situation, so we give up entirely, we stop caring altogether.

I have come to realize that this way of thinking happens to most of us. We all have ideas that we formed as children, words that were ingrained in our minds, which become self-fulfilling prophecies. Even though logic tells us these narratives are not necessarily true, the voices in our heads are too loud to be easily silenced. We don't judge the world or ourselves according to who we are, but according to what we feel. Our feelings define our thoughts and generate our actions, and the more we choose incorrectly, the more we are doomed to keep repeating the same mistakes unless we can wake ourselves up to our wrongdoings. By internalizing these ideas, we allow them to lower our self-esteem and self-worth and allow ourselves to live in a way that is beneath us.

We often go about life feeling unworthy; like we are not good enough, not smart enough, and that we therefore deserve punishment. Why? When did we forget our *neshamot* are pure, that we are made in the image of God? There is infinite greatness within us. If I had loved myself enough, cared for myself enough, would I have ended up where I did? Of course not; I would have known that I could do better and be better. When Yosef was about to sin with the wife of Potifar, the *Midrash* says he saw Yaakov's reflection in the window and immediately fled. Some say the two simply looked alike and Yosef saw his own reflection; some say it was actually Yaakov's face that he saw. But whichever it was, it produced the same thought in Yosef: How could I disappoint this image? I have forgotten who I am and this is why I'm behaving this way.

Every morning we say the blessing, "*Baruch Ata Hashem matir asurim*, blessed are You, God, who frees the prisoners." But are we in prison? Why does this blessing apply to all of us, why is it said by all of us equally? Because each one of us is an inmate of a prison we have built for ourselves. We are prisoners of our own limiting beliefs, tied to promises to which we have committed ourselves, willingly or unwillingly. We are held hostage by the things we tell ourselves, like that we will never behave in a certain way, that we will never achieve our goals, that no one will ever love us. We must break free of these beliefs and remember who we are, we must create new voices in our minds, new thoughts that are empowering and inspiring. We must find new opportunities to see the world through different lenses. Like with eyeglasses, sometimes our prescription is wrong and our perception of the world is all fuzzy and out of focus. The problem is not intrinsically us; rather, the problem is with our glasses, we just need a new prescription. Often, we make decisions, categorizing ourselves or others as selfish, lazy, arrogant. Yet, even if the behavior changes, we don't necessarily make an effort to perceive that change. But how does that way of seeing the world help us or our relationships? Why do we perpetuate these negative and damaging thoughts? What are we holding on to and when will we let it go? It all comes down to self-esteem; when we love ourselves and think highly of ourselves, then we will protect ourselves and want what is good for ourselves.

I was doing some therapy work the other day, and the exercise was to count ten reasons why I should love myself. At the beginning of the task, I was a little shaken. I don't usually say nice things about myself, and I think I often mistake low self-esteem for humility. Even though the point of the exercise was to see the good in myself, to admire my own greatness and to focus on my positive traits, the question occurred to me: Why do we need reasons to love ourselves? The Torah teaches us, "*v'ahavta l'rei'acha kamochah*, love your neighbor like yourself." That means that, by default, I have to love myself. But what does it really mean to love yourself? Torah commentaries suggest that it means to want good in your life, to want to be happy. So then, by those standards, did I love myself? Would I have consciously made the choices I did if I thought I was deserving of good? Did I treat myself with kindness, love, and compassion? We are often quick to give to others but forget to treat ourselves the same way. But beyond that, can we ever fully love others if we don't love ourselves? The verse seems to suggest that our love for others depends on the love that we have for ourselves. In order to love others, we must accept ourselves as a full vessel, must accept all parts of ourselves; we must make sure that there isn't any part of us that is unwanted or without a place.

I used to despise many parts of myself, but now I'm grateful for those same parts. I understand they exist to protect me, to guide me. I just needed to give them a voice and listen to what they were trying to tell me since they are part of me. Isn't that what we all do? We silence ourselves; we ignore the things about ourselves that we don't like. We tend to believe that in order to find happiness, we must give up our voices, surrender our inner essence, our individuality, and personality. Yet all of that is what makes us who we are. Who would we be without it? If we can learn to accept ourselves with all our faults and inadequacies, if we can learn to love them and understand them and even be merciful with them, then we can go on to love and give to others too. Everything starts at home, and we are our own homes. We need to ask ourselves: Do I feel comfortable in my own home?

I realize that so many of my problems have been because I learned to reject many parts of myself from a very young age, not realizing that those are the elements that make me who I am: a sensitive, caring, giving person. It's incredible, but consider the root of the word *rei'acha*, your neighbor; it's *ra'ah*, which is usually translated as "bad." Yet its real meaning is not "bad," but "brokenness." Therefore, what the Torah really comes to say is that you shall love your brokenness, all of your damaged parts. After all, you wouldn't be where you are today if it wasn't for them; they have propelled you and inspired you to become who you are. Similarly, we must love the brokenness of others.

Have you ever noticed what appears at the end of the verse? "Love your neighbor as yourself; I am God." Why does the reminder

"I am God" appear at the *pasuk's* end? Because it reflects the true meaning of the whole verse: God created you and your neighbor; we are all His children, all made in His image. You must love your neighbor as you love yourself, and you must love yourself as you love God because you are made in His image. How differently we would live if we always understood we were specifically crafted by God in such a way, with so much love and attention to detail. The Hebrew word for fight or discord is *machloket*, the root of which, *chelek*, means "part." We will often reduce a person to one minor element of who they are instead of seeing the whole picture. What's worse is that we even do it to ourselves. One small failure can lead us to label ourselves as wholly bad or unworthy, when really, we are so much more than that one little weakness.

Pirkei Avot teaches us that, "Any love that is dependent on something, when that thing perishes, so too does the love." Often, the love we have for ourselves depends not on one thing, but on many: success, appearances, money. Isn't it tiring, though? We place the bar for success at an unreachable height. And when some lucky few do reach it, we move it even higher. How many more conditions do we need to achieve before we can accept ourselves? And if we don't love ourselves, who will? We need to stop looking at the separate parts of ourselves and start seeing our whole selves. We are made in the image of God! That's why the word for peace in Hebrew is *shalom*, the root of which is *shalem*, which means "whole." We must see ourselves as whole to reach a place of inner peace. Reasons and conditions need not apply, it is intrinsic. Maybe if we started seeing ourselves as we really are, we will find there is nothing in us that we can't love. Like we said earlier, it's really just some dirt that stuck on, it's a misunderstanding and misrepresentation of ourselves. So, when I went back to do the exercise my therapist gave me, I wrote in big letters: I don't need reasons. I am made in the image of God. Everything else is extra. Then I wrote more than ten things, because I realized that if Hashem is the Master Creator, then everything great that I have is a direct complement to Him. Humility means being able to take complements. It is recognizing your greatness but knowing to attribute it to the Creator.

Reaching this realization was difficult, but it made me wonder about other people. What about the people who have hurt me, some of them over and over? Those who used their free will to put me down, who took advantage of me during my times of need, even blamed me for what they were doing to me. What about those toxic relationships, when we give love and expect to be loved and understood, or at least acknowledged, but it doesn't happen? And I finally understood: sometimes people want to be better, but they don't know how. Not everyone gets to experience the breakthroughs we yearn for. Sometimes God gives us opportunities, but we are so trapped in our own selves that we can't recognize the chance given to us. Sometimes, we just give up working on ourselves because we have failed so many times, we no longer believe in ourselves enough to succeed. A person can be denied love to a point at which they believe there is no love out there for them; it may be available to others, but not to them. So how do you flip years of trauma? It requires so much work, and we aren't always up to the task. I realized that no one wants to do bad things or hurt others, which is why we tend to rationalize our actions. We aren't just trying to excuse our behavior, but to justify our actions because we want to be right; we want to believe we are good.

But sometimes we are so stuck where we are, the challenge is just so big that it is like being in the sea when gigantic waves come—you manage the first few ones but then can barely catch your breath, sometimes sadly even giving up. Sometimes you are just too far away from where you want to be, and the spiritual emotional gravity is just too heavy. Most of us try to deal with this to some degree. We feel every time that "tomorrow I will be different," but then tomorrow is the same as today. How many times do we start a diet and break it because we have an opportunity to feast and then say "next week," and weeks roll and roll, and years later we are in the same place? We think that what was will always be because it has always been, but we don't realize that just because it has always been that way, it doesn't need to remain the same way. At the end of the day, we are all just trying to do the best we can with what we have. Okay, maybe not all of us are doing the absolute best we could, but I do believe we are all trying. Some of us just aren't necessarily aware of what our best actually is. Isn't that what love is at the end of the day? Love is the feeling you get when you choose to focus on someone's virtues and you identify them with those virtues.

The same goes for my feelings toward my past. I can choose to see the good, to recognize that those around me did what they thought was best. I can choose to accept that the good intentions were there but that there was miscommunication through actions. Just as we wouldn't judge the limitations of someone with a disability, we must understand that so many of us have parts that stunt our ability to be wholly good. Each one of us gives according to what we can; not necessarily what we want to give, but what we can manage to give. Once I understood that, I was able to start working on myself to try to receive what others could give, appreciate what they could give, without expecting more and being disappointed by less. And what's more—it's never too late for any of us; we don't need to be disabled forever. Everything in life is a muscle; we can change our muscle memory by giving it mobility, by stretching it in new ways. We can train ourselves to love, to judge favorably, to be kind, to be giving. One of the greatest concepts in Judaism is that of *teshuva*—often translated as repentance or regret; but it is much more accurately translated as "return." The difference is huge. Repentance means we do wrong, we feel guilty, we commit to change, but what if we aren't capable? What if that is our nature or default mode? We cannot always achieve that which we set our mind to because sometimes we are indeed handicapped emotionally and spiritually. *Teshuva* really means to return because it implies one of the greatest concepts and principles of our humanity, that we are intrinsically whole, good, divine, and pure. That we are created in the image of God and all of our deficiencies and lacking are because we deviated from our essence; we just have to get back on track. Think about it, an actor plays a character in a movie, is that who he really is? But his job is to make it so real that we can't perceive he is just acting. We have learned to play many roles during our lifetime, some of them we learned in order to survive, to ease the pain, to have control, to fit in… and some of them we play amazingly. But is that who we are? On Yom Kippur when we do the *viduy* we are not saying that's who we are, but rather we are trying to clean out the "stains and residue" that got attached to us during the year! We are pure, holy beings, full of goodness. That's the power of *teshuva*; it is never too late, we just have to realize who we are and go back to it, but most importantly we have to believe we can do it; we have to believe wholeheartedly that we are made in the image of God.

I find myself asking so many times, wouldn't I want God to believe in me, to forgive me, to give me another chance? I know I'm guilty, but that's not who I am or who I want to be. God knows what is in my heart. So too, I have to have that awareness for others. I am not God, so it is much harder for me, but it is an important point to focus on and a place to start. Some of the greatest people in the Tanach were people who were in very devious and destructive ways, but found light and chose to change their ways.

Once Rabbi Yisrael Salanter, the master of *musar*—self-work, was walking in a market very late at night when he saw a shoemaker working by the light of his candle, and he asked him what he was doing; why was he working so late? He answered, "כל הזמן שהנר דולק תמיד אפשר לתקן — While the candle is still burning, there is still time to repair." Rabbi Salanter, being the master in the art of self-work, understood the divine interpretation; as long as there is light in our souls, there is still work to be done! Even when it is late, even when it is dark, we have to believe that we can and will change.

It always amazes me that even though Noach knew he was going to be saved from the flood, the *pasuk* clearly states that he only entered the ark once the rain had started. Rashi explains that he only entered at the last moment because he didn't have enough *emunah*. The question is, after all these years building the ark, the day finally comes, and he still doubts that Hashem will deliver him? How does that make sense? But then I understood. Noach believed God would send a flood; he had no doubts about that. However, what he struggled to accept was the implication that the world would be destroyed and then rebuilt from him. That was too much for him to accept. Noach believed in God, but he didn't believe in himself. He didn't believe he was good enough to make a difference. We must not be like Noach! We must believe that we are good enough, that we can change this world for the better, that each one of us can decide how our story will be written and what changes we want to make to the script. Each one of us must know that if we are created in the image of God, it means we have His trust and His permission to be the change. As Victor Frankl wisely said, "When we are no longer able to change a situation, we are challenged to change ourselves." At the end of the day, who are we really? A body, a soul? We are our choices. That means we must own our choices in order to be who we are.

There was once a scientist working in his lab, and his little son kept pestering him. The scientist found a picture of the globe, cut it into pieces, and gave it to his son to assemble like a puzzle. The kid took the pieces happily and went to build the puzzle. A few minutes later, he returned, puzzle solved. The scientist was shocked and asked his son how he managed to assemble the puzzle so quickly, how he knew how to fix all of the pieces of the world. The child answered that he didn't know how to fix the pieces of the world, but he did notice that on the back of the puzzle pieces were the parts of a human being, and those parts he knew how to assemble. So, by fixing the human, he ended up fixing the world. That concept, of fixing the world by fixing the people in it, is called *Tikkun Olam,* and it's the Jewish view of the world. If we can fix ourselves, we can fix the world. But it starts with you; you must take the first step!

PIN IT TO YOUR HEART!

"Your soul is and will always remain pure; you just need to polish off the dirt that has settled on it during all these years."

"Being created in the image of God means that when God sees Himself in the mirror, you are His reflection."

"We need to stop looking at the separate parts of ourselves, and start seeing our whole selves."

"You must do the best you can with what you have."

"Love is when you choose to focus on someone else's virtues and you identify them with those virtues."

"Everything in life is a muscle that can be trained and stretched in new ways; we can train ourselves to love, to judge favorably, to be kind, to be giving."

"While your candle is still burning there is still time to repair."

"You are good enough; you can change this world for the better."

CHAPTER TWELVE

LET IT GO, THERE IS NOTHING HOLDING US BACK EXCEPT FOR US

The Torah ends by telling us about the death of Moshe and the end of an era. What's interesting is how the Torah chooses this moment to emphasize Moshe's greatness as a prophet and a leader by reminding us that he broke the tablets. Out of all the remarkable moments of Moshe's life, why is this moment chosen to highlight his greatness? How are we meant to understand this? Is it meant to be a reminder of the tragedy or is it meant to prove that Moshe did the right thing by breaking them? Imagine working toward something your whole life, making every decision based on whether that will help you reach your goal or not. Imagine reaching the end, reviewing your career, only to find out that what's emphasized isn't what you've been working toward this whole time at all. And not only that, but you must take your life's work and destroy it. Not so easy, right? How could you possibly wipe out all of that work, all those years of effort, all of your expectations of success? How can you simply let go of everything you thought made you who you are? Can you let go and admit it wasn't what it was supposed to be? Can you let go even if you feel like a failure, and you are completely lost and left with no direction? Yet that was exactly Moshe's test at that moment!

The Torah comes to show that the greatest thing about Moshe wasn't what he achieved, but what he stepped away from, what he let go of. It wasn't who he became, but who he chose not to be. Such actions require courage, and that kind of courage is what we call greatness. We all want to shine in life, to be recognized for our successes, but what about when that recognition doesn't come with confetti and celebration? What about when the moment of greatness is knowing when to step down, to desist, to let go and let someone else take the reins? Moshe stepped back when he understood it was time to pass on the leadership to Yehoshua. How hard must that have been? To work all of your life for something and then see someone else taking the lead to enjoy the fruits of your labor. It's not so easy to be in the spotlight at the moment in which you have chosen to stand down, and that is exactly the point. Often in life, the greatest and most difficult choice is to understand when it is time to stop and move on. The Torah wants to teach us that brokenness is a core value in Judaism, and that even when all is lost, we can always start again from zero. There is value to loss, value to pain. The greatest message the Torah gives us is that it is never too late to start over and to change directions. Just take Rabbi Akiva as an example. Imagine losing 24,000 students, all of your life's work and success, gone. What a loss, what a profound sense of failure. Yet Rabbi Akiva didn't feel that way about his circumstances. He was able to let go and start over. He learned from his mistakes, learned to start again, and achieved greatness as a result. No great person could ever reach prominence without understanding one salient point: loss is part of life; you mourn, you get up, you move on.

Here is a parable to illustrate my point:

> There was once a horse that went down river to drink some water. As he lowered his head to the stream, he noticed another horse trying to drink from the same exact spot. He tried grunting and groaning to shoo off the other horse, but the other horse did the same thing and refused to move. So, the horse moved a few meters downstream only to find the other horse now in that spot too. Angrily, he kept trying to scare away the other horse, but the other horse was putting up a real fight, mimicking him and refusing to move. Of course, what was really happening was that the horse was seeing his own reflection in the water. He was unknowingly his own obstacle in achieving that which he wanted and needed. He couldn't move past his own ego; he couldn't let go.

So often we are our own worst enemies. We will analyze a situation in circles, asking the same questions over and over, seeking a specific answer instead of recognizing the truth and moving on. As we discussed earlier, when we question God, we are admitting that we believe that His way is not the best way of doing things. Whatever our perception is, those grudges get in the way of our progress; they prevent us from advancing, they keep us stuck in the past.

Like we said earlier, holding grudges is like allowing someone to live in your head without paying rent. The apartment of my mind was certainly overcrowded with squatters, and it was taking over my ability to think and be in control. I was holding grudges against Hashem, unable to understand how He could treat me so badly. I still can't fully understand, but in writing this book, I have gained clarity and healing. I can suddenly see things from a more objective place instead of from subjective experience. I was always convinced I had *emunah* and a beautiful relationship with God, but there was one thing getting in the way and that was my lack of acceptance for what He sent my way. I held grudges against everyone from my parents to my husband, and I still haven't healed completely; it is a lifetime effort. I thought that if I were not always aware of my pain, if I didn't make those who hurt me pay for what they did by at least reminding them of how mad or hurt I was, then I would lose myself. I thought that if I let go of my pain, it would be like letting go of my experiences, making it as if nothing happened, as if I didn't exist and the harm was never done. I was holding onto so much anger and resentment about the disadvantages of my childhood and the opportunities I was never given. My life just felt like a broken record, repeating the same scratched tracks on a loop, constantly expecting more and more bad things to happen. We hold on to our pain because we think that's what keeps our memories and identity alive when, in reality, it is nothing but a ticking bomb of self-destruction. We need to understand that we attract what we believe. When our glasses are dark, then the whole world is going to lose color. If what we believe is negative, then we will only find negativity.

There was once a king who had an eye problem. He was told that in order to cure his sight, he should only see the color green. So, the king sent his officials to paint everything in the palace green; the furniture, the walls, the people, even the food had to be green. When the doctor arrived, he was surprised to see what the king had done and asked why.

The king answered, "You told me I should only look at green, so I painted everything green."

Surprised by the king's explanation, the doctor asked, "But, your highness, wouldn't it have been easier to just get green glasses?"

We are like that king; we try to change the whole world around us when we only need to make a small change to ourselves. There is no point in holding others responsible for what happens to us because they are simply messengers from God. Changing them won't change our circumstances. But changing how we see our circumstances will change how we experience them. Our only choice is whether we will be a messenger for expressing God's will in this world.

Understanding this idea was incredibly helpful to me. It made me less judgmental of others, helped me care less about who does what and instead put all my trust in God and not people. *Sefer Orchot Tzaddikim* writes that life "is like a hundred blind people walking in single file and each one›s hand is on the shoulder of his companion, but at the head of all of them there is a man who sees, and it is he who leads them all." Hashem is categorized as the seeing man. We are all blind and being guided by Him. Even though it is important to know that we can lean on each other for guidance, we must also know that we are not required to stay in that line, we do not need to remain leaning on the other blind people around us. We can step off the line and skip to the front, grab directly onto the one who sees.

When I didn't get the help I wanted and expected after the dissolution of my marriage, I was gutted. I was disappointed; I had imagined that specific people I thought cared about me would gather together and get me out of this mess. Of course, there were many angels, but not necessarily did the help come from those who I thought and hoped would have been the providers. People get busy and are dealing with their own things. It is sometimes hard for us to accept that, especially when there is an emergency, but we don't run the world; we can't control others' choices, reactions, or willingness to help. I felt they weren't helping even when they had the means and opportunity. It felt like they simply weren't in tune with my pain how I wanted them to be. Until I realized, God was going to send me whatever He wanted to send me, however He wanted to send it. He doesn't need anyone specific to be His messenger; it is us who lose by not giving. But Hashem will not abandon me simply because the people I count on aren't ready to be counted on; He will find someone else to deliver the help He wants to send me. At the end of the day, whatever God wants will always come to be. It is very hard work to learn to expect less from people. I need to allow myself to remain open to receive whatever anyone chooses to give me. I have learned to accept from God, to use a band-aid appropriate to the size of the cut, but to remove it once it has scabbed over.

All of that overthinking was overwhelming me, filling me up with unhealthy emotions and doubling my already heavy baggage. It's like a hitchhiker who is picked up on the side of the road. After a while, the driver notices that the hitchhiker is still wearing his heavy backpack on his shoulders. The driver asks his passenger why he is still wearing the backpack. The hitchhiker replies, "I feel bad. You're already carrying me; I didn't want you to have to carry my backpack too." Amazed at the foolish response, the driver exclaims, "I am already carrying you and the backpack in my car. You are putting extra weight on yourself for nothing!" That's what I was doing to myself, holding onto unnecessary baggage. I decided it was time to let go of all the needless weight, to become a lighter, happier, simpler human being.

When Lot and his family were running away from Sodom, they were instructed by the angels not to look back. Lot's wife chose to look back, and she was turned into a pillar of salt. Why was that the consequence of her disobedience? And why were they commanded not to look back in the first place? Perhaps Lot wanted to look back, not at the city, but at his past choices: Why did he separate from Avraham? Why did he go to Sodom? Why, why, why? If only he could go back and change his choices. But the message is clear: you can't look back; you can only look forward. If you look back, you will become like a statue, frozen in place, unable to move on. Your guilt, regret, and anxiety will take over. That's exactly what happened to the wife of Lot. She was turned into a pillar of salt because salt absorbs everything, and when we live in the past, it slowly begins to absorb our future. We just need to let it go; the past is in the past. As Rafiki says to Simba in *The Lion King*, "The past can hurt. But the way I see it, you can either run from it, or learn from it." That is the message behind the greatness of Moshe breaking the tablets, because sometimes we need to be broken so that we can move forward to something better for us. That's why we carried both the first and the second tablets in the *Mishkan*. The broken tablets had value; they were a reminder of the past but also an opportunity for the future. You can either run from it or learn from it.

Women especially have a tendency to live in the past, feeling guilt about everything, hoping and wishing we could just turn back time. There is a famous joke that goes, women only cry for two things: everything and nothing. We live in the past feeling embarrassment, and in the future feeling anxiety and pressure, but we are never really living in the present. That was the power and the downfall of Chava. The snake's venom was the power to *l'nachesh*, to guess, the power to ask, "What if?" Think about it, when the snake tried to entice Chava, it said, "because God knows the day you will eat from it you will be like God." The snake knows how to get you to wonder, to want something else, to rethink where you are in life and whether there is always something better. What if I would have done things differently, married differently, gotten out earlier…? I have asked myself those questions many times. But really, what's the point of wallowing? It only adds more and more salt to the wound. It's not like we have a magic wand that could undo what has been done, and that's the truth, whether we like it or not. And it's all from God; nothing can happen if God doesn't want it to be. Once I accept that, I can become a messenger for something else, I can become a vessel to express God's will in this world. We must remember Yosef's comforting words to his brothers when they worried about the repercussions of their actions toward him: "You thought you sold me; but I wasn't sold, I was sent." We are all "sent" by God on a mission; we are all messengers of God's will. For example, I wouldn't be writing this book if I wasn't a messenger. At the end of the day, that is all we have, the choice of attitude and perspective. We can be sold as victims or sent as messengers on a mission.

In her book *The Choice*, Dr. Edith Eger vividly describes how she was taken to Auschwitz as a 16-year-old girl. She had already lost everything: her dreams, her hopes, her loved ones… She was going to be in the Olympics, she was going to be a prima ballerina. Yet there she was, having stood in the selection line where she and her sister were sent to work, and her mother was sent to death. That night, as they shivered in the icy barracks, Josef Mengele, the "Angel of Death," entered, on the hunt for entertainment. He demanded that a girl step forward and dance for him. Being a dancer, the young Dr. Eger was obviously pushed forward. But how could she possibly dance for the man who had just murdered her mother? However, she knew that if she refused, it would mean the end for her too. So, she began to dance, and suddenly she magically felt like she was floating on the stage of the Hungarian Royal Opera House. She describes how free she felt in that moment, how full of life she felt. She wrote that in Auschwitz, she was free because of the thoughts she placed in her own head, and outside of Auschwitz she was a prisoner because of the thoughts she placed in her own head. After her release from Auschwitz, she couldn't let go of her suffering; she couldn't let go of the life she never had, of the dreams she never fulfilled. She goes on to describe how she was in prison in Auschwitz for four years, but she remained a prisoner for forty years because the worst prison is the one we build in our minds. When we allow past sufferings to live in our heads without paying rent, we are imprisoned by them. Eventually, she understood she must learn to forgive.

Ah, forgiveness. One of the most difficult undertakings in life. How can we forgive someone who caused us such harm? And do we forgive but not forget? How does it help us? When you don't forgive, when you don't let go, you remain chained to your suffering; permanently tethered to the people that hurt you, taking them and their actions with you through life. They live in you and perpetuate the fears, regrets, anxiety, and panic that they caused. We never wanted any of that to begin with, yet here we are inviting them to take over our existence, allowing them to take over the most intimate corners of our minds. We end up giving them way more screen time than they deserve. We don't manifest forgiveness for their sakes; we do it for our own. We forgive them because we want to break the chains bonding us to our pain and end the cycle; we want to break free and move on. As Dr. Eger writes, "forgiveness is letting go of the hope for a better past." Just let it go.

This is why women were given the most beautiful mitzvah of all, the mitzvah of *mikvah*, of immersing in purifying waters. The world can be so heavy for women, and we try to carry all of it at once. We think we are in control; we want to be in control, and we won't let go of control. But it gets heavy and overwhelming; we often regret and resent carrying all that weight. Maybe this is why women tend to suffer more from anxiety and depression. But when entering those holy waters, they tell us something about ourselves; they whisper of our beauty and power. I remember a chemistry lesson from school where we were taught about all of the elements. The description of water was: a liquid with no odor, no color, no taste; it has no shape but takes the shape of its container. You want to live a happier, lighter life? Learn to be like water!

Water always flows; it is matter, yet has no form. Water teaches us humility; it has the ability to be shaped, to form itself according to its surroundings. To be like water, we must retain our individuality, but we must also learn to let go of our exactitude; we must learn to shape ourselves according to the world around us. We must be humble enough to allow ourselves to be carried to whatever destination we need to reach. The water knows how to let go. Maybe that's why nothing holds weight in water. What makes our load so heavy is that we want to carry it constantly. But if you let go, if you adapt to your surroundings, suddenly everything is lighter. When you accept that you are a messenger for God's will, then He carries you where you need to go. Your burden becomes lighter; you can suddenly carry it all because you aren't carrying it alone. It is interesting to note that the word *simcha*, happiness, includes the letters *mem*, *chet*, and *hei*, which is the root word *macha*, which translates as "eradicate." The degree to which I eradicate my ego, my expectations, my demands for control is equal to the degree of happiness I will achieve. We must learn how to be like water, to accommodate, to be more flexible in who we are.

Water is spontaneous; it is flexible, it moves around, always finding space in which to exist comfortably. That's how I want to live my life; that's the only way of really being happy.

I have always struggled with the need for control. The enormity of fear in my life fueled this illusory state where I thought that the more I could hold it together, the more perfect I could be. There was nothing I yearned for more than security and stability, and being in control made me think I could have that. But it was exhausting just trying to keep on top of it all. I was tired of trying to keep up with myself, of always having everything together, and keeping up with my own inhuman demands of myself. I started to notice that this need for control was beginning to affect my children, too. When we fail to control everything, it all spills out, spreading everywhere and eventually soaking into those around us. Being flexible means receiving that which God wants me to have at this moment. We think *emunah* means everything is going to turn out for good, the way we want it to be, but that isn't true. We've said it before, and we'll say it again here: *emunah* means everything will be the way God wants it to be and that is good. I realized that sometimes God wants me to fail and to be humbled; that is also part of my journey. There is a time for everything, a season for every stage of the year. We may wish to skip the less enjoyable seasons, but they are necessary to complete the year.

The *Mishna* states that in the *Beit HaMikdash*, a miracle would occur in which "the people stood pressed together, yet bowed down and had room enough." In fact, it is said that it was so packed in the *Beit HaMikdash* that people would be even lifted from the ground as they were pressed in together. But, at the moment of bowing, there was a two-meter circumference around each person. This incredible miracle provides priceless advice for living. When we stand firmly to our own ideas, when we refuse to budge, refuse to give up even a bit of control, the whole world feels tight and restrictive. There is no space in which to move around because we are refusing to give ourselves that space. But when we bow down, when we give our ideas some wiggle room and flexibility, when we give up some of our control, then there can be space for us to breathe and live freely. Suddenly, it is easy to make things work. Once we can accept that we don't need to have tight control over our lives, we can move on; we can work with it, build from it, turn it into a blessing. It is what it is. That is what I keep reminding myself. There is no point in questioning or wondering.

The Torah tells us to always be happy, even in a state of pain or loss. How? The answer is that happiness doesn't mean smiling or being cheerful. Happiness is acceptance; it means being at peace with our reality and receiving whatever comes our way with open arms. Happiness is a state of contentment, an inner calm based on the knowledge there is someone else running the show and I need to let them do their job. And let me tell you, when we do achieve this real happiness, then we allow God to surprise us in the most incredible ways. Our rabbis teach us that we will never again reach the same state of complete happiness and calmness as when we were in our mothers' wombs. In the womb, there are no worries, everything is taken care of, it is utter bliss. You know why? Because we couldn't do anything for ourselves and therefore there was no limit to what could be done for us.

Rav Aryeh Kaplan writes that the *mikvah* is a "water-filled place which envelopes us and in which we are unable to live with our own powers." As our sages teach us, a prisoner can't free himself from prison, but to submerge in the water of life can set you free from that which contains you in life. It is like we are telling God, "Hashem, who am I? What am I? Am I not just a creation? I am Your creation, Your child, a part of You. You take care of me like a mother takes care of the baby in her womb." And just like that, the weight of our burdens lessens, the load lightens, the grudges and pain fade away, and we finally find freedom. This is why the word *mikvah* comes from the word *tikvah*, hope. Hope is always available to you, even when there is nothing else. The beauty of hope is always surprising; it is not limited to what we know; it goes beyond all expectation.

There is a beautiful quote from *Mishlei* that says, "Just as a face reflects on water, so too the hearts of men reflect each other." In other words, what we give is what we get; our hearts are reflected back to us by others. If we are like that stubborn horse who approaches the stream ready to fight, we will find a fight. But why does *Mishlei* refer to a face reflected in water and not a mirror? Because, for the face to reflect in a mirror, you can stand up straight and see your reflection eye to eye; but for the face to reflect on water, you must bend down and lower your head. We must not look at the world with arrogance, with defiance, as if it is out to get us and we want to get it first. It's not a contest; it's a dance. Give yourself over to the rhythm, learn to partner with it, and there will be beautiful harmony in the movement. As it is said, "The arrogant person is busy with who is right; the humble person is busy with what is right." We must ask ourselves, what kind of life do we want to live, what kind of relationships do we want to have?

The State of Israel once ran a major campaign to help reduce the number of pedestrian accidents and casualties. Israel is infamous for its risky and speeding drivers, so even crossing the street at the right place could potentially put a pedestrian in danger. The campaign slogan became one of the greatest lessons I've learned in life. It goes: "It is better to be wise than it is to be right." So, you were right—what did you gain, what did you lose, was it worth it? What is your goal at the end of the day? Are your decisions helping you reach your destination, or are they holding you back from growing? It's incredibly difficult to let go, extremely hard to forgive. But wisdom means knowing that to move forward we must stop looking backward and that the reward will be greater than the sacrifice.

PIN IT TO YOUR HEART!

"We hold on to our pain because we think it is what keeps us alive, when in reality it is nothing but a ticking bomb of self-destruction."

"Whatever God wants will always come to be; our only choice is whether we will be a messenger for expressing God's will in this world."

"When our glasses are dark then the whole world is going to lose color."

"We don't have a magic wand that could undo what has been done."

"If you look back you will become like a statue, frozen in place, unable to move on."

"We must learn to be like water. Water teaches us humility; it has the ability to be shaped, to form itself according to its surroundings."

"Forgiveness is letting go of the hope for a better past."

"Emunah means everything will be the way God wants it to be, and that is good."

"It is better to be wise than it is to be right."

CHAPTER THIRTEEN

READY TO ENJOY

The Torah teaches us that man was created to experience enjoyment. In fact, the opening paragraph of *Mesillas Yesharim—The Path of the Just* tells us that this is the only reason we were created: to derive pleasure from God and to enjoy His light. The question is, where is this so-called enjoyment? Life is hard, and anything enjoyable generally comes to us through hard work and challenges. Most of us can't just touch something and turn it to gold; we must exert ourselves to live a healthy life, to have good relationships, to have a good job, and to make a decent living. We can understand if this enjoyment is to be found in the world to come, but we are told that it is in this world. We certainly have many blessings for enjoyment: when we smell pleasing aromas, see beautiful views, eat, or derive any kind of pleasure from this world. It seems to be that God wants us to have a good life, an enjoyable life. Otherwise, why would He have made such a colorful, beautiful world? Why would He have created so many types of food and animals and landscapes? It's one of the questions He will ask us when we go up to *Shamayim*: "Did you enjoy My world?" So, when did we get confused and lose the whole picture? How do we end up leading lives in which we only feel hardship, in which we believe we are meant to struggle, and fail to find enjoyment?

We mentioned earlier that what we need to understand is that we attract what we believe. If our perception is negative, life becomes sour. The Torah, in relating the story of the *meraglim*, the spies, says that when they entered into the Land of Israel, they saw the giants roaming the land and felt like grasshoppers in their own. Rashi explains that because they felt that way, they were seen that way. As we said, if we look at the world through our own distorted lenses, we are seeing the world with our emotions, not our logic. At some point, I realized that many of us are just waiting for the next bad thing to happen. We automatically decide that whatever we are going to get in life is going to come with more hardship, and therefore we might as well be prepared. Why expect good only to be disappointed? Then again, there are all those people that seem to have exactly what it is you want, those whose lives seem so much easier, who seem to be blessed with so many of the things you desire… yet they are just as unhappy as you are. They are also constantly complaining about what they have, what they don't have, and how hard it is. Have you ever noticed that people who already have what you so badly want have a tendency to say, "Enjoy it while it lasts," and "Once you get it, everything changes."

I remember when I was single, all my married friends would tell me, "Enjoy being single. Live, party, enjoy. Once you're married, that's it." Maybe sometimes it was just pushing you to enjoy the highs of every stage in life, but often it was also in the form of a complaint. And I would think to myself, "Don't you like your husband? Aren't you happy you got married?" Like that song played at bachelor parties, "Another one bites the dust," which makes it sound like the groom is digging his own grave. When I finally got married and I couldn't get pregnant, every woman with kids would tell me, "Enjoy not having kids while you can. Take advantage of sleep. Enjoy your body now because you'll never get it back." And again, I would ask myself, "Don't you enjoy your kids? Aren't you grateful for them?" Now don't get me wrong, children are hard, I know. I feel it even more so now as a single mother to four young kids. Yet, I would never tell another woman to "enjoy while you don't have them." I heard people go so far as to say that they "can't stand their kids," which is just hurtful, adding salt to the wound.

I like to think I would choose my words more carefully and make sure not to seem ungrateful for the blessings I have been granted. But maybe that's it; maybe we don't see these things as blessings. I think we've kind of come to expect certain things in life, we see them as a given and therefore don't stop to consider the miracles. We don't consider how grateful we should be and that we are so blessed to be able to have what we do have. We don't think about how many people are lacking those same things and would give anything to have them. How many couples would love to be kept awake by a baby crying in the middle of the night? How many single women would love to have a husband who leaves their dirty socks on the floor? We need to stop for a moment and realize that what we complain about is often reflective of the blessings in our lives. So how can we prevent ourselves from becoming jaded? How can we become more grateful, more conscious, more aligned with the good in our lives?

We came into this world to experience enjoyment, but what is enjoyment? Let's rethink our definition. Enjoyment is the feeling we get when something we are lacking is provided. Think about it; we would enjoy a buffet far more if we haven't eaten in a few days, right? That's why the blessing after meals goes, "*v'achalta v'savata u'verachta,* we shall eat and be satisfied and bless God." We never want to be full in life because when we have it all, then there is nothing left to give us the satisfaction of enjoyment. When we want to be satisfied, we really only mean mostly satisfied because we want to leave room for dessert; we want to be able to enjoy the good surprises.

If enjoyment is the feeling of satisfying a deficiency, then it's safe to say, however much we may not like it, that the greater the deficiency, the greater the ultimate enjoyment. For a starving child in Africa, eating a plain, old apple is a greater enjoyment than it would be for us to eat at a fancy restaurant. Because when you have little, then every bit more is appreciated. If we understand this, then we can understand that these same deficiencies are actually triggers of enjoyment; they generate pleasure. Oftentimes, we can't avoid pain, but we can choose how we experience that pain. We can choose to not feel the pain but to see it as an opportunity for something greater. Suddenly, we can appreciate these deficiencies. Obviously, I would have loved to have had kids right away, but it didn't happen for me. It goes beyond that though, because it is precisely the experience of not having children for all of those years that allowed me to appreciate my children more, to really enjoy every moment, even the hard ones. And what do I gain by being depressed because I'm not where I want to be in life? Nothing. It's hard to say this and risk sounding callous, but the show must go on. Like we said, it is what it is, and we can either choose to dwell on it or grow from it. Because let's be honest, there will still be challenges even when we do get what we want.

I remember when I had my first baby, Shevy, and we would have those "Shevy moments" in class to just appreciate her and I never thought anyone could ever compare to her. And then I had Shira, that special soul; she was Heaven, I loved her every bit as much as Shevy. Then came the twins, and people kept saying, "You must have had such a hard time," and "Be honest, newborn twins must be a nightmare." But I didn't complain, not even once. I don't think I had a "hard" day with my twins until they became toddlers. I yearned for my children so much for so long that I saw them as the greatest gifts. That doesn't mean it wasn't hard; babies are always a lot of work. But I saw motherhood the way Yaakov saw his seven years of working for Lavan: as a necessary obstacle in achieving the greatest gift, his wife, Rachel. Therefore, like for Yaakov, the "days went by quickly." When my babies would wake up in the middle of the night, I saw it as a gift, an opportunity for bonding. It was bliss to hold them close, nurse them, bond with them, alone in the night. I celebrated each burp, each dirty diaper, each outfit, each accessory. I came to be grateful for those years of not having because they ultimately allowed me to experience the having in a fuller, more wonderful way than I could have imagined. Of course, given the option, I still might have chosen the easier and quicker road, but it didn't happen that way and instead, I am choosing now to look at the half full cup and see the good. Once we know what it›s like to feel emptiness, a glass half full feels like it's overflowing.

There is a famous question in the book of *Iyov*: "Why should man complain, isn't it enough that he is alive?" As if to say that living is good enough and it doesn't matter what kind of life you have. I'm sure many of us would disagree; it is simply not enough to be alive. We think to ourselves how this isn't the life we asked for and that there are times we would rather not be alive than experience a life of suffering. How can the *pasuk* make such an absolute declaration in its question? Is the Torah trying to preach toxic positivity? Imagine a bride wearing her white wedding dress, standing by the chuppah on the happiest day of her life. Suddenly, the groom comes and says he has cold feet and is calling off the wedding. Would you look at her and say, "It's ok, isn't it enough you are alive?" I'm sure that bride would want to punch you for saying that. In that moment, her life doesn't seem worth living anymore; it feels unbearable, unworthy of carrying on.

I can't tell you how many times I have had the same feeling, like the weight of life was too heavy to carry for one more second, like I needed to give it up for my own sake before it squashed me to a pulp. You know those people who disregard your challenges or make you feel guilty for feeling the weight of those challenges because they believe you should "look at the good," when you are obviously having a hard time and it's only human to have those feelings? They are the worst to have around in those moments. But then when is positivity welcomed and when is it too much, or even toxic, to have? Is the Torah telling us to let go of our human feelings because to be alive is good enough? Because if that's it, then I'm out! It's impossible.

I once had a student who inadvertently taught me one of the greatest lessons of life. She was an unusual person, always happy and joyful, but hiding a lot of darkness inside. This girl had had a difficult life, full of challenges left, right, and center. One time, in class, I was teaching about gratitude and positivity, and I asked my students if the glass was half empty or half full and then I answered, "It is both. But if you see it half empty, you will be sad, and if you see it half full, you will be happy." I then went on to say how for every negative there is a positive; all it takes to go from negative to positive is a 180-degree turn. It all depends on how you look at it, and that's our choice. Suddenly, this girl raised her hand and said, "Is the glass half empty or half full? It doesn't matter, we should be thankful that we have a glass to fill; some people don't even have a glass." It was like a mic drop, what a statement. Some people don't even have a glass to begin with. It puts the Torah's comment into perspective and shows us that it comes to teach us something powerful indeed. It is enough to be alive because that means that at any given moment everything can change. Life is a vessel; it can be filled. I'm coming to understand that optimism doesn't only mean seeing the good in what is happening, but also being able to see the good that can happen. It means believing there is a possibility for a better tomorrow. Life is an opportunity, a gift; as long as you have life, you have time to fill your glass. If the glass is empty, it can be filled with anything—not only water, but orange juice, coffee, milk; who knows what else life can bring you and what you are destined for. If we can learn to be grateful, we can attract goodness because we can look for the good; and if we can't find it, then we will transform what we do find into something good. In order to appreciate good, I have to be aware of what is good. If I don't have what to appreciate, then it means I'm not doing enough to manifest the good.

I was so traumatized when everything happened. Why did it have to happen in that way, why did it have to be so difficult? Yet slowly, I've come to be appreciative, not only because God removed me from a bad situation, but because He made it happen so I could not doubt myself or any of the choices that had to be made. It was just clear—I was alone, and the path was set. Those same circumstances which I thought were so difficult and unnecessarily hard allowed me to have an easier time with the process of my divorce agreement. So many people spend years and a fortune of money coming to terms on a divorce. I ended up with full custody of my children, without a fight. Yes, it's hard raising them on my own, but I would never want my children to be away from me. How blessed I am to have my children with me all the time, to not have to share them for weekends and holidays, to not spend simchas apart! How blessed are we that we can stay in our home, remain a part of the community we love, and receive such support from the schools. It may have been an incredibly traumatic experience, but that doesn't mean I can't recognize the good in it. You see, sometimes we are so blinded by the pain that everything looks like the end of the world. Yet, the truth is we can't just throw black paint over our colorful canvas and cry that it is ruined. It wouldn't be fair to us and it wouldn't be fair to the master artist, God. Why deny the beauty of the painting just because there is a black spot? Even if the spot is big and even if it covers the lovely colors, the beauty of the painting remains; we just need to look beyond the black to see it.

So often we cancel out everything in our lives because we are having a hard time; suddenly nothing feels worth it anymore. But it is still worth it. Through the hardships, we can magnify the good. I have such helpful, mature, generous children. They let me sleep late on Shabbat morning and play on their own because they know I'm exhausted. My five-year-old makes the bed, and my seven-year-old will sometimes shower her little siblings. My children are special children, and it is because of their difficulties in life that they have risen to the occasion. I have learned how to be completely independent, to do things I never thought I could do. I feel like Bob the Builder, fixing everything around the house. I can take my four kids to the beach on my own, and we can all enjoy ourselves. It used to be extremely difficult, sitting at the Shabbat table on our own. It was so hard being the only one to clean up and pick up the house all the time. I didn't have anyone to talk to other than my young kids. I would sometimes cry and tell myself that I would take him back just to have company, just to have another adult to speak to and commiserate with. But now I love spending Shabbat alone with my kids. It's like getting to know them on another level. All the work is still there, and I'm still cleaning the whole time, but we hold hands, we sing *shalom aleichem*, and we dance, we share beautiful things with each other, we make jokes, and we thank Hashem for being our Father and not leaving us lonely. The silence and solitude at night, which were so hard at first, I am now grateful for.

I'm sitting here, at one a.m., thinking about life, healing, and writing. While it would be nice to have company, to have companionship full of love and enjoyment, I first needed to enjoy my own company. I need to appreciate being with myself, not being afraid of the silence or the pain of being alone. I felt like a nebach, but I am learning to see the beauty in the thoughtfulness of others, and I've come to enjoy all of the cookies that we have been sent. There has been a lot of black lately, but the colors on the canvas are so much brighter. I remember one time watching an artist in a painting competition who painted all black onto a white canvas. The judges thought it was ugly and disturbing, and they all gave the artist a big X. But the artist gave the camera a wink and a knowing look, and I knew something awesome was coming. Suddenly, the artist turned the canvas upside down to reveal the most beautiful painting. He knew what was there all along, but the judges didn't. I didn›t. It was a life lesson for me. We don't know what will be revealed from the black in our lives; we must wait and choose to see the hidden beauty.

There is a beautiful story about Rabbi Akiva and his wife, Rachel, who were so poor that they used to live on a pile of straw. Eliyahu HaNavi wanted to reward their sacrifices for the sake of Torah. One day, he presented himself to the holy couple as a poor man in urgent need, whose wife was giving birth, and he didn't have straw for her to lay on. Rabbi Akiva and his wife looked at each other, recognizing that there were those in this world who had even less than they did, and immediately gave the poor man some of their straw. They were overwhelmed with gratitude at their newfound wealth. Is that really Eliyahu HaNavi's idea of a reward? I have a better idea—give them a bed, or a caravan, or at least some pillows! Not only did he not give them anything, but he actually took from the little they did have. Are we missing something? Yes, and the answer is life-changing. Eliyahu HaNavi did indeed give them the greatest gift: the gift of gratitude. He gave them the power of being satisfied with what they had. If he had given them something more than what they already had, they might have asked why they didn't get more and therefore may never have been satisfied. But by making them realize their own wealth compared to others, they were gifted with endless gratitude and happiness with their share, no matter what. This comes to teach us that if we aren't grateful for what we have right now, then we will never be happy. We will always excuse our lack of happiness on a deficiency in our lives and never really be content and appreciative of what we have. That's the gift of gratitude; it allows us to see all the colors on our canvas and distracts us from the black.

In Hebrew, the word for blemish is *nega*, and the word for pleasure is *oneg*. The only difference is the location of the letter *ayin*, representative of the eye. What are we focusing on? What are we choosing to magnify? We can be in a cycle of negativity and stuck in place, or we can work toward opening our eyes to the beauty that does exist. Even if it is just a silver lining, we can allow it to guide us toward gratitude and positivity. As we learn in *Pirkei Avot*, "Who is rich? The one that is happy with his share." I am coming to understand that wealth is not about what you have, but about what you don't have. Some people have much but feel like they lack so much more. And some people have little, yet are satisfied and therefore do not lack anything. It's not about your share in life, everyone has a different share; it is about accepting your share.

After the fire, people kept telling me that fire brings wealth, that I was going to get wealthy from it. When my students set up the Go Fund Me campaign, people assumed that was it. But then I had my twins, and oh boy! That was the real wealth for me. I am coming to understand today that I am incredibly wealthy: I have an army of people supporting me. I have a relationship with God that only grows stronger with every test He sends my way. I have a treasure trunk brimming over with unparalleled *emunah*, wisdom, and inspiration. For all of this, I thank You, God; for believing in me, for testing me, for pushing me, and then pushing me even more. I had no idea who I could be, but You always knew I could be more. Thank you for showing me the way.

We spoke about pleasure being the feeling that we get when we feel a deficiency in our lives. In that sense, it seems that a person who doesn't have anything lacking in their life cannot experience true enjoyment. If a person always gets A's and his friend always gets C's, then once he gets an A, he will have far more pleasure from that A than his friend who always gets A's, right? But it occurred to me that there is a disclaimer that should go along with this idea. There is, in fact, a way of experiencing enjoyment without having to experience deficiency, and that is through gratitude. You see, gratitude allows us to experience what it would feel like to have the deficiency without having to actually experience the insufficiency. Therefore, we can enjoy satisfying the deficiency, but we didn't have to physically and emotionally experience it. We use our hearts and minds to visualize what it would be like to not have something, which allows us to feel so much more joy and gratitude for having it. The more I concentrate on the details and the "extras" that I have, the more thankful I will feel in my heart. Eyes aren't only eyes; we have lashes and eyebrows to protect them, tears to keep them moist, and glasses to regain lost vision. What a marvelous creation, how grateful we are to have our eyes, and all the details that make them work. We could go on and on about the things we have, and we would feel overwhelmed with gratitude for our lives. This is why, in Hebrew, the word *l'hodot* means "to thank" as well as "to acknowledge," because in order to be thankful we have to acknowledge the good, we have to be aware of the blessings, and count all of them.

When a parent gives their kid a chocolate, the parent will often ask the child, as they give them the treat, "What do you say?" You'd think it's done to teach the child manners, to say please and thank you, but it actually comes to teach us much more than that. That kid is in "entitled mode," or as I like to call it, "*magiah li* mode"—I deserve it mode. But when the parent asks for those magic words of thanks, suddenly the child realizes that the parent can choose whether or not to give the chocolate. You know what happens when he does give it? The child recognizes that the parent chose to give, chose to make him happy, and therefore he develops appreciation for the parent. The parent's prompt is the switch in the child's brain that generates love and gratitude. It's the same with God. He makes us pray for what we want—not because He needs us to pray, but because we need to realize that He is choosing to give to us because He loves us, and that will generate love in us toward Him. When we pray for something, we allow ourselves to really want it, which generates yearning within us. Therefore, when we are finally given what we desire, we feel so much more enjoyment and appreciation for it.

Yet so many of us would rather be ungrateful. We prefer to be blind to our blessings; we prefer to focus on what we lack. We don't want to acknowledge that we've been given anything, and we don't want to feel like we owe anything in return. Acknowledging the good would mean acknowledging that we have no right to complain, no right to be victims. Many times, we don't feel the enjoyment because we feel entitled to it, like it is our right to have it. Let's talk about that for a minute. Ours is certainly an entitled generation; we feel we deserve the goody bag like everyone else. The thing is, when we expect to receive, we can't recognize the genuine love and kindness that has been given to us. Judaism—and the same goes for all relationships, for that matter—is based on gratitude. Our challenge is to notice what was done and how it was done, all for us. Often in life, we feel that we should get whatever we want, like that's just a part of life, and everyone is getting what they want, so we should too, right? But when it doesn't come as easily as you expected, you suddenly realize, "I don't deserve anything, and I haven't been promised anything. But I have received so much anyway." That right there is how us achieve love.

I didn't deserve kids; none of us do. We said it before: we don't deserve anything in life. We are incapable of repaying God for even the smallest kindness that He has done for us. So, when we stop and realize not only the greatness of the blessings themselves, but all the extras that came with them, we are overwhelmed with gratitude and love for the Creator who gave them to us. It doesn't matter how hard my day has been; I need only to see the faces of my pure, beautiful angels smiling, and I feel like it is all worth it. I look at them and think, "Hashem, why did you have to make them so cute? It would have been enough to just have a child, but You made them so special, so pure, so well-behaved," and automatically my day takes a turn for the good. That's choosing to go from zero to 180 degrees.

Imagine if one day someone were to randomly gift you one million dollars. I bet you'd feel like the luckiest person in the world, like all your dreams have come true, right? But at the same time, you could never have imagined such a scenario even in your wildest dreams. You would be so grateful, dancing with joy. But then, imagine if a few minutes later the same person were to turn to your friend and give him ten million dollars. How would you feel then? You'd probably feel like you were just stabbed in the chest, like darkness has surrounded you. You'd probably think to yourself that you should have been that friend. If he had another ten million dollars to give, why didn't he give it to you? You were the first one he gave anything to; it should have been yours. Now you are angry, hurt, disappointed... What changed? Do you not still have your million dollars? Aren't you still a million dollars richer than you were five minutes ago? Why can't you appreciate that? Because now you feel entitled to more, so now you feel like you've been cheated. The gift is no longer a source of joy; it is actually the source of pain. Why? Because you decided that you should have gotten more, and now you feel rejected.

That's what many of us do to ourselves every day of our lives. Because we feel we should have more, we suddenly become blinded by and resentful of all that we do have, despite the fact that it is not a given that we should have gotten anything in the first place. Who says we are entitled to life, friends, family, health, marriage, children, etc.? These are all free gifts from God. But because we think we could have been given more, everything we have been given subtracts from our happiness. Why do we do this to ourselves? Why can't we appreciate the free million? Open your eyes; count your blessings! Every one of the morning blessings refers to something priceless in our lives, but we take it all for granted. These prayers force us to stop and recognize what we wouldn't give to be able to see, to be able to stand up straight, to be free. And we already have all of that. We should feel like we are overflowing with wealth!

It is said that no one ever thanked God until Leah gave birth to her son and named him Yehuda, which means "to be thankful." But how is it possible that no one had ever thanked Hashem before this point? Was it so hard to be grateful? Had no one ever received any kindness from God until then? What about the major kindnesses, like when Hashem saved Noach from the flood or stopped Avraham from sacrificing Yitzchak? Were none of them thankful? You see, we often receive something in life, or something happens to us, and we automatically feel inspired to say thank you. We feel and live that gratitude in that instant, but then the momentum is lost, and we forget how we felt at first. Adam himself complained to God about Chava only a short time after asking for her. We're all like that. We want kids and then complain they make a mess. We want husbands, but then complain they leave their socks on the floor. We want a job, but then complain that it is too demanding. Is there anything we don't complain about?

But you see, Leah had done some math and realized she was really only meant to have three children, so when she had a fourth child, she was aware it was an extra kindness from God. The seeds we plant in ourselves will flourish in our children through how we raise them. How we choose to see the world will be expressed in the outcome of all our actions. Leah chose the name Yehuda because she never wanted to forget how she felt at his birth, never wanted to forget the joy of that moment. She knew that it was only a matter of time before, like all babies, Yehuda became another weight on her shoulders: a baby that cries, a toddler that makes messes, and a teenager that talks back to her. She named him Yehuda so that one day, when she forgets how much she wanted him and how grateful she was for his arrival, and she yells, "Yehuda!" in anger, she is reminded of the gift she was given. In that moment, she will turn to thank Hashem and choose to live a life in which she expresses that gratitude. This is one of my favorite *divrei Torah*. So much so, in fact, that it is actually the reason I chose that name for my son. After such a long wait for children, and all the struggles that went with it, I knew my son would be called Yehuda. We took it further and called him Yosef Yehuda, meaning "to add praise." That was my hope for my children: that they should grow up knowing they were gifts, they were wanted, they were waited for.

I didn't grow up feeling like that, and I often felt like a bother or a burden. I was always one of those people saying sorry for every little thing because, on the inside, we think we have to be sorry we even came into this world to begin with; maybe we don't feel we are wanted or chosen. Yet the first words we say every morning are *"modeh ani l'fanecha,* I am thankful in front of you, God." Have you ever made plans for next week, next month? How do you know you will even be here? How can you guarantee there is a future for you? We don't know or control anything. But we wake up every morning and acknowledge our existence, acknowledge that God is choosing to give us life, and it is the forefront of His actions. He wants us here; He is involved in our lives and wants us to be present and to report for duty every day! The prayer continues, *"raba emunatecha,* Your belief in us is great." Imagine, out of every person in the world, Hashem chose you; He woke you up today; He chose you as part of the Jewish people. Shouldn't we wake up every day feeling like a million dollars? I mean, we were chosen!

Every day, I tell my students that the fact that we woke up this morning means that there is something we have to do that no one else can do. God doesn't need backdrop extras in His movie. We aren't background characters that can easily be written off or forgotten; we are the main characters. That's why we start the morning with the word *modeh*, thanks. I'm not here for me; I am here for You. I acknowledge that You are giving me life, and I want to thank You for that by being *l'fanecha*, by being consciously aware that I stand before You because You have chosen me. I will show my appreciation by doing Your will, by living a life that is full of meaning, so that my whole existence is in praise of You. God gives us life because He believes in us; it's about time we start believing in ourselves too. And you know how we do that? By living and breathing gratitude through meaningful choice. This is why the opening verse of *Tehillim* begins with, *"ashrei ha'ish,* happy is the person." Because there is no greater happiness than being a person who has used their choice the right way.

I am coming to understand that while my life is hard, every part of it expresses God's personal involvement in it. In a way, things get so crazy that it can only be God behind the scenes. Clearly, He wants to be involved in my life; He is choosing to run the show Himself. Who says *hashgacha pratit*, divine providence, can only be found in the good things we get in life? All of God's involvement is part of His providence; it is Him telling us that He believes in us and He is cheering for us more than we will ever understand. The moment we start paying attention to the details, we can start to develop a meaningful, positive relationship with God. Finding God in the small things shows the greatness of our relationship with Him. We expect the big things, but it's the small things that show how much someone really cares, how attuned they are to our needs. Gratitude is what gets us to this destination. Because the more we say thank you, the more we are choosing to see God's love in our lives.

I like to call these moments "I just called to say I love you" moments. Occasions where God does something for me with such swift, unassuming beauty that makes me think, "He's just calling to say He loves me." Like the cookies that were brought to our house to remind us we are loved when we were feeling alone, or the envelopes of money that magically appear in my mailbox when I need it most, or the supermarket gift card that was given to me two days before the *Chag*. All of the amazing, beautiful messengers that Hashem has sent my way: the rabbis, the rebbetzins, the therapists, the siblings, the parents, the family, the friends. The rebbetzin who took my kids to buy gifts before the *Chag* so they could have *simchat* Yom Tov and filled my freezer with meat and chicken so that we would have an abundance of food for the holiday. The sister who randomly showed up at my house with sushi three days after it all happened, just to cheer me up. The sister who sent me a box of chocolate the day I received my *gett* because she knew I would need a pick-me-up. The rebbetzin who took me out for a margarita because she knew I could use a drink. All of the people who came with me to receive my *gett* so that I wouldn't sit there on my own, and who stayed with me for hours even though I told them it was okay to leave and they need not waste their time.

They only repeated that they were here to support me and there was nowhere else they would want to be at that moment. The rabbi who messaged me almost every single day to see how I was feeling and to let me know that I am a hero and I should be amazed at my own strength; who went to the Kotel to *daven* for me. The brother who came to babysit my kids every day for weeks so that I could have time for myself and go to the gym. The friend who constantly invited me for Shabbat and would come to my house to help me and my kids climb up the hill to her house. The friend who would come over at two a.m. so that I wouldn't cry alone. The friend who sponsored therapy from the other side of the world and the wonderful therapist who gave me time with so much joy and a happy disposition. And who can forget the person who took it upon herself to come up with my mortgage payment every month so that I wouldn't drown in debt in addition to everything I was going through? The ones who believed in me and told me I would make it out, who encouraged me to believe in myself and write this book. The students that joined together to send me Shabbat food and assembled a "help group." The neighbor who sent her daughter to babysit every week, and the school that embraced my daughter and surrounded her with support. The calls, the texts, the visits, the cookies, the meal trains, the hugs, the *chizzuk*, the tolerance, the shared tears—all of it. I couldn't possibly mention it all in such a short space as this book. Yet all of this was Hashem calling to say He loves me through those who chose to bring His light to dispel my darkness.

As I remember and write all of this, I can feel my face glowing with a big smile that I can't control. If only I had taken note of each individual kindness, of every generous person, so as not to forget it. But I have it in my mind and in my heart. As I write, I am overcome with happiness. I even feel like, in a way, it was all worth it, if only to be able to witness such kindness, to have received such generosity. It seems that gratitude really can change our perspective. If we only open our eyes, we can turn bitterness into sweetness. All of the deficiencies I felt then have allowed me to take joy in the small things, the minor gestures, to have awareness of them, to be grateful, and inspired by them.

I have often thought I wouldn't be able to handle everything on my plate—not physically, emotionally, or spiritually. I remember waking up to thousands of messages just a few hours after the house fire, seeing the Go Fund Me campaign, and realizing that Jewish people are going to pull me through. Because we are one, and if I hurt, they hurt. That same feeling is what kept me going this time, too. It was clear from the beginning that I couldn't possibly do everything on my own, but I knew that I had an army of people behind me, supporting me, cheering me on. It saddens me to think that there are those who don't have such a support system. How could anyone survive such challenges without having others to believe in them, backing them up? It reminds me of a story where a non-Jew attacked a rabbi, claiming that the Jews believe the gentiles are subhuman because the Torah only uses the word *adam*, man, in reference to the Jews.

"So what are we?" the non-Jew asked. "Why do you degrade us?"

To this, the rabbi answered, "It is not that you aren't human like us, but can we call all of you non-Jews, *adam*, one man? Do all of you hurt when one of you is hurting, as if you were the same person? Do all of you get together to pray for and support each other?"

Whenever tragedy has hit the Jewish people, we can always see how our differences go right out the window. At the end of the day, we all know that the size of our kippah doesn't matter; it's the size of our hearts that counts, and we have huge hearts. I couldn't possibly mention every single person who supported me in my time of need, yet the impact each one made is unforgettable. Know that you have the ability to give life to others; all it takes is a kind word, a smile, a plate of cookies, supporting a campaign… It might seem small, but for those in pain, every gesture is a huge hug that carries them one step further.

We spoke about Leah and how she thanked God, but my name is Rachel, and I want to share what Rachel Imeinu taught me about gratitude. When Rachel had Yosef, the Torah teaches us she called him Yosef because "*asaf Hashem et charpati*, Hashem has gathered my shame." Rashi explains that during the time that Rachel could not conceive, she had no reason for not being the best wife. I mean, who could she blame if the house wasn't clean or if she didn't have dinner on the table? A baby is a great excuse for poor housekeeping. You can't help but read this and wonder if it's some kind of joke. Rachel couldn't have children for fourteen years, and once she finally had a child, all she could think is, "Hashem has gathered my shame of not being a good enough housewife?" I mean, if we're already talking about shame, maybe focus on the real shame that Hashem is taking away from you: the shame of not having children, of being barren all these years. But to have someone to blame for not having dinner ready is just ridiculous.

However, I think Rachel wants to teach us a lesson on gratitude and the choice in our perception. Of course, she was grateful she had a child. She had been barren for so many years, embarrassed in front of her sister and maids. She didn't just want to thank God for the big milestone of having a child; that's an obvious one. She wanted to express gratitude for the smallest, most insignificant details of her sufferings; she wanted to focus on all of it, to appreciate what she had gained even more. Not only for the obvious gift, but for the collateral that came with it. So, she chose to focus on the mundane aspects of her pain. Who would even think of that? No one; it just sounds absurd. But that's the point. If you can notice the tiniest details, then your level of gratitude, and therefore happiness, will increase exponentially. The greater the deficiency, the greater the enjoyment. We must be aware of everything we lack in our lives so that we can fully appreciate the enjoyment that comes from the fulfillment of that deficiency. Never let go of even the most minute detail because each one is a gold coin that makes up the treasure of life.

One year, on Rosh Hashanah, I was thinking about the symbolic foods we eat and the blessings we say, and I thought of the most famous of them all: apples and honey. Why do we eat an apple dipped in honey? To have a sweet year? Is that really the best choice of foods to symbolize sweetness? Isn't there anything a bit more inspiring than apples and honey? If it was me, I would have suggested chocolate and strawberries. I had to come up with an answer to satisfy my question, and what a rewarding answer I found. Honey is the only kosher food in the world to come out of a non-kosher being. You can go to a beehive, put your hand in, take some honey, and eat it—no problem with kashrut at all. But what if there were bees stuck in the honey? How could that be okay to eat? It turns out that honey has a unique chemical property that causes anything placed in it to become honey, literally transforming it into more honey. So much so that if you were to put a piece of pork in a container with honey, once it reaches a point that it can no longer be seen, you can eat that honey. The pork has literally become honey.

I think we all want a good, sweet life, but many of us think that in order to have a good life we need to have sweet things. However, not all of us are dealt good hands, and we need to work really hard to play those hands and still win the game. Winning the game by playing a hand made up of jokers and luck does not give you wisdom. Wisdom is earned by learning to play whatever terrible cards we are dealt and managing to make the best of our hand. In other words, having a sweet year is not about having sweet things; it's about trying to be like the honey and turning everything into sweetness. The same bee that stings also produces the sweetest thing in nature. So too, it is often the most painful stings in life that bring out the greatest light in us. I will also note that this chemical property of honey will only decompose what is already in pieces; it only works if what is put into the honey is already broken. If we want to grow in life, e have to allow yourself to be broken, to let go of your ego, and surrender ourselves to a greater power that is here to guide you on your journey.

So, we now understand why honey, but why an apple? I feel like an apple is such a boring fruit. It seems to be always available wherever you are in the world, and it's often the cheapest option for fruit. It's like the one fruit you can always count on; it's always there. What's so special about the plain, old apple? Why not kiwi, or strawberry, or pineapple? That's exactly it. We think, "if only" I could have a kiwi or a pineapple or a strawberry, then I would be happy. If I could have more, if I could have better. But an apple is not only good enough; it is too good to be true. The *apple* has so much nutritional value, so much flavor and goodness packed into one little fruit. Happiness is to be found in the simple things, like learning to see the beauty in an apple. You don't need much; you just need to recognize what you already have.

This is actually one of the beautiful explanations for why kosher animals chew their cud. They chew and digest, and then it comes back up, and they chew and digest again. This comes to teach us that sometimes we want to "eat" more, to digest more; we think we don't have enough, yet really all we need to do is revisit what we already have. We've already received the blessings; we just didn't digest them enough. All we need to be happy is right here, available to us whenever we choose to digest it properly. As it is written in *Mishlei*, "All the days of a poor man are bad, but a good-hearted person feasts perpetually." This verse is not referring to a materially poor man, but a man who is poor in his *emunah* and his relationship with God. Such a man has only bad days; he can't find good in anything; everything is an issue, there is always a complaint. But the person who has a relationship with God and a heart full of gratitude, his entire life is a party; everything is good. This man is seeing the world through rose-tinted lenses; everything has become beautifully colorful; he perceives life in a positive light. Happiness is learning to see the beauty in the apple; we don't need more than what we already have, we already have it all.

They say the grass is greener on the other side, and I once read a version of that saying which left me thinking: Sometimes the grass is greener on the other side because it's fake. But really, the grass is not greener on the other side; it's simply greener where we water it. While we are busy looking at someone else's grass, we neglect our own; we forget to water it and to watch it grow. The time has come for us to water our blessings. When we can do that, *b'ezras Hashem*, we can be guaranteed that we will see them blossom into beautiful gardens, and our lives will be filled with enjoyment.

PIN IT TO YOUR HEART!

"If you can notice the tiniest details, then your level of gratitude, and therefore happiness, will increase exponentially."

"Optimism doesn't only mean seeing the good in what is happening, but also being able to see the good that can happen."

"We attract what we believe."

"God is constantly calling to say He loves you."

"The grass is greener where we water it."

"Know that you have it in your power the ability to give life to others."

"The greater the deficiency, the greater the ultimate enjoyment."

"Happiness is not about your share in life; it is about accepting your share."

"We are adam; one nation with one heart."

"Life is about being like the honey and turning everything into sweetness."

"The same bee that stings also produces the sweetest thing in nature."

CHAPTER FOURTEEN

BECOMING GODLY BY CHOOSING GOOD

The most important questions a person must ask himself are: What am I doing here, what do I want to do, and who do I want to become? Am I pursuing the correct path to being that person, or do I keep getting lost and distracted along the way? Sometimes there are hard choices in life, but wisdom is measuring what we gain in exchange for what we lose. We tend to think that the right choice should be the easy choice, but it's often the opposite. The *satan* knows what happens if we choose the right thing, so he makes it difficult for us; he lays obstacles in our paths, clouds our minds with confusion and fear. We often wonder what the right thing to do is. We are not always clear on our own values, let alone society's values, and we can get lost in the chaos, blinded by our needs and our fears. Well, in the Torah, right and wrong are clearly defined, just not in a way that we are used to. The Torah describes "good" as that which brings us closer to Hashem, and "bad" as that which moves us away from Hashem. At the end of the day, we are here to be godly, and our goals should be to make godly choices. But how do we know when we are doing the right thing? We need to ask ourselves, what does Hashem expect from me in this moment? Who am I trying to serve, and what needs am I trying to fulfill?

Pirkei Avot teaches us that the correct path a person should choose for himself is "that which makes him look good in the eyes of God and in the eyes of others." I like to ask myself the following questions: If I were to leave this world right now, would I be proud of who I was, of who I became? Would I want to marry me? Would I want me as a mother? Can I look in the mirror and feel love and pride, or am I embarrassed by my own reflection? We often forget what our goal really is; we forget why we are being tested and why we are put in specific situations. The Torah way of life is to understand that our lives are meant for growth; everything is a setting for us to learn, to develop ourselves as human beings, and to reach our highest selves. When we understand this, then our whole view of the world changes; we see people and situations as opportunities, as moments in which to practice what we've learned, moments to flex our developing muscles.

There were plenty of times in my marriage where something would happen, my husband would ask for my forgiveness, and I would jokingly respond, "Maybe don't do something wrong, and then you won't need my forgiveness." His response would be to play the religion card and remind me that God forgives, to which I would answer, "But I'm not God." Then I would think about what I just said and wonder, who do I want to be? To what do I aspire? I would realize that while I am not God, I want to be like God. Therefore, I must learn to forgive and forget, to be kind and compassionate, even when I feel like I have nothing left to draw on, even when I've been hurt by others. Because I'm not doing it for others; I'm doing it for myself, to fulfill my own purpose of being godly. Over time, I am coming to realize that real giving must be selfish in nature. Not in the sense that it stems from ego, but in the sense that giving benefits me just like it benefits the person I am giving to. We have bodies that always want to be satisfied, to be comfortable, to fulfill desires, but we also have a soul that wants to be satisfied, to be filled with kindness. Many of us give to others because we see there is a need; we are hurt by seeing other people hurt. Yet, we can totally choose to avoid giving if we wanted to because we can choose to blind ourselves to the pain of others; out of sight, out of mind. We can choose to be so self-involved that we fail to recognize the existence and the needs of others outside of ourselves.

When a baby boy is given a *brit mila*, we bless him with the words, "*zeh hakatan gadol yehiyeh*, may this little one be big." A strange blessing, to say the least, but it does come to show us something significant. Babies are physically small because they are emotionally small; they are only aware of their own needs. They are selfish in the extreme; they can't think about whether they are bothering others or being annoying. As the infant grows, he becomes physically bigger, and it should be an expression of him growing spiritually as well. The greatest rabbi of a generation is not merely called a *talmid chacham*, but rather a *gadol hador*, the greatest of his generation. Why? Because the definition of a *gadol*, one who is great, is someone whose definition of self expands to include others. They don't see you as an outside entity; they see you as part of themselves, and they feel for you like they feel for themselves. There is a famous story of Rav Aryeh Levine, who accompanied his wife to see a doctor because her leg hurt, and he said to the doctor, "Our leg hurts." Every relationship should be like that, not only marriage; I should see you, feel for you, and be there for you, as if it were me.

Avraham was personified by his quality of *chessed*. The word *chessed* tends to be translated as "kindness," but that is not an accurate definition. In fact, the Torah uses the word *chessed* to describe immorality too; the absolute term "*chessed*" is defined as a lack of boundaries. Unlike the negative use of *chessed*, where our boundaries are loose and we show no control over ourselves, reducing our "self," the positive use of the word *chessed* is when we are very aware of our "self," but our boundaries are not limited to ourselves; specifically, when our definition of self expands to include others in a positive way. This is beautifully illustrated in the custom of the *chattan* extending his *tallit* over the *kallah* under the *chuppah*, symbolizing an extension of his self, his heart, and his protection to his wife, as they become one.

At the beginning of any crisis, people often rush to help; they make an effort to be more available right away. But slowly, as time passes, and the emergency becomes everyday life, the urgency of their help dies down, and they tend to forget; they go back to being involved in their own lives. The hardest part is when the storm has finally calmed and you try to get back into a routine, but you are still carrying all the weight of the world on your shoulders. It is at that point when you turn around and realize that you are now carrying your burden alone. Everyone has moved on, and you are left on your own. As I have often been reminded, everyone has their own life to worry about; everyone is busy. But can we ever be too busy to recognize the pain and needs of others? Of course, everyone is busy with their own lives, but there are different kinds of busy, and the Torah instructs us, "Do not stand idle by your brother's blood." In other words, don't be indifferent; there is so much more that you can do.

Pesach came very soon after my personal storm hit this year. In Israel, Pesach is family time, and I wanted to give my children a real Pesach, with fun trips and activities, just like everyone else. Even though I did my best, I couldn't help but feel out of place among the other families. Seeing other families in the park having fun and bonding while I was just trying to keep my own family afloat, working hard to smile for my kids and give them a good time made me feel isolated. All I wanted at that time was to be embraced, to be taken care of; I wished someone could adopt my family and welcome us in so that we could feel a sense of belonging, to feel that we are wanted, that we are seen. So often, people experiencing pain feel invisible; they wonder if anyone understands what they are going through, if anyone can feel them, hear them, see them. We also want to belong; we also want to have fun; our kids also deserve what other kids have. They didn't choose it; we didn't choose it, so have us in mind; don't forget us.

As much as we are all trying our best , I'm taking from this to try to be like Avraham, who sat outside his tent looking for guests to invite into his home, even when he had a great excuse. I mean, he was ninety-nine years old and had just had very delicate surgery, yet he understood that the act of *chessed* is for his own benefit, his own godliness. He had surgery without anesthesia, yet he still chose to keep others "in sight and in mind," to step outside himself and be great. If someone is in pain, we should feel their pain. You and I are one; therefore, I need to take care of you because taking care of you is taking care of me. That's what the Torah teaches us: Happy is the Jewish people because we are *adam*; we are one person, one body, one soul! Real kindness is selfish, but the good kind of selfish, the kind of selfishness that takes care of the soul.

It's pretty incredible that when Avraham saw the angels approaching his tent, he was mid-conversation with God, and he literally left God on hold so that he could do a *chessed*, and only came back when he finished. Hashem recognized Avraham's greatness in that act and thus chose to share with him the plans to destroy Sodom and Gomorrah to give Avraham the opportunity to pray. Hashem not only approved of Avraham interrupting their conversation but was actually proud of him for it. That's truly astonishing, if you ask me. How could he possibly have the nerve to put the King of Creation on hold? Avraham understood that it is greater to be like God than to be with God. To be like God is to really love God because it stems from a true appreciation of His greatness and the desire to emulate Him. Do you know what happened when Avraham ran out to greet his guests? The *Midrash* tells us that his bandage fell off and he was completely healed from the circumcision. His body had been elevated to such a degree by the act of *chessed* that it made him whole like an angel because his act was angelic; he was able to overcome his pain and his human selfishness in such a way and with such alacrity.

Rav Aryeh Levin was known to visit houses of mourning in order to cry with those grieving because that is what is needed by someone experiencing loss: to really have someone who can empathize with their pain. Sometimes we feel like we have enough on our plates as it is; we can't possibly carry anyone else's weight in addition to our own. Yet physics teaches us the exact opposite. If two people are built with the same weight and strength and carry a 60-kilogram bag between them, you would assume that they are each carrying half, thirty kilos each, right? However, interestingly enough, some of the weight becomes "dead" weight and basically gets lost somewhere in the middle. In other words, when you help someone carry their weight in addition to your own, the weight is divided between each of you, and it's as if Hashem Himself is so moved by the kindness that He also joins and carries some of the weight as well. This is what Judaism calls "bearing the yoke with one's fellow man."

At my most trying time, I was convinced I didn't have the strength to make it through in one piece. But I was reminded that I'm part of the greatest people in the world, and that we are responsible for each other and we care about each other. Most importantly, we must allow ourselves to give to each other. When I started opening up about what was happening and I saw how others cared—how they got together to help—I had a moment of realization that helped me pick myself back up. I realized that I don't need to pull through on my own; the Jewish people were going to help pull me through. With that amount of power and will, I couldn't possibly fall; the Jewish people wouldn't let me; they would make sure I made it through. Just like when *B'nei Yisrael* were in the desert and only four people were needed to carry the whole *Mishkan*. Our sages tell us that this was possible because, in fact, the *Mishkan* carried those who carried it. I realized this is true of our nation today. The moment I choose to carry what God has given me, He will send messengers to help me. This is the very quality that defined every great person in the history of the Jewish people, like Moshe or King David. The care they showed toward everyone and everything, down to their flocks of sheep, was a direct expression of the kind of leaders they were. They understood the meaning of oneness.

In telling the story of Moshe's youth, the Torah says, "The child grew and was brought to Pharaoh's daughter." In the next *pasuk*, the Torah writes, "Moshe was grown and he went out to his brothers." Rashi asks, didn't the *pasuk* already mention that he grew? How fast is he growing that it needs to be repeated in such close succession? Rashi answers that the first mention of growth refers to his physical size; the second refers to his spiritual greatness. When Moshe went out to his brothers, he didn't see himself as a stranger even though he could have been indifferent to their strife; he was enjoying life as a prince of the palace, yet he chose to go out and be one with the Jewish people, to carry their burden even though it was not his own.

There is a famous *Gemara* which tells of a Roman who came to Rabbi Akiva with a question:

"Doesn't it say in your Torah that God is good?" he asked.
Rabbi Akiva answered, "Yes, He is great. Why?"
The Roman replied, "Well, if God is so good, why did He create so many poor people?"
Rabbi Akiva answered, "In order to allow the rich to give."

Maybe you have asked yourself this same question a few times, as have I. If God is so good, why is there so much pain in the world? Why is there so much hardship? Rabbi Akiva offers an inspiring answer. We came into this world in order to be godly, and God's essential trait is that He is a giver, as the *pasuk* in *Tehillim* says, "*olam chessed yibaneh,* the world is built by *chessed.*" We need to realize that, in order to give, there has to be someone to give to, someone who can be the receiver of our giving. When Adam was created, he was perfect. How could he not be when, after all, he was made in the image of God? Yet right afterward, the *pasuk* tells us that he wasn't good, as "it is not good for man to be alone." So how can Adam be perfect but not good? What makes something good? Well, good means it is able to fulfill its purpose, and a perfect man cannot give because he doesn't understand what it means to need. Therefore, in answer to Adam's request, God didn't just create another Adam; He created Chava, a woman, because real giving means recognizing and fulfilling that which is lacking. It's not about what we want to give, but what others need to receive from us. The Torah teaches us that it is not that we love and therefore we give, but rather that we love those to whom we give. Hashem, in all His greatness, created all of us with many deficiencies so that we can give to each other and bond with each other. It is not that the rich give to the poor, but that the poor give to the rich by giving them the opportunity to become givers, to become godly. They are the ones biting the bullet, so to speak, experiencing hardship and challenges so that we have an opportunity to perfect ourselves by helping them. Poor, in this case, doesn't necessarily mean financially; instead, it refers to parts of life in which we are lacking.

I have constantly been put in situations in which I depend on others, where I have had to allow others to take care of me because I couldn't possibly do it all myself. To be honest, plenty of times I am stubborn, refusing to ask for or accept help. There is a part of me that is embarrassed, that feels that I am somehow lesser now because I am needy, because I depend on others. But part of my growth is understanding that receiving is also a way of giving, and that often it can be harder than giving. Being a receiver means taking a passive position; it can feel like giving up on a level of self-sufficiency or accepting failure. When my house burned down, I got to see what true greatness really is: people going out of their way to help us, to be there for us. A meal train had been arranged to help us, but I specifically remember this one amazing woman who not only brought us food but went the extra mile to make it an enjoyable meal. She said that we had been through a hard enough time already and she wanted us to feel special and pampered. So, along with the food, she brought a tablecloth, nice dishes, refreshing drinks, and all of the odds and ends that make a meal more luxurious and festive. That is the definition of having empathy, of being sensitive to the needs of others.

I remember how, after the fire, the first night out of the hospital was one of the most difficult nights of our lives. We were staying in someone's apartment, and it wasn't too comfortable. Our whole family was packed into one tiny room, and I started to panic. I was crying, overwhelmed with the sense of loss, when suddenly someone knocked on the door. I still remember coming down, still crying, and seeing all of my students there. They had come with balloons and chocolate to cheer me up. When I found out that they had started a fundraising campaign for us, I was so embarrassed. Was I now a *tzedakah* case? How could I possibly accept charity? It was putting my independence and all of my successes at risk. Our rabbi explained that "Your *avoda* right now is to accept. Accept any help that's being offered so that you can get back on your feet again feeling strong."

It was now my job to accept, to receive for others. That's how I was meant to serve Hashem during that time. *Tzedakah* is a mitzvah; it is a mitzvah to give to others "*asher yechsar lo,* whatever they are lacking." What I had failed to understand until then was that I had become a channel through which others could perform the mitzvah of *tzedakah*, and do it happily. I was the conduit for hundreds of people to become givers. What an honor, what a gift! People were giving to me, but I was also giving to them by providing them the opportunity to choose good, to be godly. Once I understood that, I was able to shift my perspective. How can we be givers if there is no one to give to? It's hard to be on the receiving end. But that's the thing; it's not about ego; it's about being the medium through which others can do *mitzvos*. Instead of being sad for my circumstances, I became grateful for the opportunity it presented for directly experiencing what it means to choose to do the right thing even when it's hard.

There was a little boy who had heard someone mention that there had been a fire and that a little girl was now homeless. I will never forget the rabbi bringing us this massive *Playmobil* set because that little boy said he wanted to give it to the girl who had lost everything. The opportunities for *mitzvos* didn't stop there. Even though we are not allowed to do laundry during *Pesach*, people were coming here to collect and wash our smoky clothes before the odors and stains set in. They didn't do their laundry on *Pesach*, but they did ours and returned it all folded and organized by color. These are the moments when we realize that we really are one people. When one of us hurts, we all hurt. All of these experiences have made me so much more sensitive to others. Maybe I too was blind and indifferent to others' pain; maybe I was too busy with my own life to focus on others. But once you are the one experiencing the hardship, suddenly your heart opens in ways it never did before. The Torah teaches us that we have a heart made of stone because if it were made of flesh, we wouldn't be able to live from all the pain it would sustain. At the same time, we can't allow ourselves to become such stones that nothing moves us. We must open our hearts and make a mark, drop by drop, like Rabbi Akiva as he watched a trickle of water form a crater in a rock.

Rav Noah Weinberg asked how the Torah could possibly expect us to love others like we love ourselves. The answer he offered was to imagine you are chopping vegetables with one hand and accidentally cut your other hand. Would that hand then take the knife and cut the other one in return? Of course not, because then you would have two bleeding hands. From where we sit, it may seem that our hands are separate entities, but if we were to look from afar and see the whole picture, we would see that they are part of the same being. The same goes for how we may seem to be individual beings, but really, we are all one nation, connected at the core. How can we bleed from one hand and not use the other to stop the bleeding with a bandage?

Howard Schulz, the founder of Starbucks, once mentioned a story that was told to him by a rabbi describing the sufferings of those in the concentration camps. It was said that as many as six people had to share one thin blanket to survive the bitter winters. How did they manage to cover six people with a single blanket? The answer is that when each one considers how the blanket can be extended to cover the person next to him, then they can all be covered. There is another story of two men in a cattle cart, a young man trying to keep an older man warm by embracing him. Both of them survived the bitter cold because providing for another creates a sense of purpose and a responsibility in a person and motivates him to keep going. Like Viktor Frankl said, "Success, like happiness, cannot be pursued; it must ensue, and it only does so as the unintended side effect of one›s dedication to a cause greater than oneself." The more we give, the more we get. Giving feeds our souls; it helps us be more alive. Even a small child can understand that the pleasure of giving is much greater than the pleasure of receiving. Like my little toddlers who don't want to share their *Bamba*, even with their mommy. After reluctantly sacrificing one piece, they could see my joy and their faces light up. Suddenly they don't just want to give me one piece; they want to stuff the whole bag in my face. Giving allows us to emulate the greatness of God, and what could be better than to allow for that aspect of us to be expressed!

There was once a teacher who asked his young students, "Do you believe in God?" His students all responded, "Yes, of course we believe in God." Then the teacher said, "Well, if you believe in God, then the God you believe in must be very evil because look at all of the evil that exists in the world."

The students were silent until one young boy raised his hand and asked, "Can I ask you a question?"

The teacher said he could, so the boy continued. "Teacher, do you believe in cold?"

"Yes," said the teacher.

"If you believe in cold," said the boy, "then you're mistaken because in physics you can't measure cold; you can only measure the lack of heat."

The teacher was silent as the student went on.

"Teacher, do you believe in darkness?"

The teacher answered that yes, of course he did.

"Well," said the student, "you are again mistaken! In physics you can't measure darkness, only the absence of light."

The teacher still didn't answer, so the student asked one last question.

"Teacher, do you believe in evil?"

"Of course," said the teacher.

"Then you are mistaken again!" exclaimed the student. "Evil is simply a lack of *godliness* in the hearts of men!"

The reason there is bad in this world, the reason there is poverty and pain, is because it is hard for us to constantly choose good and overcome our *yetzer hara*; it is hard to be Godly. We want comfortable lives full of meaningless things, but we are supposed to choose good, to choose Godliness. When Hashem created man,

He said, "*na'aseh adam,* let us make man." The obvious question is, who is the "us" He is referring to? There are many famous answers; specifically, Rashi's explanation on the *pasuk* is that Hashem consulted with the angels on whether or not He should create man. But my favorite answer is that the "us" refers to you and me. God was speaking to each and every one of us. He says, "I'll give you life, talents, health, family, and friends. I'll give you all of the raw materials, but you have to make a human being out of that." As the famous saying goes, "Who you are is God's gift to you; who you become is your gift to God."

PIN IT TO YOUR HEART!

"It is greater to be like God than to be with God."

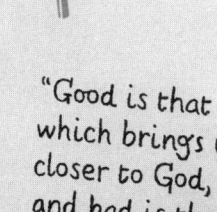

"Good is that which brings us closer to God, and bad is that which moves us away from God."

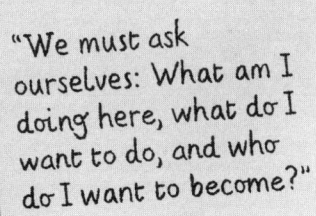

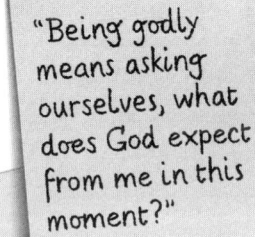

"We must ask ourselves: What am I doing here, what do I want to do, and who do I want to become?"

"Being godly means asking ourselves, what does God expect from me in this moment?"

"God gives us talents, tools, and all the raw materials; our job is to make a human being out of that."

"Evil is simply a lack of godliness in the hearts of men."

"Who you are is God's gift to you; who you become is your gift to God."

CHAPTER FIFTEEN

LEARNING TO LISTEN

We are all looking to heal ourselves in some way, but the question remains: how? We discussed how God has a master plan for us and that everything in our lives is moving us in that direction, but manifesting it is our job. It seems that it all comes down to how much we choose to include God in our lives and how much we are willing to become a vessel for God's will in this world. At the end of the day, if I am here to develop my soul, does it really matter if my body is not as comfortable? The best scenario for me is the one in which my soul achieves everything that it can possibly achieve in this life, pain and hardship aside, right?

When Avraham was ready to sacrifice Yitzchak, a voice called out to him from Heaven and said, "Avraham, Avraham... Do not raise your hand against the boy, or do anything to him. For now I know that you fear God." After being tested by God ten times, how is it only now that God recognizes Avraham's devotion? Were none of the other tests good enough? And why is Avraham's name said twice? Often in the Torah, the names of great people are mentioned twice in succession to signify their greatness. Avraham's name is mentioned twice here because, at that moment, the Avraham of this world had reached his peak and aligned himself with the Avraham of the next world. In other words, Avraham had reached the ultimate level of his own potential because of those ten trials. *Pirkei Avot* teaches us that, "With ten tests Avraham, our father, was tested—and he withstood them all; in order to show how great was the love of Avraham, our father." All of the trials were an expression of God's love for Avraham in order to help him become who he was destined to become, and only after the completion of the ten tests did he become Avraham Avinu, our father. Avraham didn't resist the hardships that God sent him. He gave all of himself to God, even when it meant letting go of the greatest part of himself, what he was most attached to. Tests are an expression of your potential; the more you are tested, the more light you can bring into the world, and the more is waiting to be revealed.

Hashem knew that Avraham was a man of *chessed*; how could He put him through such a trial which is the antithesis of *chessed*? And with his own son! The very son He promised would become the father of generations, and when he himself fought against the practice of idol worshippers who sacrificed children! The sacrifice of Yitzchak was significant because it went against Avraham's nature, against his logic. The true greatness of *Akeidat* Yitzchak is that Hashem expected Avraham to let go of that which he loves the most. The long-awaited son, the heir to Avraham's spiritual pursuit and purpose, meant to realize God's promise of nationhood. And suddenly Hashem tells Avraham to give him up as a sacrifice? For Avraham, it was the most difficult of all ten trials.

We only get to have one "number one" thing in life. Yet often, we only know what it is when we are forced to let it go; we only recognize our number one when everything becomes number two in comparison. God doesn't need us to have Him as our "number one." But we need it for ourselves because the degree to which we have God in our lives is the degree to which we will be happy, in tune, and aligned with ourselves. We need Hashem to be our "number one" to a degree at which there is no separation between us and Him, no obstacles or resistance in our service of Him. We need to become one with Him; that oneness is what makes us whole. In Hebrew, the words for peace and wholeness are the same because we can only feel peace when we feel whole with ourselves, and we only feel whole with ourselves when we are one with God. When we have full acceptance and harmony with what is going on around us and within us, then we can feel complete. That's why the test of *Akeidat* Yitzchak is the greatest of all of Avraham's tests, because it is the one in which he is able to fully let go of everything holding him back from being one with God. As soon as we can let go of that which we love the most, we can achieve oneness with Hashem, and only then can we reach a point of fulfilling our ultimate potential in both worlds.

The greatest pain in life is to fail at becoming who we have the potential to be, to cut short our potential. I dread getting to *Shamayim* and Hashem saying to me, "Raquel, this is who you could have been, and this is who you were." I am terrified of the fiery shame that I will feel in that moment. That is who I could have become, and this is all I've managed to be? That is the level of potential I had? To know that there was so much greatness waiting for me and I didn't get to scratch the surface of it because I was too lazy and too resistant with my spirituality. That is our true test in life: reaching our full potential, and we will be tested continuously until we achieve it. We all have our own *Akeidat* Yitzchak; that one big hurdle in our path, the one thing we can't do, can't give up. Yet our seemingly impossible mission is always possible; we just need to want it enough to make the necessary sacrifice. We must ask ourselves, what am I doing in this world at the end of the day? We must tell ourselves that we want to be God's vessels.

Every day, when we say the Shema prayer, we say, "And you shall love the Lord your God with all of your heart." Rashi offers a beautiful commentary on the prayer: loving God with all your heart means "your heart should not be fragmented with God." In other words, we must not be in a state of discord with God; rather, we must be one with Him. To love God with all your heart means to accept His decrees and His choices for you because you know He loves you, and therefore you give yourself over to Him entirely. Don't fight with God; don't fight with the place you are in life. As Hashem said to Moshe, "The place where you stand is holy." I know it doesn't feel that way sometimes. I know it can feel like the sand is burning your feet or the thorns are nipping your toes, but the place where you are standing is holy. You are exactly where you need to be. And if you can't see it, it is because you haven't reached that level of love for God; you are not one with Him, not seeing eye to eye; there is discord between you. When we can accept where we are, we have succeeded in life. Hashem can only do for you that which is good for you because God is all good. God has no selfishness; He doesn't gain from your pain; everything He does is purely for your sake. We will only be as happy as our understanding of that. We are sent on a mission to help, to inspire, to give strength to others. That's what keeps me going every day, hoping that I can, *b'ezras Hashem*, inspire and help so many people. It's why the Jewish people find comfort in loss; we understand that it was for the sake of something greater than ourselves.

There is a powerful idea in *Parashat Ki Tavo* when the Torah describes the hardships that the Jewish people will experience if they don't listen to God. We're talking real hardship here—extreme pain, all written in explicit detail. Most surprising is the reason the Torah gives: "All of this will happen because you didn't serve God with happiness and a good heart." Hold on, all it takes to be met with punishment is a lack of happiness? Not that the commandments weren't kept, not that we did not follow the Torah or do *mitzvot*, but only that we didn't do so happily? What is the big deal with that? We all struggle with doing the *mitzvot* with complete happiness. Some of us might be a bit resentful of the inconvenience of keeping Shabbat; some of us might wish we could eat at a non-kosher restaurant, but we're still keeping the *mitzvos*. We all have a *yetzer hara*, so what's the big deal if we're missing some happiness in our actions? Do we deserve all of that pain and suffering simply because we didn't follow through on the commandments with the required level of happiness? Why does it all come down to happiness?

When I was studying in Neve Yerushalayim, I had a friend who was a small child when the USSR disintegrated, and she remembered her family having to flee the country. I asked her if she was scared, and I wondered where they slept and what they ate. She just said that she knew her parents were going to take care of her, so she wasn't worried. Little kids don't think about anything too much; they don't worry; they are not depressed or anxious about the big things in life. They may stress about their candy, but that's it. Why is that? Because they know whatever they need, Daddy and Mommy are there to provide. What's interesting is that one of the sources for how we learn to pray comes from the same idea. The *pasuk* says, "You must be perfect with God." In other words, just as a baby relies on its parents and trusts them to deliver their needs, so too, we should be innocent, pure, and dependent on God. We shouldn't accept a "no"; we must instead fixate on our visions and keep asking because we know that He loves us and wants to deliver. That's what parents do; they create a sense of security for their children, providing stability even when it means sacrificing their own needs.

One of the greatest movies I ever saw as a child was a Holocaust film called *Life Is Beautiful,* about an Italian Jew and his son who were taken to a work camp. To protect his son from the horrors they faced, the father pretended their experiences were all part of a game with a special prize at the end. He would purposely mistranslate the Nazi orders for his son and present them as rules for the game; he would clown around to amuse the boy and play "hide and seek" with him to protect him from witnessing traumatic scenes. I am still amazed and inspired by that film because it is a true representation of what we do for our kids; we take care of their physical, emotional, and spiritual needs. The young boy in the film was able to survive the concentration camp without necessarily understanding the severity of his situation simply because his father worked so hard to protect him—physically, mentally, and spiritually. When we know we have a father who loves and cares for us, our worries are fewer; we know we will be taken care of and that it will all work out. But what happens when a kid gets lost, or God forbid, is taken away from their parent? He has no one to protect him; suddenly he is vulnerable to all danger; his greatest nightmares become possible.

That's how I understood the curses that would befall the Jewish people in the event that they did not serve God with *simcha*, happiness. It is, in itself, the curse; it means that we weren't living with God; we didn't feel His care and protection. To live with God means to live with happiness because I know, not believe but know, that everything He does for me is for my own good. No one is saying that it's not painful, but pain and bad are not the same. When you have dental surgery, you may experience lots of pain, but you are still grateful and willing to undergo the procedure because you understand that it is necessary. In an email with Rabbi Y.Y. Jacobson about my struggles, I shared how I was feeling alone and overwhelmed by pain. He told me the following story:

A young woman who was going through hard times began to pray to God for help. Suddenly, in her mind's eye, she saw two sets of footprints, side by side on a sandy pathway. Immediately, her spirits lifted because she interpreted this to mean that God was with her and was walking beside her.

Then the picture changed. She now saw the footprints located in a vast desert wilderness, and instead of two sets of footprints, there was only one. Why was God no longer beside her? As despair settled back over her, she began to cry. Then the inner voice of God softly spoke and said, "I have not left you. The one set of footprints is mine. You see, I am carrying you through the wilderness."

"*Imo Anochi b'tzarah,*" we are not alone; we are being carried. We just may not see it sometimes because we are too lost in our own darkness. If you had to say which is the most prominent of all prayers in Judaism, which would you choose? I think it's safe to say that *Shema Yisrael* is an iconic prayer, an anthem for every Jew. "Hear, O Israel, Hashem our God, Hashem is One." What is it about this verse that has moved us, guided us, and been our final words for thousands of years? We know there is a commandment to say this verse twice a day, in the morning and at night, and that this is a statement and testimony of God's kingship. But what does it mean to be "one"? Is the verse simply referring to numbers?

The third of Rambam's Thirteen Principles of Faith teaches that we are obligated to believe that God is one. However, it would be too obvious if that statement was simply referring to a number. It would be too obvious a statement to necessitate being its own principle; even someone limited in intellect can understand that two means division, duality, limitation, and if there were two or more gods, it would mean none of them are omniscient, omnipresent, or unlimited. Then what does it mean that God is one? Our sages teach us, "*ein od milevado,* there is no one else but Him." It's not one in the sense of numbers; rather, it is one in essence. There is no one else. God is only one, but He is also the one source of everything. Furthermore, why is it necessary to begin the verse with the command to "hear"? Is hearing the sense that we most trust? I wouldn't think so; we like to say "seeing is believing" because we tend to trust our eyes more than anything else. So then why don't we say "See, Israel" or "pay attention, Israel"? Why "hear"?

In Israel, there is a Blind Museum and a Deaf Museum, and interestingly enough, the former has many more visitors every year than the latter. It makes sense because we tend to value our sense of sight more than our sense of hearing. However, in the Torah, the sense of hearing is of significantly more value, considered to be worth more when lost. Why? Well, we all want to be heard. We will pay therapists just to feel heard. We feel the need to voice our opinions, share our thoughts, and know that what we say is being paid attention. The Torah teaches that in this world, we can't see God; we can only hear Him. But that can't be it because we know we can't see God, and we also can't literally hear God. So, what is this trying to teach us, and why is *Shema* at the core of Jewish belief?

We live in a world where we think that what we see is what we get, simply because we don't want to work harder, and it's easier to trust what we see. Eyesight gives you an instant understanding and grasp of reality. We believe that seeing something gives us the whole picture; therefore, we trust and depend on what we see with our own eyes. However, we're wrong to think that way: what you see is not always what you get. Seeing doesn't necessarily mean you are getting the whole picture; you may only be seeing what fits into the frame.

Think about it: if seeing is instantaneous, hearing is exactly the opposite. With hearing, you need to wait from the beginning until the end before you can understand what you heard. That's exactly the point: when you interrupt someone while they speak, you prevent them from expressing their full thought, and as a result, you may not understand them fully. Hearing requires patience; it means connecting with what you are hearing and internalizing its meaning. Hearing is the only sense that happens internally; every other sense has an external catalyst. What's more, hearing is the most subjective of all our senses. We may hear the same thing, but we may process it differently. How we process it depends on our personal mentality and understanding; it depends on who we are.

It's like connecting the dots: when you trace the line from one dot all the way through the hundredth dot in order to get the image. Imagine if at dot seventy-five you saw that it was an image of an elephant, so you stopped and moved on to the next image. But that first image wasn't just an elephant; it was actually an elephant standing on a ball. Those final, incomplete dots change the whole picture, but you didn't have the patience to wait to make it to the end. Therefore, your understanding of the picture is lacking.

The reason we all want to be heard so much, the reason why many of us will even pay someone to just listen to us, is that we feel like we are not being understood through our image. Our hearts are yelling from within, "I am not only that which you see, so don't reduce who I am to one scene in my life! I am a whole human being, made out of so many parts, and you are only seeing a tiny part of me. Don't judge me because you don't really know me." The sad truth is that we often condense others to the actions and reactions that we see; we judge them based on external moments and deficiencies. Yet, we are all much more than what is seen on the outside; we are entire human beings created in the image of God. As we said earlier, we can't judge a person even when we think we have been in their place before. Every one of us is composed of different emotional, physical, and spiritual makeup, which influences how we experience and relate to everything in our lives.

Think about your favorite song. What is it about that song that makes it so special? Maybe it's that one note that gives you goosebumps every time you hear it. But there are a bunch of notes in the song; what is so special about that one note that makes the whole song special to you? It's the buildup—everything that comes before, leading up to that moment, and then everything that comes after it. A note is just a note, but in the context of other notes, it becomes art. The same goes for life; we are made up of so many little details that create the music of our lives. And if we, as people, need to learn to listen to ourselves and others, how much more so do we need to learn to listen to God? We say not to judge others, yet we often judge God. We reduce Him to that one detail, that one moment in our lives, and we automatically reject that He is a loving Father because He sent us something painful. If we want to have a relationship with God, we must hear Him in order to connect the dots; we must have patience. That's why God says *Shema*, hear, "Listen to Me. You can't see Me now, but I'm here; I'm always here. I have a vision, I have a goal; you just can't see it. *Lo yirani adam v'chai,* no person can see Me and live. It's not that I don't want to show you, but you are limited by your humanity; you couldn't understand even if you wanted to."

Have you ever wondered why we cover our eyes when we say the Shema? Sephardic Jews cover their eyes in a specific way, using their fingers to create the shape of the three letters of the name of Hashem: *shin, daled, yud*. This is the name attributed to the sufficiency of Hashem. Why is this name focused on here? Reciting the Shema is making a statement, offering testimony for God's oneness, the all-encompassing source of everything. It is an admission that everything comes from God, and therefore, everything is God. Yet sometimes, when we look at the world, we can't understand it; we can't find God. Where is His goodness, His kindness, His mercy? We see the world, and we ask so many questions. We want to be honest; we want to fill our hearts with hope. Therefore, we cover our eyes and we say, "God, I don't see You; all I see is my own darkness. I would be a fraud to say that I see You and believe You, that

I feel You close and that I understand You. Still, I close my eyes, and I know that even though I can't see You, I can always hear You. I know that what I see is not necessarily what is; I know I cannot see the whole picture. Therefore, I refuse to reduce You to this."

Often, the verse will appear in such a way that the *ayin* in the word *shema* and the *daled* in the word *echad* are formatted larger than the rest of the letters; we see this in the Torah, of course, and many *siddurim*. This is because the ayin represents the eye, and the *daled* represents the four corners of the world. Thus, as we close our eyes, we state that the eye cannot see everything in this world and understand it; therefore, we will not trust our eye and will not let it define our beliefs and relationship with God. That is why many people form the name of God with their hands; it comes to say that we know that God is sufficient, that He is capable of delivering. Even if we can't see Him, can't see how our problem will be resolved, we know He can pull us through. There are plenty of times we can't see God, and it is often better not to try because our eyes can deceive us. But even if we can't see God, we can always hear Him.

Hearing is different from seeing in its intention. In order to see, you must open your eyes and concentrate on what is before you. If your eyes are closed, you'll never be able to see anything, no matter how hard you concentrate. But with hearing, your ears will pick up on all of the sounds around you, even those you may not be listening to; you just need to be attuned to your surroundings. In the second paragraph of the *Shema*, we say, "*v'haya im shamo'ah tishma'u,* and it will come to pass that if you listen, you will hear." The phrasing may seem redundant, but it's not. If you listen, if you choose to actively listen, if you choose to tune your radio to the right station, then you will be able to hear what God is saying. But if you refuse to listen, then no matter what, God will not be able to get your attention. Some people may be blind, but others choose not to see.

One story in the Torah always amazes me. When Yosef is sent to prison, he sees two people who are sad and miserable, and he asks them why they are feeling that way. Isn't that how we expect people to feel in prison? Yet we find that Yosef's jail experience was a relatively positive one. That's because he imbued it with God's presence, thereby creating a positive environment. How did he manage to do that, though? How can he sit in such a dark, lonely place and not only retain his good spirits but lift the spirits of others as well? It is because Yosef lived with God, and he was able to "hear" Him in every situation.

The Torah tells us that when Yosef was sold to the Yishmaelim, they were carrying good-smelling spices, even though they normally carried foul-smelling merchandise. From here we learn that God will never give you more than what you need or deserve; God is precise, down to the last detail. Yosef didn't need to suffer the added anguish of foul smells, so Hashem didn't give him that experience. My question is, do you think Yosef even noticed the nice smell? I mean, who in his circumstances would think about that? On the days when everything is going wrong, do we stop to smell the flowers? Of course not! We're in a rotten mood, and therefore everything feels rotten. Our attitude is negative, and we're only thinking about the next thing that could go wrong, the next bad thing God will send your way. But that wasn't Yosef's attitude. He did, in fact, notice the pleasant aromas, and he realized that it was not the norm and recognized that God was doing it for his sake, as a kindness. He recognized that God didn't want him to feel alone, and this was how He showed Yosef that He loves him and will follow him into exile. Yosef carried those thoughts with him the whole way through. God will often whisper to us, "I am here, do you hear me? Do you see me in all the little details, moving things around for you?" We just need to listen for Him.

I remember when I was looking for a new place to live after the fire; I was so frustrated, so lost, so stressed out. I had looked at dozens of apartments, but they were all so expensive. I raised my eyes to Hashem and said, "This is the last day; if You want me to get an apartment, it's now or never." The next property I checked out was replace with really great, so we grabbed it. Turns out that life doesn't have to be good or simple for us to know that God is running things. Sometimes we just have to pay a bit more attention, see the silver lining, so to speak. Maybe God is hiding; sometimes we need that, or deserve that, but it doesn't mean He isn't there. It simply means that He can only be found if we look for Him. Like when I spent an entire school year petitioning my daughter's school to provide therapy for her. They kept dragging their feet, claiming there was more paperwork, more bureaucracy; it would take time to make anything happen. Suddenly, magically, the week everything fell to pieces for us, she got approved for therapy. That was God letting me know He didn't forget me, even though I can't see Him.

It's interesting to note that the *parasha* in which the Torah is given to *B'nei Yisrael* begins with the words, "*Vayishma Yitro,* and Yitro heard." The obvious question is, does that mean only Yitro heard? In fact, we know that when Hashem gave the Torah, all the nations of the world knew about it because they had witnessed everything going on around them. So, even though Hashem technically revealed Himself only to the Jews, the rest of the world was aware, too. So, what happened? Why is Yitro so honored in the *pasuk*? The answer is because he actively listened. He didn't let the words of Hashem go in one ear and out the other; he heard, he internalized, and he acted accordingly. During *kriyat Yam Suf,* when the Jewish people faced the split sea, they cried out to Hashem in a panic. Hashem asked, "Why are you crying? Just go!" *B'nei Yisrael* answered, "But we are scared; shouldn't we be crying and praying?" However, they were wrong in believing so. If we believe in God, if we trust Him, we must act on that trust and just go!

I am learning to hear God in every area of my life. When I succeed at this, it has allowed me to constantly work on trying to see Him more often, even in the darkness. And though sometimes I may choose to be blind, the truth is often so loud that it's deafening and impossible to deny. Many of my students tell me, "I don't regret anything that has happened in my life. If it hadn't been for those circumstances, I wouldn't have ended up here." It makes me think to myself how there are many ways to arrive at a destination; why take the longer route when a shorter one is available? I say to myself, if only we could be humble enough and pay close enough attention, we would sooner recognize that God is our Father and He loves us; He wants us close so that He may take care of us. But to do so, we must take His hand and let Him guide us, like a child crossing the street with a parent. Life is much simpler than we think; we overcomplicate it because too much of our ego is involved. We need to learn to let go! What happens when we let go? We let in God, and God is greater than we think. He is not limited by our misconceptions or preconceptions. God can do anything for us, but only if we let Him, so we must take a leap of faith. The amount of God we see in our lives is completely dependent on the amount of God we want to see. There is a famous quote that goes, "Where is God? Wherever we let Him in." We need to invite Him in because He is waiting right outside. Let Him in; make space for Him to surprise you. I always say that God is as powerful as we want Him to be and as limited as we think He is.

Never, in my wildest dreams, would I have thought that after the fire, I would end up in my own house just a few short months later; that I would have four beautiful, precious, delicious kids to light up my life; and that I would have the merit to inspire many people. After all, who am I? I'm just little Raquel who thought she was going to sell popsicles on the street, who thought she would never make it in life. I can still remember the smile I had on my face when I went on my first international tour. I had been looking back at myself, at my low self-esteem, at the scared little Raquel who used to hide in the bathroom, when suddenly I realized that I couldn't contain my smile. I was amazed that this was my life, that I was learning to connect to God, teaching His Torah. I survived and thrived throughout so many challenges to become who I am now. How did I do it? The answer is that I didn't do it—we did it: God and me, and all the Jewish people together. All of you have been part of my journey, my growth, my dreams, and my destination.

It is said that when Hashem took the Jewish people out of Egypt, He did so "on the wings of eagles." In nature, most birds carry their offspring in their claws, under their bodies, protecting them from the predators who fly above them while unfortunately exposing them to the hunters shooting from below. However, the eagle carries its offspring on its wings because it flies the highest of all the birds and isn't afraid of predators from above, all while protecting its fledgling from the hunters below. Because the other birds carry their offspring with their claws, their babies could just wait patiently in the nest to be picked up and carried away. But this is not so for the young eagle, whose parent gets close to the nest but does not lift it up. If that baby eagle wants to fly, it must jump out of the nest and onto its parent's wings. We are like those young eagles; we have to leap from the nest onto Hashem's protective wings.

I have often taught my classes that the closer we are to God, the more He tests us. I mean, look at the patriarchs; look at King David. We think that being close to God means spiritual bliss, being "besties" with the Divine. I know I thought as much when I became religious. But the opposite is true, individually and communally as a people: the closer you are to God, the more He will challenge you to see if your love for Him is sincere or if it is conditional. It's just like how kids constantly test their parents. They want to know if we only love them when it's convenient for us, or if we love them even when it's not so convenient for us. Do we love only when the object of our love is compliant, or also when it is defiant? Hashem was testing my love for Him, and I had to recognize that this was my moment to shine, to prove my love for Him, and to really draw from within me the *emunah* I wasn't sure I even had.

PIN IT TO YOUR HEART!

"The greatest pain in life is to fail at becoming who we have the potential to be."

"The degree to which we have God in our lives is the degree to which we will be happy."

"Don't be at discord with God; don't fight with the place you are in life."

"God can only do for you that which is good for you because God is all good."

"The amount of God you see in your life is completely dependent on the amount of God you want to see."

"If you choose to tune your radio to the right station, then you will be able to hear what God is saying."

"We must connect all of the dots to see the complete picture."

"God is as powerful as you want Him to be and as limited as you think He is."

"We must be like young eagles and leap from the nest onto Hashem's protective wings."

EPILOGUE

In life, we all want to achieve happiness and success—that we have accomplished everything we were meant to accomplish. What's funny, though, is that in the entire Torah, there is only one person who was ever considered to be successful: Yosef HaTzaddik. The *pasuk* writes, "*vayehi Yosef ish matzliach,* and Yosef was a successful person." We know he became the viceroy of Egypt and that all of the Jewish people—and really the whole world—was saved because of him. But can we really say that his is a success story? Yosef had an incredibly difficult life, with lots of ups but just as many downs. And despite the heights he reached in life, he was still the first to die out of all his brothers.

Yosef wasn't the stereotypical *talmid chacham*, learning in *Kollel* all day. And even as a handsome young man, he was sold into slavery for just a few coins, eventually landing in prison. Is that really what we would call a life of success?

It's interesting to note that the *pasuk* which describes Yosef's success begins with the word "*vayehi.*" The rule of the Torah is that whenever a *pasuk* begins with the words "*vehaya,*" it denotes good news, while a *pasuk* beginning with the word "*vayehi*" denotes bad news. So, why does the Torah describe Yosef's success through negative language? The answer is that Yosef became who he was because of the many *vayehi's* in his life, because he was able to overcome his hardships. Yosef's life was a success because he kept fighting and pushing, and he never gave up. He wasn't always scoring points; sometimes he would shoot and miss; sometimes he was out of the game. No matter what, he kept showing up, kept coming back, and trying again.

We think success is hitting the jackpot every time, but that's not real success; that's simply having good luck. Being human—being a great human for that matter—means having the ability to overcome obstacles, getting up when we fall, and carrying on. I mean, think about Sarah Imeinu, who couldn't conceive for ninety years. Wouldn't we have given up? And Rabbi Akiva, who lost 24,000 students and his life's work! Wouldn't we have given up if we were him? Yet, had either of them given up, we wouldn't have the Jewish people, and there would be no Oral Torah! Where would we be if they had? Rabbi Akiva kept going against all odds, despite his tragedy. He accepted God's will and understood that as long as he was alive, then he had time to do something, to become something. Yosef was the epitome of success because he was the epitome of failure. True success is doing the best you can with what you have; it's getting up even after you have been knocked down hundreds and thousands of times.

Yosef is called a *tzaddik*, yet it seems he needed divine help when Potifar's wife tried to force him to lie with her. The *Midrash* tells us that Yosef fled because either he saw his father's image or his own reflection in a mirror and as a result was reminded of who he was. So then why is he called a *tzaddik*? Anyone else given such a direct reminder from God would have done the same, so what's the big deal with Yosef? The lesson here is that Yosef wasn't considered a *tzaddik* because of that particular moment. No, he was considered a *tzaddik* because of the many moments during his time in Potifar's house when he chose to resist temptation. Potifar's wife constantly tried to seduce him, yet he continually denied her, despite the fact that he was a young man, alone and susceptible to youthful hormones. But why did he resist at all to begin with? Who cares? Why not just give in? Yosef stuck to his beliefs and values, to who he was, and resisted until he had no more strength left in him to resist anymore. It was then, when his resilience began to wane and he almost gave in to her, that the *pasuk* tells us, "He came to the house to do his work. No man of the household was there in the house." The *Midrash* tells us that it wasn't that literally there were no men in the house but that Yosef wasn't a man anymore; he was taken over by his more carnal desires. He was overcome with temptation; there was no more will left in him, no more self-control. He had come to do "his work"; the *Midrash* suggests that this is, in fact, a euphemism for his manly desires. At that moment, Hashem chose to help him, saying to him, "You worked, you tried, you persisted, and did all that you could! Now I will do the rest; I will help you."

Success is a direct expression of effort. Yosef is a *tzaddik* because of the choices he made leading up to that moment. That's why every morning we say, "Blessed are You, God, who gives the weary strength, *hanoten laya'ef koach.*" That blessing is an odd turn of phrase. Grammatically speaking, it should say, "who gives strength to the weary." But the blessing is written this way purposefully and comes to tell us that God will give us strength but only when we are weary. In other words, once we've done all we could do on our own. When we show commitment, strength, and devotion, then God will step in and give us that final push. Success is doing the best we can with what we have; the rest is up to God. We can't control the outcome, but we can and must control our choices.

When the *Mishkan* was first built, all the princes of the tribes brought gifts and offerings, but Aharon HaKohen was sad because he didn't have this opportunity. Therefore, Hashem gave him the mitzvah and privilege of lighting the Menorah. Hashem said to him, "Don't worry, you have the Menorah, and it is eternal. Yours is bigger than theirs." These words resonate like a boom in my heart: yours is bigger than theirs. Yes, the princes brought offerings; everyone saw, everyone applauded. Aharon's offerings were hidden; no one saw them. Therefore, to Hashem, his were greater than theirs; his small light will light up the world for generations. This idea comforted me because who am I? What do I know about my own successes? All I know is that it doesn't matter how many times we get knocked down; we must get up again. We might not see it now from within the darkness, but one day we will look back and realize we were building ourselves up to reach our ultimate goal: to build the Jewish people.

I guess in that sense my life has been successful so far. I might not have the same glitz and glitter or picture-perfect life that others might have, but maybe mine is the glimmer of light in darkness, a light for the generation! Daily, I am reminded, "*Kol hazman shehaner dolek tamid efshar l'taken,* as long as the candle is still burning, there is time to repair." My candle is lit, and the flame is burning bright with the desire to rise up and do the right thing, to be close to the Creator and give Him *nachat* by doing His will. Hashem, I just want to do Your will, and it seems that this is the path You have chosen for me. Who am I to tell You what I need to achieve those goals? Who am I to tell You what tools I need in order to serve You better? It would certainly be nice to be able to serve Hashem with a full toolbox, but our challenge is to serve Him as best we can with the tools we have. That is the true reflection of our greatness and success.

There is a common factor between all of Yosef's tests. He easily could have asked himself what the point of everything was. Why work so hard? May as well give up. I, too, have often wondered if there was really a point to any of my suffering. It seems that the more I try, the more I hit a wall. I've told myself, not once but many times, to just give up. But then I always ask myself, "What if?" What if next time I try I hit the jackpot? What if there is something worth building? What if this destruction is really a magnificent beginning? A few days ago, someone asked me how I manage to carry on and not give up. I answered her that I want to show everyone how to overcome and become the best version of ourselves. I want others to see and believe that Hashem loves us no matter what, and He will push us to achieve our goals. So even when it is hard, we cannot give up on Him because He doesn't give up on us. As Chana said to Hashem when her children were taken from her, "Until now I had to divide my love between many, but now I can give it all to You."

Hashem, my love for You is not conditional. You don't owe me anything, and You've given me so much. As long as I live, I will give all that I have to You, and I will continue to choose You, not in spite of the pain, but because of the challenge.

I would like to finish with a beautiful parable:

There was once a woman who would go down to the river every day and fill two buckets of water, which she would carry back to her village on her shoulders. One bucket was fully intact and would arrive at its destination full of water. The other bucket, however, was cracked and full of holes, and the water would leak out of it along the way.

One day, the broken bucket began to cry to the woman, "I'm so sorry I can't do my work properly. I'm so sorry that I have disappointed you because I'm broken and can't give you all you want. I wish I were like the other bucket, whole and strong."

The woman answered, "The next time we make the trip back from the river, look at the road. I want to show you something beautiful."

The next time the woman walked home with the buckets of water, the broken bucket looked at the road. It noticed that on the side of the whole bucket, the road was blank earth and pavement. But on the other side, the side that the broken bucket was carried on, the road was covered in beautiful blooming flowers. The bucket turned to the woman and asked what it was seeing. The woman answered kindly, "This is what your brokenness made. Your cracks watered the road and nurtured the earth every day. You thought you were only losing water, but you have grown all of this beauty."

May beauty continue to grow from our brokenness. We must not be afraid of our cracks and holes because we may never know what seeds our tears have watered and what landscapes will flourish through our efforts. Change your thoughts, and you will change your life. Remember, "we are not human beings; we are human becomings." In other words, we are not simply going through life; we are growing through life.

I started writing this book in the hope of helping others. At the time, I didn't know that in the end, I started writing this book in the hope of helping others. I didnt know that at the end it would help *me* the most. For the first time, I have allowed myself to be seen with all my imperfections, rough parts, and edges. So often we are looking for answers in life, not realizing that the answers have been with us all along. The answer I was looking for was that the one and only way to forgive and let go, to overcome and become who I need to be, is to live a life with God. Therefore, I choose greatness, I choose healing, I choose success, I choose *emunah*.